# The Emergence of Richard Wright

# The Emergence of Richard Wright

A STUDY IN LITERATURE AND SOCIETY

*Keneth Kinnamon*

UNIVERSITY OF ILLINOIS PRESS  *Urbana, Chicago, London*

Grateful acknowledgment is made to Harper & Row, Publishers, for permission to reprint material from the following works of Richard Wright: *Uncle Tom's Children* (Copyright 1938 Harper & Row, Publishers), *Native Son* (Copyright 1940 Harper & Row, Publishers), and *Black Boy* (Copyright 1945 Harper & Row, Publishers). Grateful acknowledgment is made also to Jonathan Cape Limited and Mrs. Ellen Wright for permission to reprint material from *Native Son* and *Black Boy*.

Second printing, 1973

© 1972 by The Board of Trustees of the University of Illinois. Manufactured in the United States of America. Library of Congress Catalog Card No. 72-78023.

ISBN 0-252-00201-6

To my wife, Paquita

# Preface

This book is a study of the life, literary career, and social milieu of Richard Wright from his birth in 1908 through the publication of *Native Son* in 1940, with a glance in the final chapter at his withdrawal from the Communist movement and the beginning of his expatriation. The effort throughout has been to reconcile the varying claims of literary and social criticism, to examine Wright's early poetry and fiction both as works of the aesthetic and moral imagination and as events in the history of American racial protest. Such a dual focus may fail to satisfy the extreme partisans of the opposed camps of art and action, but it seems the only sensible approach to a writer for whom the literary and social consciences were one.

The intellectual and scholarly obligations one incurs while working on a topic of this kind are inevitably great. An early version of this work was written under the direction of Kenneth S. Lynn and Alan E. Heimert, who offered both warm encouragement and penetrating criticism. In the initial stages of planning and research, I was aided by the suggestions of Harold C. Martin and the late Perry Miller.

More than fifty persons patiently and helpfully answered, by letter or in interview, my queries concerning Richard Wright. Particularly helpful were the responses of O. Rudolph Aggrey, Samuel Allen, Guy-Claude Balmir, Arna Bontemps, Jack Conroy, Frank Marshall Davis, Ralph Ellison, Tyrus G. Fain, John T. Frederick, Donald Gallup, Walter Goldwater, Granville Hicks, Benjamin Higgins, Edward Margolies, Thomas F. Pettigrew, Kenneth W. Porter, Carl Pugh, Saunders Redding, Howard P. Vincent, Theodore Ward, Henry F. Winslow, Sr., and Peter Witt. To all of these, as well as to those unnamed, I express my gratitude.

Several of my most useful informants are now beyond the reach of thanks: Earl Browder, Langston Hughes, Adam Clayton Powell, Jr., Kirker Quinn, Ira DeA. Reid, Carl Van Vechten, and Horace R. Cayton. My indebtedness to the last-named goes beyond the scholarly aid he so readily provided by letter and tape recorder during 1964 and 1965 to the personal friendship he gave during the last sixteen months of his life. Those months were filled with work on his projected memoir of Richard Wright, to which all students of Afro-American literature had been looking forward.

I must single out for special mention, also, my friend Michel Fabre of the University of Paris III. The beginning of his own important work on Wright preceded my first efforts, and with great generosity he gave me encouragement, guidance, and judicious criticism as I carried out my investigations. After carefully reading an earlier version of this work, he sent me a painstaking commentary, drawing on his unrivaled knowledge of Wright's biography, which saved me many an error. In addition to all his other services, he permitted me to make copies of letters he had received concerning Wright from Nelson Algren, Claude A. Barnett, Gwendolyn Brooks, Marcel Duhamel, James T. Farrell, Howard Fast, Langston Hughes, Philip Rahv, and Frank G. Yerby.

My largest debt is to my wife and sons for their love, support, and patience.

# Contents

One     The Burdens of Caste and Class     3

Two     A Literary Apprenticeship     34

Three     *Lawd Today* and *Uncle Tom's Children*     75

Four     *Native Son*     118

Five     Epilogue     153

Selected Bibliography     163

Index     191

# The Burdens of Caste and Class

# ONE

The childhood and youth of Richard Wright were filled with obstacles to a career of literary distinction more formidable than those faced by any other major American writer. That a novelist rather than a criminal emerged from the racial prejudice, poverty, family disorganization, and inadequate education that afflicted his early years is a phenomenon not easy to explain. Indeed, he was at different times in his youth a juvenile delinquent. But ultimately he became Richard Wright, not Bigger Thomas. An abiding irony of Wright's life is that in spite of his belief in environmental determinism, he himself fulfilled his dream of success against more than Algeresque odds.[1]

Other American writers, of course, have suffered from one or two, or even three, of the handicaps imposed on Wright, though seldom so intensely. Several have passed their boyhoods in straitened circumstances — Emerson, Melville, Twain, Robinson — or even real poverty — Dreiser, Sandburg; Wright often suffered

---

[1] Some conservative white reviewers of *Native Son* were quick to attack the novel's sociological thesis by pointing out that the success of the novelist contradicted it. See, for example, Burton Rascoe, "Negro Novel and White Reviewers," *American Mercury*, L (May 1940), 113-16. At the same time, blacks and sympathetic whites have often exploited Wright's career for its inspirational value. See, for example, Edwin R. Embree, *13 against the Odds* (New York, 1944), pp. 25-46, in which Wright's success is shown to be even more astonishing than that of twelve other notable blacks. The very fact that his achievement is so exceptional, however, would seem to confirm, not deny, Wright's emphasis on the shaping influence of environment.

3

physical hunger and malnutrition. A number of authors received little formal education — Whittier, Melville, Whitman, Twain, Howells — though this lack was often compensated by a good family library or extensive travel. Wright attended a black Seventh-Day Adventist school and, to the ninth grade, black public schools, mainly in Mississippi; his environment was mostly indifferent to creative intellectual activity, and his travels as a boy took him only from one black ghetto to another in Mississippi, Tennessee, and Arkansas. Fatherless authors are common enough in American literature: Emerson, Hawthorne, Poe, Melville, Twain, Stephen Crane, Frost. The fathers of all of these died young, but Wright's father abandoned his wife and two sons in a penniless condition to run off with another woman, a more humiliating kind of loss for a sensitive young boy. Most black writers in America have been raised in homes of some cultivation — W. E. B. Du Bois, James Weldon Johnson, Charles Waddell Chesnutt, Ralph Ellison, Phillis Wheatley, Langston Hughes, Chester Himes — or have at least lived their childhoods in the North, thus escaping the most overtly oppressive forms of racism, as in the cases of Paul Laurence Dunbar and James Baldwin. Wright was the son of an illiterate Mississippi sharecropper.

It is important to consider in some detail each of these four basic facts of Wright's youth — his racial status, his poverty, the disruption of his family, and his faulty education — not only because collectively and individually they left ineradicable scars on his psyche and deeply influenced his thought, but also because they provided much of the subject matter of his early writing. Social reality determined Wright's literary personality, even if his successful efforts to become a writer constituted a gesture of mastery over that reality.

Richard Wright was subjected to racial discrimination and racial prejudice during the entire period of his life in the United States. The intensity of the racist assault on the integrity of his sense of self, and occasionally on his physical body, decreased, of course, from his boyhood and youth in Mississippi, Tennessee, and Arkansas to his young manhood in Chicago and finally to his attainment of fame as a writer in New York, but his suffering as a black man always remained the central fact of his American experience. After moving to France, he announced, "There is more freedom in one square block of Paris than in all of the United States."[2] He had experienced tantalizing foretastes of this liberation during brief trips to Mexico in 1940 and Quebec in 1945; in the United States this native son met only varying degrees of racial oppression.

The most severe was in his native state of Mississippi, where he was born on 4 September 1908 on a plantation where his father was farming shares, located not far from Natchez in the center of one of the most racist areas of the most racist state. On the political scene, in the year of Wright's birth James Kimble Vardaman, "The Great White Chief," had completed his first term as governor. Vardaman rose to eminence by prescribing for sound race relations in this way: "The way to control the nigger is to whip him when he does not obey without it, and another is never to pay him more wages than is actually necessary to buy food and clothing."[3] To insure the continuation of this tradition, Vardaman's aptest pupil, Theodore Gilmore Bilbo, "The Man," was in 1908 beginning his political career by taking his seat as a state senator. Thirty-eight years later, only a few weeks after Wright arrived in Paris, Bilbo, then a United States senator, said, " 'The nigger is only 150 years from the jungles of Africa,' where he cut up 'some fried nigger steak for breakfast.' "[4] If such redneck demagogues as Vardaman and Bilbo were more vocal, they were hardly more racist in theory or in practice than Bourbon aristocrats like John Sharp Williams and Leroy Percy. The general fact is that suppression of black people has been the dominant goal of Mississippi politics since the end of Reconstruction.[5] The specific fact is that the boyhood of Richard Wright was spent in those years before and during World War I when that goal was perhaps most completely realized.

Socially and economically, blacks in Mississippi during this period

[2] Roi Ottley, *No Green Pastures* (New York, 1951), p. 3.
[3] W. J. Cash, *The Mind of the South,* Vintage ed. (New York, 1960), p. 253.
[4] Quoted from *Time,* 1 July 1946, p. 22, by A. Wigfall Green, *The Man Bilbo* (Baton Rouge, 1963), p. 104.
[5] An incisive account is the chapter on Mississippi in V. O. Key, Jr., *Southern Politics in State and Nation* (New York, 1949), pp. 229-53, and a longer treatment is Albert D. Kirwan, *Revolt of the Rednecks, Mississippi Politics: 1876-1925* (Lexington, Ky., 1951).

were subjected to total discrimination. As the most rural state, the most completely dependent upon a cotton economy, it had no large urban centers, such as New Orleans or Atlanta, to alleviate the severity of the caste system and virtually no industrialization, such as was making rapid strides in Birmingham and elsewhere, to provide economic opportunity. The state's unpaved roads and inadequate communications reinforced the isolation and parochialism that supported the feudal social structure. Ethnically, the white population of Mississippi was one of the most homogeneously Anglo-Saxon in the nation, with the 1910 census listing only 9,324, or .5 percent, foreign-born.[6] As a result, both Delta planter and hill-country poor white farmer united to exploit and suppress blacks in a frenzy of racial solidarity that frequently overrode considerations of broad social and economic welfare. If the Vardamans and Bilbos could oppose the large landowners by supporting penal reform, improved public education (from which Vardaman advocated the exclusion of blacks[7]), and more equitable taxation, the white masses united with the classes to uphold the sacred dogma of white supremacy. The brief flirtation of the Populists with interracial solidarity of economic interest was a thing of the past in the first decade of the twentieth century. The pattern here so roughly sketched was common in other parts of the agricultural South, but nowhere did it operate so rigorously and with such a total absence of countervailing forces as in Mississippi.

Most black Mississippians during the years of Wright's boyhood worked as sharecroppers, often in peonage, always desperately poor. For the fortunate minority who managed to struggle upward to the ownership of small farms, there was always the inescapable confrontation with the white cotton-buyer and the white gin-owner, against whom there was little recourse in white courts if cheating

[6] Paul Breck Foreman, *Mississippi Population Trends* (Nashville, 1939), p. 3. In the 1920 census both the number and the percentage were even lower — 7,931 and .4 percent.

[7] In the gubernatorial primary election of 1903, Vardaman declared, "When I speak of educating the people, I mean the white people. . . . The negro . . . was designed for a burden-bearer. . . . Then why squander money on his education when the only effect is to spoil a good field hand and make an insolent cook." Quoted from the *Jackson Weekly Clarion Ledger*, 30 July 1903, in Heber Ladner, "James Kimble Vardaman, Governor of Mississippi, 1904-1908," *Journal of Mississippi History*, II (October 1940), 176, 177.

took place. Indeed, few blacks had the temerity to invoke legal action against whites for any reason whatever, because the threat of violence was always immediate.[8] In the towns and the few small cities, blacks worked as laborers, servants, and in other menial capacities. Wright's own jobs as a boy were typical: carrying lunches to railroad workers, carrying firewood and trays for a small café, delivering clothes for a pressing shop, sweeping floors, selling newspapers, serving as scribe for an illiterate black insurance agent, doing chores for a white family, working as water boy and bat boy in a brickyard, caddying, serving as porter in a clothing store, working in an optical shop and a drugstore, mopping floors and bellhopping in a hotel, and taking tickets in a black motion picture theater.[9]

In an effort to escape the deprivation inherent in his status as a black sharecropper in Mississippi, intensified by the ravages of the boll weevil, the father of Richard Wright loaded his young family on a riverboat at Natchez sometime in 1914 to migrate upstream. "My father," Wright recalled in *Black Boy,* "was a black peasant who had gone to the city seeking life, but who had failed in the city; a black peasant whose life had been hopelessly snarled in the city, and who had at last fled the city. . . ."[10] Well might he have failed, for the city was Memphis, in many respects an extension of the Mississippi mentality across the state line of Tennessee into Shelby County. Here Wright lived until he was almost eight, and here he first became conscious of white oppression.

This is not to say that Memphis in the years before World War I was not in some ways an attractive refuge for the tenant farmers and sharecroppers, white as well as black, and for the lumberjacks of Mississippi, Arkansas, and western Tennessee. It was enjoying an economic boom in lumber, cotton marketing, cottonseed-products manufacturing, and other industries. For blacks it offered varied, if

[8] As late as 26 March 1944, Isaac Simmons, a black minister of Liberty, Mississippi, near Wright's birthplace, was removed from his home and shot to death by a lynch mob on the charge that "he was hiring a lawyer to safeguard his title to a debt free farm through which [there] was possibility that an oil vein ran." Jessie Parkhurst Guzman, ed., *Negro Year Book* (Tuskegee, 1947), p. 305.
[9] Richard Wright, *Black Boy: A Record of Childhood and Youth* (New York, 1945), pp. 73, 112, 119, 127, 141, 142, 143, 157, 163, 170, 172, 176, 177.
[10] Ibid., p. 31.

discriminatory, employment at wages that were indeed low enough but at least better than those of Mississippi. As further inducement, the black man in Memphis could vote, though often only at the behest of Mayor Edward Hull Crump, then in an early stage of his career spanning almost half a century as political boss of Memphis. Above all, perhaps, Memphis was attractive because of its size, almost 150,000 when the Wright family arrived. The "life" that Richard Wright's father sought resided in the variety and excitement of this metropolis of the middle South, so different from the drabness of the plantation. For black people these qualities emanated from Beale Street, where at this very time W. C. Handy was absorbing — and helping to create — their musical expression.

These advantages of Memphis over Mississippi, however, were only comparative. In the city, also, white supremacy was the unalterable code, the ideal "most passionately upheld" by white Memphians, according to William D. Miller, the closest student of Memphis during this period: "It was held above religion, morality, or law by all classes, and the fanaticism engendered in its defense explains much of the violence in the city's life during the first two decades of the twentieth century."[11] "Boss" Crump himself migrated to Memphis from Holly Springs, Mississippi, and of his attitude one writer said in 1948, "He thinks he knows where the color line is: it is where it was long ago in North Mississippi. He thinks Memphis wants it to stay there."[12] One might surmise that the economic advantages were not overwhelming. As night porter in a Beale Street drugstore, Wright's father could have made little more than the fifteen-cent-per-hour wage of the common laborer that the Business Men's Club of Memphis boasted of in a 1910 brochure addressed to northern manufacturers.[13] After the father deserted his family, Wright's mother earned even less as a cook.

A special characteristic of life in Memphis in these years was a widespread, deeply entrenched violence. As a frontier river town it had long had an unsavory reputation, and its prevailing violence had manifested itself in racial conflict as early as 1866, when forty-

[11] *Memphis during the Progressive Era, 1900-1917* (Memphis and Madison, Wis., 1957), p. 19.
[12] Shields McIlwaine, *Memphis Down in Dixie* (New York, 1948), p. 377.
[13] Miller, *Memphis during the Progressive Era, 1900-1917*, p. 51.

six blacks and one white English sympathizer were slaughtered and great property damage inflicted in retaliation for the murder of one white policeman by a black mob.[14] In the years preceding the war when the Wright family lived in Memphis, it was notorious as the murder capital of the nation. In 1916, for example, it had the astonishing homicide rate of 89.9 per 100,000 population, almost three times the rate of its nearest competitor.[15] In cases of homicide or other violence by whites against blacks, no matter how flagrant, convictions were virtually unknown. On the contrary, extreme savagery was often applauded in the name of white supremacy: "When 'Wild Bill' Latura, a bemused divekeeper, strode into a Negro saloon and without provocation killed six of its patrons, his act was considered one of almost religious devotion, performed in the dramatic manner that he and his kind could appreciate. To many people of the city he became a folk hero, and when his trial was held, there was practically no sentiment for conviction, and he was shortly freed."[16] On 22 May 1917, less than a year after Wright's mother took Richard and his brother, Alan, back to Mississippi, Eli Persons, a mentally defective black man, was lynched in the classic manner some five miles from the city limits by a crowd of five thousand people, the number undoubtedly swollen by the front-page coverage the *Memphis Commercial Appeal* gave the impending event. After Persons was burned alive, his heart was cut from his body, which was then dismembered. "On Beale Street the head and a leg were thrown among a group of Negroes, and a barber shop, seeking to attract customers, displayed a charred remnant."[17] Against this background of violence, it is small wonder that Wright's initiation into a knowledge of southern race relations occurred in Memphis at the age of six when he heard of a beating

[14] McIlwaine, *Memphis Down in Dixie*, pp. 149-52.

[15] Miller, *Memphis during the Progressive Era, 1900-1917*, p. 92.

[16] Ibid., pp. 19-20. Even mild objections to the recreational murder of black people followed the curious logic of white supremacy. After Latura was acquitted, the *Memphis Commercial Appeal* of 12 December 1908 editorialized that the practice was "being overdone" and should cease "because it was wrong in itself" and, more significant, because "those white men who kill negroes as a pastime . . . usually end up by killing white men." Quoted in Miller, *Memphis during the Progressive Era, 1900-1917*, p. 96.

[17] Ibid., p. 194.

administered by a white man to a black boy.[18] When he returned to Memphis several years later, he was to receive further lessons in "The Ethics of Living Jim Crow."

If Memphis shared the fervent devotion of Mississippi to the code of white supremacy, Phillips County, Arkansas, where Wright moved with his mother and brother in the summer of 1916, was virtually indistinguishable in appearance, economy, and social customs from Coahoma County, Mississippi, on the other side of the river. Like the adjoining Delta area of Mississippi, this part of Arkansas had the heaviest concentration of black population, consisting mostly of sharecroppers, and thus the strictest system of white domination in the state. Here white violence struck close to young Wright.

The Wright family went to the small town of Elaine, Arkansas, upon the invitation of his mother's sister Maggie Hoskins, whose husband, Fred, operated a profitable black saloon. In late 1916 or early 1917 Uncle Hoskins was shot by whites who envied his lucrative liquor business, and the terrified family, fearing for their lives, fled twenty-five miles north to West Helena, also in Phillips County, where they hid in rented rooms for several weeks, afraid to venture into the streets. As Wright recounts the episode in *Black Boy,* it is clear that the vague white threat had now become an immediate actuality: "This was as close as white terror had ever come to me and my mind reeled. Why had we not fought back, I asked my mother, and the fear that was in her made her slap me into silence."[19]

In an effort to reorganize the shattered life of the family, Wright's mother and Aunt Maggie took the two boys to Jackson for a period of several months in 1917, but they were back in West Helena by the winter of 1918. Again in Arkansas Wright felt the pervasive white terror. Growing older, he began to work for a few extra pennies to supplement the impoverished family's income, Aunt Maggie having fled to the North and his mother often too ill to work. On one occasion he attempted to sell his dog in a white neighborhood, but fear and resentment caused him to back down from

18 *Black Boy,* pp. 20-21.
19 Ibid., p. 48.

a prospective buyer.[20] At this time racial tensions were increasing as the war was ending, and the effect on young Wright as he reached his tenth birthday was intense and permanent: "The hostility of the whites had become so deeply implanted in my mind and feelings that it had lost direct connection with the daily environment. . . . Tension would set in at the mere mention of whites. . . . It was as though I was continuously reacting to the threat of some natural force whose hostile behavior could not be predicted. I had never in my life been abused by whites, but I had already become as conditioned to their existence as though I had been the victim of a thousand lynchings."[21] If one is tempted to consider such feelings as merely the inflated product of the restlessly active imagination of a prepubescent boy, he should recall that in the first week of October 1919, only a short time after the Wrights left Phillips County to return to Richard's grandparents' home in Jackson, a "race riot" — more accurately, a small-scale effort by whites at genocide — took place in and around Elaine in which more than one hundred black men and "several white men" were killed.[22] If young Wright's fantasies of racial violence were in part subjective, they could hardly have been more grotesquely horrible than the all too objective reality of life in Mississippi, Tennessee, and Arkansas from which they sprang.

The twentieth-century Mecca of blacks in the lower Mississippi valley has always been Chicago. A common folk expression ran, " 'We'd rather be a lamppost in Chicago than the president of Dixie!' "[23] Even before the second decade of the century the migra-

[20] Ibid., pp. 60-62.

[21] Ibid., p. 65.

[22] *Arkansas: A Guide to the State,* American Guide Series (New York, 1941), p. 354. The conflict resulted from an attempt by black sharecroppers of the Elaine area to form a union. This episode may have contributed to the background of Wright's "Bright and Morning Star," though the setting of this story is near Memphis in the 1930s. In *Black Boy,* pp. 64-65, Wright relates his hearing, while he lived in West Helena, a story of a black woman who shot some of her husband's lynchers with a shotgun she had concealed in a winding-sheet. Wright used this story, with some modifications, as the conclusion of "Bright and Morning Star."

[23] Richard Wright, *12 Million Black Voices: A Folk History of the Negro in the United States* (New York, 1941), p. 88. Earlier, in his first novel (published posthumously), Wright had given a slightly different version: " '*Lawd, I'd ruther be a lamppost in Chicago than the President of Miss'sippi. . . .*' " *Lawd Today* (New York, 1963), p. 154.

tion had started, consisting chiefly of some 10,000 educated blacks, many of whom had held political office during Reconstruction, fleeing from the repressive measures instituted with the return of white supremacy. This group represented only a trickle compared to the flood that followed. Black workers poured into Chicago to meet the severe labor shortage brought about by the advent of World War I. Whereas some 10,000 migrants had come between 1890 and 1910, 50,000 arrived in the following decade, most of them after 1914. At only a slightly lower rate the flow of immigration continued in the twenties and thirties.[24] To consider the case of a single state, in 1890 only 1,363 blacks born in Mississippi were living in Illinois, but in 1930 the number had increased to 50,851, most of them in Chicago. The exodus from Mississippi to Chicago sometimes, as in Wright's case, was made in stages, with Memphis and St. Louis as midway stations. In 1930 these cities had, respectively, 35,400 and 30,600 black inhabitants born in Mississippi.[25]

After the foregoing discussion of social conditions pertaining to race in Mississippi, Tennessee, and Arkansas, it is hardly necessary to dwell upon the motives of the black migration to Chicago. They were essentially two: to escape racial discrimination in the South and to find economic opportunity in the North. The question remains, however, of how well Chicago met those expectations.

If not the promised land dreamed of by blacks in southern bondage, Chicago was a measurable, in some ways a dramatic, improvement over the Deep South, especially when Wright reached the city at the end of 1927. By this time the bitterness in race relations brought about by the race riot of 1919 and the strikebreaking activities of black workers in the stockyards in the early twenties had subsided in the economic boom that began in late 1924 and provided full employment for both races. Black political activity was not only

[24] St. Clair Drake and Horace R. Cayton, *Black Metropolis: A Study of Negro Life in a Northern City*, rev. and enl. ed. (New York, 1962), I, 53, 58, 76. See also Allan H. Spear, *Black Chicago: The Making of a Negro Ghetto, 1890-1920* (Chicago, 1967), especially chap. 7.

[25] Foreman, *Mississippi Population Trends*, pp. 113, 117, 120. It should be pointed out that the white emigration from Mississippi has also been great. The difference is directional. As Foreman shows, pp. 106-17, the black characteristically goes due north — to Chicago; the white goes due west — to Texas.

tolerated but also actively encouraged, and some political power had been achieved, as was dramatically demonstrated within a year after Wright's arrival in the city by the election of Oscar DePriest as the first black congressman from the North. In many sectors of public life de jure equality of the races had been attained, and in some sectors — public transportation, retail buying, access to sports events and theaters — a substantial degree of de facto equality prevailed.[26] In all these respects Chicago was in marked contrast to the Egypt from which the black migrants had fled.

But Chicago was not Canaan. Discrimination was severe in the crucial areas of housing and employment. For the most part, flats could be found only in the Black Belt on the South Side, a ghetto whose inevitable expansion under the pressure of the migration was contested by bombs and by less violent but more effective restrictive covenants. Much of the Black Belt, especially the area north and northwest of Washington Park, with which Wright was most familiar, consisted of appalling slums with all the usual indices of social and economic deprivation — high rates of juvenile delinquency and adult crime, illegitimate births, infant mortality, disease, and the like. Discrimination in employment was equally overt and equally damaging. Comprising 8 percent of the city's population in 1930, blacks held only 2 percent of the white-collar jobs, 9 percent of the manual-labor jobs, mostly unskilled, and 34 percent of service occupations.[27] However discriminatory, employment was at least readily available during Wright's first two years in Chicago. The effect of the Depression, however, was catastrophic: "In January of 1931, the Unemployment Census revealed that over half of the Negro employable women (58.5 per cent) and nearly half of the employable men (43.5) were without jobs."[28] Throughout the thirties about half of Chicago's black families were on relief.

In areas other than housing and employment, the color line in Chicago, if less clearly demarcated than in Mississippi, was no less real. Wright could marvel happily at the natural, casual quality of his relationship with white waitresses when he worked as dishwasher

[26] Drake and Cayton, *Black Metropolis*, I, 77, 342-43, 367-68, 99-108.
[27] Ibid., I, 178-79, 184-87; II, 604-5; I, 213-19.
[28] Ibid., I, 217-18.

in a North Side café,[29] but "social equality" in any meaningful sense was proscribed. De facto segregation prevailed in schools and in public recreational areas, particularly bathing beaches. In such "private" amusement enterprises as dance halls, skating rinks, and bowling alleys, the color line was absolute, as it was in churches and social clubs. Some restaurants, many bars, and most hotels discriminated against blacks.[30] To the recent southern immigrant to Chicago, the psychological tension the color line produced was greatly augmented by the element of uncertainty in its application:

> While working in Memphis I had stood aghast as Shorty had offered himself to be kicked by the white men; but now, while working in Chicago, I was learning that perhaps even a kick was better than uncertainty.... I had elected, in my fevered search for honorable adjustment to the American scene, not to submit and in doing so I had embraced the daily horror of anxiety, of tension, of eternal disquiet. I could now sympathize with — though I could never bring myself to approve — those tortured blacks who had given up and had gone to their white tormentors and had said: "Kick me, if that's all there is for me; kick me and let me feel at home, let me have peace!"[31]

Wright was to find neither peace nor an "honorable adjustment to the American scene" in New York, where he moved in 1937. Later Wright lived in Brooklyn and Greenwich Village, but his first home in New York was Harlem. As the Harlem correspondent for the *Daily Worker* and as a member of the staff of the Federal Writers' Project working on the Harlem sections of *New York Panorama* and the *New York City Guide,* Wright came to know intimately the condition of black people in New York both from close observation and from bitter personal experience.

In some ways life in New York and Harlem was better for Wright than life in Chicago and the Black Belt. For one thing, like the city

[29] Richard Wright, "Early Days in Chicago," *Cross-Section 1945,* ed. Edwin Seaver (New York, 1945), pp. 313-15. This essay, originally part of an autobiographical manuscript of which the first two-thirds was published as *Black Boy,* is reprinted, with minor changes, as "The Man Who Went to Chicago" in Wright's *Eight Men* (Cleveland, 1961), pp. 210-50.

[30] Drake and Cayton, *Black Metropolis,* I, 103-4, 106, 107-8.

[31] "Early Days in Chicago," pp. 308-9. Throughout this study, unspaced ellipses indicate Wright's punctuation, and spaced ellipses are mine.

of which it is a part, Harlem is a cosmopolitan place. In the late thirties, before the success of the movement toward nationalism in Africa, Harlem was an unofficial capital not only for black America but also for blacks throughout the world. The black population of Chicago when Wright left was almost entirely native-born, mostly from the middle South, but the more than 250,000 people in black Harlem in 1937 included, in addition to southern migrants mainly from the Atlantic coastal states, tens of thousands of British West Indians from Jamaica, Trinidad, Barbados, and the smaller islands, some two thousand Africans, and several thousand French-speaking immigrants and students from Haiti, Martinique, Guadeloupe, and French Guiana.[32] Adjoining and merging with black Harlem on the south and southwest, Spanish Harlem consisted of 100,000 Puerto Ricans, many of varying degrees of African descent, and smaller groups of Cubans, South Americans, and Mexicans.[33] Due south of black Harlem was Italian Harlem. In black Harlem itself lived small numbers of Chinese, East Indians, Japanese, and Filipinos.[34]

In addition to its cosmopolitan composition, Harlem was attractive as an intellectual center. The Harlem Renaissance of the middle and late twenties was now only a fading memory, but in 1937 Wright was collaborating with Dorothy West and Marian Minus on a literary quarterly, *New Challenge,* intended to serve as an outlet for black writing in the context of the social urgency of the time.[35] In politics Harlem was, encouragingly from Wright's point of view, growing increasingly more radical. The cause of the Scottsboro boys, with which the Communist party was closely involved, was receiving almost universal support in the community. The substantial Harlem vote in the thirties and early forties for such candidates as Mayor Fiorello La Guardia, State Assemblyman Oscar Garcia Rivera, Congressman Vito Marcantonio, and City Councilman Benjamin J. Davis, Jr., a black Communist, augured well.

But for all this, Harlem was still a black ghetto in America. Per-

[32] Roi Ottley, 'New World A-Coming' (Boston, 1943), pp. 44, 41, 49.

[33] [Richard Wright], "The Harlems," in Federal Writers' Project, New York City Guide (New York, 1939), p. 266.

[34] Ottley, 'New World A-Coming,' p. 53.

[35] Richard Wright, "Negro Writers Launch Literary Quarterly," Daily Worker, 8 June 1937, p. 7.

haps even more congested than the Black Belt of Chicago, it suffered from the same syndrome of disease, criminality, drug addiction, alcoholism, and infant mortality. Poverty was endemic among New York blacks: "Though today they account for only a little more than five percent of the city's population, Negroes comprise more than 20 percent of the total number of persons on relief rolls."[36] These conditions, resulting directly from the same kind of discrimination in housing and employment found in Chicago, had led to the eruption of Harlem in the riot of 1935, the first but not the last such outbreak in Harlem history. After the riot and the subsequent report of the Mayor's Commission on Conditions in Harlem, correctly identifying the cause as "resentments against racial discrimination and poverty in the midst of plenty,"[37] the conditions persisted, as Wright reported in such *Daily Worker* articles as "Negro, with 3-Week-Old Baby, Begs Food on Streets" (4 August 1937), "Harlem Women Hit Boost in Milk Price" (3 September 1937), "Insect-Ridden Medicine Given in Hospital" (4 September 1937), "Opening of Harlem Project Homes Shows How Slums Can Be Wiped Out in New York" (8 October 1937), "Ban on Negro Doctors Bared at City Probe" (14 December 1937), and "Gouging, Landlord Discrimination against Negroes Bared at Hearing" (15 December 1937).

Nor did Wright escape the humiliation of personal encounters with Jim Crow, for the insults a black man faced in New York outside of Harlem, against which James Baldwin was to utter his anguished protests twenty years later, were both more widespread and more severe during Wright's residence in the city. On his first trip to Manhattan in the spring of 1935 as a delegate to the first American Writers' Congress, he had difficulty finding lodgings, for hotels refused blacks, and white Communist ranks were not free of what was quaintly called "white chauvinism."[38] Even the acquisition of fame and money with the popular success of *Native Son* did not

[36] [Richard Wright], "Portrait of Harlem," in Federal Writers' Project, *New York Panorama* (New York, 1938), p. 139. In *'New World A-Coming,'* p. 156, Ottley cites "more than twenty-five per cent" on the relief rolls as blacks.

[37] Ottley, *'New World A-Coming,'* p. 153.

[38] Richard Wright, "I Tried to Be a Communist," *Atlantic Monthly,* CLXXIV (August 1944), 69-70. This essay was reprinted as Wright's contribution to *The God That Failed,* ed. Richard Crossman (New York, 1949).

insulate Wright from racial discrimination. Returning from a vacation in Mexico in 1940, he was separated from white passengers as the train crossed the Texas border, and three years later the experience was repeated as he traveled by train to Nashville for a speaking engagement at Fisk University.[39] He suffered from discrimination in Greenwich Village and when trying, unsuccessfully, to buy a house in New Hampshire.[40] Restaurants were a constant problem. One white acquaintance recalls the problem this way:

> As a sad sidelight I do remember that in those days I had my office along with those of Story Magazine on Fourth Avenue. Of course I had always looked forward to meeting Richard Wright having long admired him as an author and having been shaken to the core when I saw his NATIVE SON on the stage. Then when we finally met we always had terrible trouble finding a restaurant where we could go and not be rejected or molested. It always ended up being some Armenian place, I seem to recall, that he liked particularly and where we would retire to.[41]

When one considers the long road of racial suffering in America down which Richard Wright fled, from Mississippi to Arkansas to Memphis to Chicago to New York, and when one considers also his extreme sensitivity and self-consciousness, his emotional vulnerability, very little hyperbole seems to remain in the remark, summarizing his treatment in his own land, that he made to Carl Van Vechten not long before he left for Paris: "I never left my house to walk two blocks without being made to feel a Negro."[42]

Of the four handicaps young Wright faced, racial prejudice was undoubtedly the most difficult, but the other three — poverty, family disorganization, and poor education — were quite formid-

---

[39] Richard Wright, "How Jim Crow Feels," *Negro Digest,* V (January 1947), 44-53; Horace R. Cayton, "The Curtain," *Negro Digest,* XVIII (December 1968), 11-15.

[40] Ollie Harrington, "The Last Days of Richard Wright," *Ebony,* XVI (February 1961), 90. See also William Gardner Smith, "Black Boy in France," *Ebony,* VIII (July 1953), 36.

[41] Letter from Peter Witt to the author, 3 December 1964. For a detailed account of a discriminatory incident in a Brooklyn restaurant involving Wright, Horace R. Cayton, and Elmer Carter, see Constance Webb, *Richard Wright: A Biography* (New York, 1968), pp. 210-14.

[42] Interview with Carl Van Vechten, 2 April 1964.

able. In fact the four were interrelated, for the latter three were at least partially caused by his racial status. Thus the poverty of his childhood and youth resulted from discriminatory employment practices compounded by inadequate education, itself a result of the separate but unequal schools for blacks in Mississippi and Arkansas. The disruption of Wright's family was a typical, if extreme, example of a widespread social pattern related to racial prejudice, poverty, and ignorance among blacks. Wright's four handicaps intensified and reinforced each other in a cruel and frustrating manner.

During most of Wright's years in the South, he lived in a poverty so complete that hunger was normal and adequate nutrition exceptional. Again and again Wright's autobiography iterates this fact. His father's desertion of the family in Memphis in 1914 first brought to the five-year-old boy the persistent, debilitating pangs that were to remain with him for years: "... I would feel hunger nudging my ribs, twisting my empty guts until they ached. I would grow dizzy and my vision would dim. I became less active in my play, and for the first time in my life I had to pause and think of what was happening to me." The resentment toward the father typical of many American authors had more justifiable motivation in Wright's case than in some others: "As the days slid past the image of my father became associated with my pangs of hunger, and whenever I felt hunger I thought of him with a deep biological bitterness." Whites, as well as his father, became the object of the boy's animosity on this score, for he was often forced to eat scraps, if any were left, from the tables of white homes where his mother worked as a cook. Eventually the family's situation became so desperate that Wright and his brother were placed in an orphanage, where two skimpy meals were served each day. Later in the same year, 1916, the family moved to Elaine, Arkansas, to live with Aunt Maggie and Uncle Hoskins. For the first time in his short life, in the Hoskins house Wright had enough to eat. Indeed, he was so amazed at the abundance of food that he took bread from the table at night to ward off any future scarcity, until he finally became convinced that food would be available at each meal.[43]

Such largesse was too good to last. After the death of Uncle Hos-

43 *Black Boy,* pp. 13, 14, 17, 25, 44-45.

kins, the family was once again reduced to the verge of starvation, particularly after Aunt Maggie left. Wright's attempt to sell his pet dog was provoked by hunger. When his mother suffered a stroke in 1919, the family was forced to return to Jackson, where the boy subsisted for several years on two meals a day — "mush and gravy made from flour and lard" in the morning and "a plate of greens cooked with lard" in the afternoon. Only occasionally was he fortunate enough to obtain a job in a white home where he could have — or steal — decent food. After graduating from junior high school and taking a full-time job in 1925, he was able to eat somewhat better, but even then he skimped on food in order to save money to go to Chicago. In Memphis, for example, he was accustomed to "a pint of milk and two sweet rolls for breakfast, a hamburger and peanuts for lunch, and a can of beans . . . at night. . . ." At the age of fifteen Wright weighed less than one hundred pounds. The poverty he endured in his youth took many forms, but above all it meant physical hunger.[44]

Poverty also exposed young Wright to cold and clothed him in rags. The opening sentence of *Black Boy* presents him huddling over a fireplace warming himself while a chill wind blows outside. When no coal was in the house, he was forced to remain in bed during the day for warmth. While living in Arkansas he gathered stray pieces of coal from railroad tracks in the mornings for use as fuel. Clothing was an even more persistent problem. Aside from the shame they induced in the boy, his clothes were often too ragged to permit him to attend school.[45]

Hunger and physical exposure were the most brutally obvious consequences of the impoverishment of the Wright family, but the slum conditions to which it led, combined with segregation, were likewise corroding to the boy's spirit. Living conditions in Natchez and Memphis were bad enough, but after the father's desertion the family's situation deteriorated rapidly. The nadir was reached in

[44] Ibid., pp. 60-62, 90, 198, 141. A notion of the extent of this hunger and the depth of the impression it left may be gained from the fact that in addition to the passages already cited, Wright refers to hunger or to its alleviation on pp. 23, 24, 26, 29-30, 32, 39, 40-41, 53, 67, 68-69, 71, 73, 75, 77, 83, 87, 89, 98, 107, 110-11, 117, 119, 120, 125, 127, 128-29, 130, 131, 143, 144, 151, 175, 188-89, 192, 196, 202-4, 217, 218, 221.

[45] Ibid., pp. 3, 20, 73, 21, 71, 107, 125-26.

West Helena, where the family, now consisting of Wright, his brother, his mother, and Aunt Maggie,

> rented one half of a double corner house in front of which ran a stagnant ditch carrying sewage. The neighborhood swarmed with rats, cats, dogs, fortunetellers, cripples, blind men, whores, salesmen, rent collectors, and children. In front of our flat was a huge roundhouse where locomotives were cleaned and repaired. There was an eternal hissing of steam, the deep grunting of steel engines, and the tolling of bells. Smoke obscured the vision and cinders drifted into the house, into our beds, into our kitchen, into our food; and a tarlike smell was always in the air.

The other half of the house, as the nine-year-old boy soon learned by direct observation, was occupied by a prostitute who conducted her business there. When Aunt Maggie left to go north and his mother's illness forced her to stop working, the family moved, several times, to progressively cheaper quarters. His maternal grandparents' house in Jackson, in which Wright lived for most of the time from 1919 to 1925, was considerably better, but it became crowded in 1923 when Uncle Tom and his family moved in.[46]

Crime was another direct result of Wright's poverty. Black thievery was an accepted part of southern race relations,[47] but Wright himself had proudly held aloof from it until in 1925 the pressure of his need to escape became too great to permit him to wait the two years necessary to save the stake of one hundred dollars he had decided upon. Working as a bellboy in a Jackson hotel, he first engaged in bootlegging. Then he gained employment as a doorman in a black motion picture theater, where he became a party to swindling the owner. Finally he stole a gun from a neighbor's house, pawned it, and then stole cases of food from a black college to sell to restaurants.[48] With the money thus attained he was able to board a train for Memphis, the first lap of his journey in quest of a life richer — in all senses — than he had found in his nightmarish childhood.

[46] Ibid., pp. 52, 55-56, 73, 136.
[47] "So, pretending to conform to the laws of the whites, grinning, bowing, they let their fingers stick to what they could touch. And the whites seemed to like it." Ibid., p. 175.
[48] Ibid., pp. 176, 177-80.

Wright was to experience poverty again in Memphis and in the Chicago of the Depression, and his first years in New York were hardly affluent. Not until the success of *Native Son* in 1940 did he become financially secure. But he suffered most from poverty, as from his other afflictions, in the Deep South of his youth.

The extreme disorganization of Wright's family left an even more permanent impression on him than did its poverty. Common in lower-class black life, the phenomenon of family disorganization is brought about by poverty, slum conditions, discrimination in employment against the black male, the mother-centered tradition inherited from slavery, and migration. The effects of such familial instability on the personality of a black child are inevitably great. Juvenile delinquency is only the most obvious of these. An insecure home life also leaves the child more vulnerable to the assaults of a racist environment.[49]

The first stage in the disintegration of Wright's family was the father's desertion. After the family moved to Memphis, he became a stern and unattractive figure, offering little except blows and reprimands to his two sons. Retrospective bitterness caused Wright to exaggerate his father's defects, but their reality seems clear enough: "He was the lawgiver in our family and I never laughed in his presence. I used to lurk timidly in the kitchen doorway and watch his huge body sitting slumped at the table. I stared at him with awe as he gulped his beer from a tin bucket, as he ate long and heavily, sighed, belched, closed his eyes to nod on a stuffed belly. He was quite fat and his bloated stomach always lapped over his belt. He was always a stranger to me, always somehow alien and remote." This man's desertion caused little diminution of emotional warmth in the boy's life, for little was being contributed, but it did have marked immediate effects. As noted above, it brought physical hunger to the family. It also exposed the children more fully to their slum environment. When Wright's mother at last found employ-

[49] For a concise account of family disorganization and its effect on black personality, see Thomas F. Pettigrew, *A Profile of the Negro American* (Princeton, N.J., 1964), pp. 15-24. Professor Pettigrew has remarked to me that Wright's account in *Black Boy* is "a textbook case" of family disorganization among blacks.

ment as a cook, Wright, then five years old, and his younger brother were left alone during the day to shift for themselves. Wright amused himself by spying on a row of outdoor privies with exposed backs or by frequenting a neighborhood saloon, where he begged for pennies, learned an extensive vocabulary of obscenities, and began to cadge drinks. He became, at the age of six, a drunkard. Only with great difficulty was his precocious taste for whisky overcome.[50]

Wright's mother's legal efforts to force his father to provide support for the family were unavailing. In typical southern fashion, the Memphis court that heard this case was reluctant to take the domestic difficulties of a black family seriously. When Ella Wright subsequently became ill, her only recourse was to place her sons in a squalid orphanage, where young Wright was so miserable that he ran away. With the purpose of getting enough money to move to her sister's home in Arkansas, she then took the boy to appeal to his father. They found him with his mistress "sitting before a bright fire that blazed in a grate." The appeal for money was denied. Wright was long to remember the hellish vision of this night in 1916: "Many times in the years after that the image of my father and the strange woman, their faces lit by the dancing flames, would surge up in my imagination so vivid and strong that I felt I could reach out and touch it; I would stare at it, feeling that it possessed some vital meaning which always eluded me."[51] Wright was to see his father only once after that occasion. In 1940, returning from Mexico, the now famous writer stopped in Natchez, where his father had returned to resume sharecropping. The elder Wright no longer seemed formidable, but merely a worn and stolid peasant. The son could pity his father, but he could not bridge the gulf that separated them. There was no communion; the two were still strangers.[52]

Ella Wright and her two sons were finally able to move to Elaine, Arkansas, after a visit in Jackson. But the lynching of Uncle Hoskins again disrupted the family, as did Aunt Maggie's subsequent departure and the ensuing frequent changes of residence. But the cruelest blow was yet to come. In the spring or summer of 1919, Ella Wright, for many years in poor health, suffered a severe para-

[50] *Black Boy,* pp. 9, 14, 16-19.
[51] Ibid., pp. 29, 30.
[52] "How Jim Crow Feels," p. 49.

lytic stroke. For the rest of her life she alternated between slow, painful recovery and agonizing relapses. The example of her unmerited suffering was seared indelibly into her son's mind and became symbolic to him of the general human condition,

> gathering to itself all the poverty, the ignorance, the helplessness; the painful, baffling, hunger-ridden days and hours; the restless moving, the futile seeking, the uncertainty, the fear, the dread; the meaningless pain and the endless suffering. Her life set the emotional tone of my life. . . . A somberness of spirit that I was never to lose settled over me . . . a somberness that was to make me stand apart and look upon excessive joy with suspicion, that was to make me self-conscious, that was to make me keep forever on the move, as though to escape a nameless fate seeking to overtake me.[53]

After their mother's stroke, the responsibility for her sons fell upon her relatives. His younger brother had the good fortune to be sent to Detroit to live with Aunt Maggie, but Wright himself was sent to live with Uncle Clark and Aunt Jody Wilson in Greenwood, Mississippi. After a time he became frightened and unhappy and was returned to Jackson. Except for a trip to Clarksdale, Mississippi, to accompany his mother while she had an operation,[54] Wright was to live in his grandparents' Jackson home for the following six years, from early 1920 to late 1925.

His position in the household was painful. Persecuted by members of the family for his independent spirit and his inability to accept the rigorous Seventh-Day Adventist family faith, he was often made to feel an unwanted outsider. And he was not slow to return the family's hostility, especially that of Granny, Aunt Addie, and Uncle Tom. So intense was the conflict between the latter two and Wright that the boy was forced to defend himself from their beatings by means of a knife and razor blades. Severe arguments were commonplace in the household, and physical violence was frequent. Wright's characteristic position was that of the pariah; his Uncle Tom went so far as to forbid his children to associate with their cousin living under the same roof.[55]

[53] *Black Boy*, pp. 74, 87.
[54] Ibid., pp. 77, 85, 86.
[55] Ibid., pp. 93-95, 139-40, 151.

After Wright's expatriation, critics were quick to utter the familiar warnings about the dangers of a writer's cutting himself off from his roots.[56] The truth is that Wright never remained in one place long enough to put down any roots. *Black Boy* records nineteen changes of residence in his first nineteen years. Possibly there were still others. Wright's father had deserted and humiliated the family while the boy was quite young. His mother, to whom he was more closely attached than to anyone else, was forced to neglect him, first because of financial exigencies and then because of a catastrophic illness. The generally unsympathetic relatives among whom he lived were eager to administer punishment and admonitions, but slow to offer understanding or companionship. The stability and warmth of a united family were completely absent from Wright's childhood and youth.

The fourth handicap imposed on young Wright by his environment was a shamefully inadequate opportunity for education. In a very direct way this handicap was a function of each of his other handicaps — racial status, poverty, and family disorganization. That a boy whose formal education ceased at graduation from the ninth grade of a Mississippi public school for blacks should become the author of *The Outsider,* the friend of Gunnar Myrdal and Jean-Paul Sartre, is a miracle of the human will.

The educational disadvantages for southern blacks in general and those of Mississippi in particular are too familiar to require extensive citation here. A few statistics from Wright's final school year should suffice. At that time the school term for blacks in Mississippi consisted of 112 days, compared to 140 days for whites. The average value of public school property per black child of school age was $6.00, compared to $32.57 per white child. The average annual educational expenditure per black child of school age was $5.62,

[56] See, for example, Nelson Algren, *Chicago: City on the Make* (Garden City, N.Y., 1951), pp. 63-64. Saunders Redding develops the thesis fully in "The Alien Land of Richard Wright," *Soon, One Morning: New Writing by American Negroes, 1940-1962,* ed. Herbert Hill (New York, 1963), pp. 50-59. The question is debated by a number of black writers in Hoyt W. Fuller, "A Survey: Black Writers' Views on Literary Lions and Values," *Negro Digest,* XVII (January 1968), 10-48, 81-89.

compared to $25.95 per white child.[57] Until 1925 there was no black high school in Jackson, the state's capital and largest city.[58] Howard Institute in Memphis, where Wright sporadically attended the first grade in 1916, and the black schools of Phillips County, Arkansas, could hardly have been much better. Of these Wright remembered chiefly the obscenities that he learned from the older boys and the painfully acute self-consciousness that seized and paralyzed him when called upon to recite.[59]

Quite aside from discrimination against blacks in educational opportunity, Wright suffered the additional handicap of extreme poverty. Because his mother was unable to buy him the necessary clothing and books, his schooling was frequently interrupted. Even when he was able to attend, hunger often distracted his attention. When he began working mornings and evenings, he had difficulty staying awake in the classroom. Together with his unsettled family life, the boy's poverty prevented his completing one full, uninterrupted year of school until he reached the age of twelve.[60] Young Wright's education was greatly disrupted by the disorganization of his family. The frequent moves prevented any sustained contact with one school until he was able to begin more or less regular attendance in Jackson in 1921. His mother's illness elicited his mental preoccupation and at times required his physical presence.[61]

Moreover, his family was not only unstable but also narrow in its attitude toward education. His father, totally illiterate, "had never been inside a school."[62] His mother's family valued education, especially as a means of achieving social status, but as a fanatical Seventh-Day Adventist, his semiliterate grandmother, who dominated the Jackson household, hated works of fiction. In the summer of

[57] Monroe N. Work, ed., *Negro Year Book* (Tuskegee, 1925), pp. 293, 295.

[58] "Black Boy in Brooklyn," *Ebony*, I (November 1945), 27. See also Charles H. Wilson, *Education for Negroes in Mississippi since 1910* (Boston, 1947), p. 120. In its chaotic organization and faulty grammar this book is itself a sad witness to the deficiencies of the education it treats and exemplifies. Formerly head of the department of social sciences at Alcorn Agricultural and Mechanical College, the author at the time he wrote the book was principal of the Smith-Robinson School in Jackson, which Wright attended.

[59] *Black Boy*, pp. 21-22, 66-67.

[60] Ibid., pp. 21, 65-66, 110-11, 131, 107.

[61] Ibid., p. 24.

[62] Embree, *13 against the Odds*, p. 26.

1916, when Wright was visiting Jackson after leaving Memphis and before going to Arkansas, a young schoolteacher boarded in his grandmother's house. Intrigued by her constant reading, he questioned her about it. Reluctantly she spoke to the boy about novels and began to tell him the story of Bluebeard. The effect on the novelist-to-be was immensely exhilarating: "The tale made the world around me be, throb, live. As she spoke, reality changed, the look of things altered, and the world became peopled with magical presences. My sense of life deepened and the feel of things was different, somehow. . . . My imagination blazed. The sensations the story aroused in me were never to leave me." The narrative was abruptly halted by the appearance of Granny, who shouted, " 'I want none of that Devil stuff in my house!' " The schoolteacher was forced to look for new lodgings, and Wright was threatened with damnation for his interest in stories. His grandmother burned the "worldly" books that the boy was to bring into her house when he was older.[63]

Some of the other members of the Jackson household were also less than helpful in encouraging his literary inclinations. Wright's first full year of schooling was spent in a crowded Seventh-Day Adventist school under the instruction of Aunt Addie, who was teaching for the first time. Because of the inadequacy of the school and the violent antagonism between the boy and his aunt, the year was a total loss. When Wright published his first story, "The Voodoo of Hell's Half-Acre," in the *Southern Register,* a black newspaper in Jackson, his grandmother pronounced it "the Devil's work," Aunt Addie deemed the use of the word *hell* sinful, and Uncle Tom ridiculed the piece.[64] Even his mother, who had taught occasionally in black country schools in the Natchez area in Wright's early childhood[65] and had instructed him in reading before he began school, reacted to her son's literary effort by advising him to be more deferential to white opinion: " 'You're growing up now and you won't be able to get jobs if you let people think that you're

[63] *Black Boy,* pp. 34, 35, 40, 112-13.

[64] Ibid., pp. 96, 147.

[65] The fullest account of Ella Wright is in Webb, *Richard Wright,* especially pp. 16-18. See also "How Jim Crow Feels," p. 49, and Embree, *13 against the Odds,* p. 26.

weak-minded. Suppose the superintendent of schools would ask you to teach here in Jackson, and he found out that you had been writing stories?' "[66]

Outside the family the boy's environment was mostly indifferent to intellectual curiosity or a literary bent. His first effort at fiction was a melancholy story about an Indian girl who commits suicide. Afraid to show it to his relatives, he read it to a neighbor. The blank incomprehension with which it was received gave him a strange sort of satisfaction, for it signified an aspect of his apartness in which he could take some pride rather than undergo torment: "My environment contained nothing more alien than writing or the desire to express one's self in writing. But I never forgot the look of astonishment and bewilderment on the young woman's face when I had finished reading and glanced at her. Her inability to grasp what I had done or was trying to do somehow gratified me." During his first nineteen years his literary interests were generally ignored, suppressed, or ridiculed, with the notable exceptions of the teacher who told him the story of Bluebeard and the editor of the *Southern Register* who accepted his story for publication. In school "the literature of the nation or the Negro had never been mentioned." Before his discovery of Mencken in 1927, Wright's reading consisted of such pulp fiction as Zane Grey, *Flynn's Detective Weekly,* the *Argosy All-Story Magazine,* Horatio Alger, and the Get-Rich-Quick Wallingford series.[67] Even for such a bright and inquisitive boy as Richard Wright, these were the limits of literary taste possible in the black neighborhoods of Jackson, Mississippi, in the twenties.

What were the effects on Wright's personality of the racial discrimination, poverty, family disorganization, and faulty education of his formative years? Such lacerating afflictions obviously cannot leave a sensitive spirit unscarred.

In a real sense an answer to this question can be reached only at the end of this study, so pervasive were the effects of his early ex-

---

[66] *Black Boy,* pp. 20, 147.

[67] Ibid., pp. 105-6, 146, 112, 116, 147-48. See also Richard Wright, "Alger Revisited, or My Stars! Did We Read That Stuff?" *PM,* 16 September 1945, magazine section, p. 13.

perience on his later life and work. Certainly any brief answer runs the risk of glibness, but two chief effects may be mentioned here — fear and alienation.

Fear characterized Wright's relations with virtually all his relatives. His earliest memories were of terror. After he set a fire at the age of four that burned down his house, a traumatic punishment was administered:

> I was lashed so hard and long that I lost consciousness. . . . I was lost in a fog of fear. . . . Whenever I tried to sleep I would see huge wobbly white bags, like the full udders of cows, suspended from the ceiling above me. Later, as I grew worse, I could see the bags in the daytime with my eyes open and I was gripped by the fear that they were going to fall and drench me with some horrible liquid. . . . Time finally bore me away from the dangerous bags and I got well. But for a long time I was chastened whenever I remembered that my mother had come close to killing me.

The possibilities of Freudian interpretation are tempting, but the important point here is that this beating came from his mother, the member of his family to whom he felt closest. His father, as has been noted, was an awesome figure to the young boy. During his Jackson years he was beaten by Granny and Aunt Addie. He was able to stave off a thrashing by Uncle Tom only by threatening to slash him with razor blades. Even an attempted joke could have terrific consequences, as when Uncle Hoskins drove his buggy into the Mississippi River, telling the appalled boy that he intended to have his horse drink in the middle of the river. While living in Greenwood, Mississippi, with his Uncle Clark and Aunt Jody, Wright was so badly frightened when he learned that the room he slept in had been previously occupied by a boy of the same age who died that he begged to be sent back to Jackson.[68]

Even more scarifying than the fear of his relatives and the danger of the black ghettos in which he lived was the overwhelming fear of the white world outside. Some of the conditions of racial discrimination that evoked this fear have been described, and some of

[68] *Black Boy*, pp. 6, 45-47, 81-83. Constance Webb claims that the incident concerning Wright and Uncle Hoskins did not actually happen, but was based on a somewhat similar story involving Ralph Ellison. See her *Richard Wright*, p. 409.

Wright's reactions have been indicated. An additional instance or two may be cited here to illustrate the impact of fear of whites upon his early life.

While living in Arkansas, Wright once became involved in a gang fight against white boys with cinders and broken bottles used as projectiles. During the melee he was struck behind the ear with a broken bottle, causing a deep cut. Seeking sympathy from his mother when she returned home from work at the end of the day, he was instead stripped and beaten with a barrel stave until his temperature reached 102 degrees: "She would smack my rump with the stave, and, while the skin was still smarting, impart to me gems of Jim Crow wisdom. . . . I was never, never, under any conditions, to fight *white* folks again. And they were absolutely right in clouting me with the broken milk bottle. . . . She finished by telling me that I ought to be thankful to God as long as I lived that they didn't kill me." His reaction was similar to that earlier one after the beating following his setting the house afire. The nightmarish vision returned, but now the "white bags" had become "white faces": "All that night I was delirious and could not sleep. Each time I closed my eyes I saw monstrous white faces suspended from the ceiling, leering at me."[69] A decade later, in Memphis, his emotional life was still concentrated on this pervasive feeling of fear, now even more intense: "My days and nights were one long, quiet, continuously contained drama of terror, tension, and anxiety."[70]

Without attempting psychoanalysis, one may speculate that the fear Wright experienced in his childhood and youth, brought about both by the brutality of his family and by racial oppression, may account for the extreme self-consciousness to which he testifies frequently in *Black Boy*. It may also be at the root of the reserve he often demonstrated in his personal relations after reaching maturity.

Closely related to this fear was a deep and abiding sense of alienation — from other blacks, from whites, and from society in general.

[69] Richard Wright, "The Ethics of Living Jim Crow," *American Stuff* (New York, 1937), pp. 40, 41.

[70] *Black Boy*, p. 222. Drawing heavily upon Wright's experience, Horace R. Cayton presents a suggestive discussion of fear among blacks inspired by white oppression in "A Psychological Approach to Race Relations," *Présence Africaine*, no. 3 (March-April 1948), pp. 418-31, and no. 4 (n.d.), pp. 549-63.

So thoroughgoing was his isolation, so lasting were the effects of his almost homeless childhood, so persistent was his sense of apartness, that he made his condition a way of life; he embraced the role of the outsider. Rather desperately protesting his allegiance to a concept of nonallegiance, he wrote in 1957:

> I'm a rootless man, but I'm neither psychologically distraught nor in any wise particularly perturbed because of it. Personally, I do not hanker after, and seem not to need, as many emotional attachments, sustaining roots, or idealistic allegiances as most people. I declare unabashedly that I like and even cherish the state of abandonment, of aloneness; it does not bother me; indeed, to me it seems the natural, inevitable condition of man, and I welcome it. I can make myself at home almost anywhere on this earth and can, if I've a mind to and when I'm attracted to a landscape or a mood of life, easily sink myself into the most alien and widely differing environments. I must confess that this is no personal achievement of mine; this attitude was never striven for.... I've been shaped to this mental stance by the kind of experiences that I have fallen heir to.[71]

As a child he lived in black communities, but he was hardly a real part of them any more than he was a functioning member of a family. Each new school he attended and each new neighborhood he moved to presented a new problem of adjustment, solved often with his fists. In Jackson his grandmother's fanatic religiosity set the family apart from the general black community. Pork, veal, catfish, and baking powder were excluded from the household diet. Saturday was observed as the Sabbath, and for several years he was not permitted to work on this day. As a result he was unable to earn money to buy clothes presentable enough to reduce his self-consciousness in school. Nor did his skeptical spirit and varied past enable him to find a niche in the small group of Seventh-Day Adventists that claimed the fervid loyalty of Granny and Aunt Addie. When his mother began taking him to a Methodist church and thus into the mainstream of black southern life, it was too late to develop a valid affiliation: "I had been kept out of their world too long ever to be able to become a real part of it."[72] In 1939 he wrote to Joe C.

[71] *White Man, Listen!* (Garden City, N.Y., 1957), p. 17.
[72] *Black Boy*, pp. 90, 132.

Brown, an old boyhood friend teaching in Jackson. "How do you find Jackson?" he asked. "I have been wanting to get down into that section of the country. . . ." In 1945, twenty years after he left Mississippi, he asked Brown, "Just what in the name of God do they [young blacks] think about from morning to night down there?"[73] So estranged did he become from black life in the South that his evaluation of it acquired a harshness in which there reverberated a painful note of longing for an emotional richness that had been denied him:

> . . . I used to mull over the strange absence of real kindness in Negroes, how unstable was our tenderness, how lacking in genuine passion we were, how void of great hope, how timid our joy, how bare our traditions, how hollow our memories, how lacking we were in those intangible sentiments that bind man to man, and how shallow was even our despair. After I had learned other ways of life I used to brood upon the unconscious irony of those who felt that Negroes led so passional an existence! I saw that what had been taken for our emotional strength was our negative confusions, our flights, our fears, our frenzy under pressure.[74]

Alienated from blacks by the individual circumstances of his early years, he was alienated from whites during the same period by the rigid caste system of the South. Some of the fervor with which Wright attached himself to the Communist party was owing to the warmth of interracial fellowship — comradeship — that it offered. During the middle and late thirties the party seemed to offer him the emotional warmth and security of the home that he had not known.

But the party, too, failed him. Perhaps the habit of isolation had become too deeply ingrained for even so cohesive a faith to overcome it fully. In any case, he made his alienation a virtue; he embraced it by rejecting, for himself, both Communism and anti-Communism. It was no accident that Sartre and de Beauvoir became his friends and that he wrote the patently existential novel *The Outsider;* all his prior life and experience had prepared him to

[73] Richard Wright, *Letters to Joe C. Brown,* ed. Thomas Knipp (Kent, Ohio, 1968), pp. 8, 13.
[74] *Black Boy,* p. 33.

sympathize with the ideas promulgated by this postwar philosophy of man's terrible independence, existential agony, and social isolation. During his last years he became deeply interested in the upsurge of anticolonialism among the dark peoples of Africa and Asia, to which he was sympathetic by reason of racial affinity and of historical and social thought. But no real identification was possible, as he learned from his trips to the Gold Coast and Indonesia. The pragmatic spirit of the West was too intrinsic a part of his mental equipment for him to respond to what he considered the irrational dominance of religion in the Eastern mind. Alienated from the West by the searing experiences of his youth, from the Communist world by painfully acquired conviction, and from the Asian-African nations by a cultural gulf, he was indeed an outsider. The process that had begun in the sharecropper's shack in Mississippi and the orphanage in Memphis had become alienation on a global scale.

Though exceptional in the severity of their operation, the fear and alienation that characterize the life of Richard Wright are not untypical of the plight of the twentieth-century intellectual. Indeed, his case may be viewed as a radical example of the sense of dislocation and isolation, the terror, the violence, the quest for value through shifting ideologies, the restlessness, and the emotional deprivation so often experienced and expressed by modern writers. More than that, one may even venture to suggest that the history of the last half-century reveals that Wright is a radical example of the situation not only of the contemporary writer, but indeed of contemporary man.

It should not be thought, however, that Wright was morose and embittered in his adult personal relations. On the contrary, he seems deliberately to have compensated for the psychological damage suffered from fear and alienation by cultivating a pleasant, if somewhat distant, personality. The testimony of his friends and acquaintances clearly supports this point.[75] Both blacks and whites enjoyed his company but usually found him somewhat reserved. It

[75] This assertion is based on interviews with Horace R. Cayton, Ira DeA. Reid, and Carl Van Vechten, and letters from Samuel Allen, Gwendolyn Brooks, Frank Marshall Davis, and Langston Hughes.

appears that the mature Wright coped with the fearful isolation of his early life by asserting his kindness and amiability, but this effort could not entirely overcome the psychological residue left by fear and alienation — the intensity, seriousness, self-consciousness, shyness, and reserve remarked by so many of his friends.

More important, of course, are the effects of fear and alienation upon his work — the literary uses to which he put them. All that follows in this study attempts to trace these effects, for they are thematically central to his early fiction. Such Wright protagonists as Jake Jackson, Big Boy, and Bigger Thomas are men driven by fear of a hostile environment. In this respect they mirror the experience of their creator. To no American author does Ernest Hemingway's maxim apply more truthfully than to Richard Wright: "Writers are forged in injustice as a sword is forged. . . ."[76]

[76] Quoted, in a somewhat different connection, by Robert A. Bone, *The Negro Novel in America* (New Haven, 1958), p. 1.

# A Literary Apprenticeship

# TWO

The question remains: How did Richard Wright the writer and intellectual emerge from the fearful and alienated youth described in *Black Boy?* What were the countervailing forces that permitted him not only to survive but also to achieve literary distinction, turning the materials of his suffering into the stuff of his art? For one thing, *Black Boy* is a portrait of the artist as a young man that conceals as well as reveals the real self and experience of its author. The literal recording of fact often gives way to the imaginative re-creation of feeling. To convey his sense of what it was like to grow up as a black boy in the South, to impart to the white reader the full horror of the racist assault on the human personality, Wright found it artistically expedient to deemphasize the very elements that made for survival — both his individual resources, to some degree, and, to a larger extent, his human ties.

Wright was a brilliant child. If he was precocious in learning to fight, drink, and curse, he was also precocious in learning to read. Too poor to begin school at the usual age, he learned to count to one hundred in a single afternoon and learned to read by looking at other children's school books and by quizzing his mother. Despite his irregular school attendance and his difficulties in making social adjustments, he found his studies easy. Leaving his aunt's tutelage in the Seventh-Day Adventist school, he entered the Jim Hill School in Jackson in September of 1921. As on other occasions, he had to win the acceptance of his schoolmates by fighting, but he found life in a public school invigorating after the stifling atmosphere of religious fanaticism: "I knew that my life was revolving about a world that I had to encounter and fight when I grew up. Suddenly the future loomed tangibly for me, as tangible as a future can loom for a black boy in Mississippi." Assigned to the fifth grade because of his age, he immersed himself in his studies and within two weeks had received promotion to the sixth grade, despite his spotty prior preparation. He even began to dream of a career in medical research.[1]

His success continued the following year when he entered the seventh grade, changing from Jim Hill to the Smith-Robinson School.[2] In his last school year, 1924-25, his grades were so high that he was given the honor of part-time supervision of his class. As the school year ended, Wright was selected valedictorian of his class, but the assistant principal presented him with a speech carefully prepared so as not to offend the white school officials who would be present at the graduation exercises. Wright refused this prepared speech and insisted on delivering his own, and neither the blandishments of the assistant principal in dangling before his eyes a teaching job, nor the officious urgings of his schoolmates, nor the promptings of his Uncle Tom could sway him from this position. He was determined not to be an Uncle Tom in either the specific or the generic sense. Borrowing money from Mrs. Bibbs, his white employer, to make a down payment on a suit — much against his will he had been wearing short pants, the last boy in his class to do so — he delivered his own speech on the night of 20 May 1925 and graduated from the Smith-Robinson School — tense, defiant, estranged from his black world and fearful of the white world he was about to encounter, but taking a grim satisfaction in his own integrity.[3]

There can be no doubt of the inadequacy of the education Wright received at Jim Hill and Smith-Robinson. His native ability quickly

[1] *Black Boy*, pp. 19-20, 107, 110, 109.
[2] Wright himself does not mention changing schools, but when the W. H. Lanier High School was constructed in 1925, the seventh, eighth, and ninth grades were transferred to it from Smith-Robinson. Jim Hill seems to have been strictly an elementary school. See Wilson, *Education for Negroes in Mississippi since 1910*, p. 120.
[3] *Black Boy*, pp. 152-56.

outstripped the opportunities offered by the curriculum, and boredom was the inevitable result. "I sat in classes, bored, wondering, dreaming," he writes in *Black Boy* of his eighth-grade year, and he repeats the complaint about the ninth grade. All the same, one surmises that in *Black Boy* Wright somewhat exaggerates the deficiencies of his education in Jackson. Edwin R. Embree reports a less unfavorable estimate Wright made in the early forties:

> He remembers the Smith-Robinson School with some gratitude. The teachers tried their best to pump learning into the pupils. "They realized," Wright says, "that this was all the schooling the colored kids of Jackson were likely to get. So they gave all they had." He remembers having algebra for two years, United States history, civics, even a little botany and physiology. He learned to rattle off the names of all the bones in the body. "But I didn't learn anything worth knowing," he says. "I didn't even learn how to read with any skill, certainly not with any pleasure or understanding."[4]

But Wright's final comment to Embree seems to protest too much. Though he perhaps owed little to the schools he attended for his interest in reading, the interest was undeniably intense. For young Wright, literature was a transcendent experience. From the restrictive and oppressive atmosphere of his actual life, he turned avidly to the imaginative and emotional liberation that reading could bring. As has been noted, his response to his first encounter with fiction, the story of Bluebeard narrated to him by his grandmother's boarder, was strong, and the fanatical opposition of his Grandmother Wilson had no effect on the boy's awakened interest: "I hungered for the sharp, frightening, breath-taking, almost painful excitement that the story had given me, and I vowed that as soon as I was old enough I would buy all the novels there were and read them to feed that thirst for violence that was in me, for intrigue, for plotting, for secrecy, for bloody murders. . . . Ella's whispered story of deception and murder had been the first experience in my life that had elicited from me a total emotional response. . . . I had tasted what to me was life, and I would have more of it, somehow,

[4] Ibid., pp. 144, 152; Embree, *13 against the Odds*, p. 27.

someway."[5] He made a similar response years later to his first serious literary experience, the reading of Mencken's essays. Perhaps the significant fact about Wright's early reading is not that it consisted of subliterary pulp fiction by such writers as Zane Grey and Horatio Alger, but that any reading at all provided an emotional release from the pain of his life.

Reading constituted an escape from reality, but writing could give a kind of creative mastery over reality. At the age of twelve Wright began to write verses for hymns and then the melancholy tale about an Indian girl who commits suicide. It contained "no plot, no action, nothing save atmosphere and longing and death," but the creative act brought its own valuable psychological reward. By the time he was fourteen, he hoped to become a writer. Of all his youthful conflicts with whites, one of the most humiliating occurred when his employer attacked his literary ambition:

> "You'll never be a writer," she said. "Who on earth put such ideas into your nigger head?"
>
> "Nobody," I said.
>
> "I didn't think anybody ever would," she declared indignantly.
>
> As I walked around her house to the street, I knew that I would not go back. The woman had assaulted my ego; she had assumed that she knew my place in life, what I felt, what I ought to be, and I resented it with all my heart. Perhaps she was right; perhaps I would never be a writer; but I did not want her to say so.

A year later, seeking relief from boredom and idleness, he wrote, in three days, "The Voodoo of Hell's Half-Acre" and submitted it for publication to the *Southern Register,* a black newspaper in Jackson. The editor encouraged him and printed the story in three installments. Disappointed that he was not paid, Wright at least had the satisfaction of seeing his work in print, however much his puzzled family and friends disapproved of his literary efforts.[6] The pleasures of authorship as well as the delights of reading had become for Wright a tactic for survival.

Further help was given by the sustaining love of his mother and the close friendship of several schoolmates. Young Wright undoubt-

---

[5] *Black Boy,* pp. 35-36.
[6] Ibid., pp. 105, 129, 144-46.

edly felt isolated and alienated, though again not as much as the reader of *Black Boy* is led to believe. Like that of many other American writers, the psychological pattern of Wright's childhood was clearly Oedipal. Chastisements from his mother were doubly painful because of the source, separations from her were agonizing, and her illness became for him the symbol of all human suffering. Under the difficult circumstances of their lives, Ella Wright did her best for her son. Even after her devastating illness, she often attempted to defend her son against the hostility of her mother and her sister Addie. Most important for his subsequent literary career, Wright's mother, herself a somewhat dreamy woman according to Constance Webb,[7] encouraged Richard's response to the imaginative. It seems a strange coincidence that the narrator of the Bluebeard story, "a colored schoolteacher . . . a young woman with so remote and dreamy and silent a manner that I was as much afraid of her as I was attracted to her,"[8] has the personal characteristics and the profession as well as the name, Ella, of Wright's mother. There may indeed have been such a schoolteacher boarding in the Wilson house in Jackson, but no other boarders outside the family are mentioned in *Black Boy*. It is at least possible that this Ella is actually Ella Wright. In any case, Wright's inscription to *Native Son* reveals directly the extent of his mother's influence on him, the strength of his attachment to her, and the connection between these and his emergence as a writer: "To My Mother who, when I was a child at her knee, taught me to revere the fanciful and the imaginative."

It is with regard to his friends that Wright's fictive shaping of autobiographical fact in *Black Boy* is most striking. In order to stress his isolation, Wright underplays the role in his life of friendships with his peers. As the biographical investigations of Constance Webb and Thomas Knipp have recently shown, Wright had several close friends in Jackson with whom he kept in touch for years afterward. As the leader of the "Dick Wright Klan" — "an exclusive club . . . of boys from middle-class families who had a certain status in the community but very little money"[9] — Wright seems more

[7] *Richard Wright,* p. 16.
[8] *Black Boy,* p. 34.
[9] Webb, *Richard Wright,* p. 54.

a black Tom Sawyer than a black Huck Finn. This group, consisting of Wright, Joe C. Brown, Richard "Squilla" Jordan, Lewis
Anderson, Perry "Conkey" Booker, and Frank Sims, played boyish
pranks, misbehaved in school, and swam in a creek not far from the
Wilson house. What Wright called "a somberness of spirit" that
made him "stand apart and look upon excessive joy with suspicion"
did not preclude such activities. The youthful masculine camaraderie that so often recurs in Wright's fiction — *Lawd Today,* "Big
Boy Leaves Home," *Native Son, The Outsider, The Long Dream*
— has its autobiographical origin in the "Dick Wright Klan."

Whether Wright discussed his literary ambitions with his friends
is unclear. Constance Webb follows the account in *Black Boy* in
denying that he did, but Wright's later correspondence with
Brown,[10] who is himself an unpublished author, is so full of literary
talk as to cast some doubt on the matter. But his friendships clearly
did provide him with literary material as well as personal satisfaction. That life for blacks in Mississippi during the twenties was hell
is attested by the fact that most of Wright's friends sooner or later
followed him in his flight north. That they also followed him in developing a capacity to endure and even prevail is attested by their
success in later life.[11]

When Wright boarded the Jim Crow car of a Memphis-bound
train on a Saturday night in November 1925 to make "the first lap
of a journey to a land where [he] could live with a little less fear,"[12]
he took with him a character molded not only by racism, poverty,
a fragmented family, and a poor education, but also by the love of
his mother and other female relatives,[13] the friendship of numerous
other black boys, and a quick mind enlivened by a fertile imagina-

---

[10] *Letters to Joe C. Brown,* ed. Thomas Knipp.

[11] Joe C. Brown became a teacher in Mississippi and then a state civil ser-
vant in Illinois. C. T. Robinson graduated from the Howard University Law
School and practiced in Akron and Chicago. Essie Lee Ward taught school in
Chicago. "Squilla" Jordan and Arthur Leaner also migrated to Chicago, the
former working as a railroad cook and the latter earning great wealth as a
disc jockey and entrepreneur. Ibid., pp. 6, 5, 7, 10, 14, 15.

[12] *Black Boy,* p. 181.

[13] Michel Fabre asserts that Wright's cousin Velma "partly ignored her
father's advice [not to speak to Wright] and she was rather close to [him]."
Letter to the author, 6 February 1968.

tion. In the months that followed, he continued his education, both in what he ironically called "The Ethics of Living Jim Crow" and in the possibilities of literature.

As for racism, he learned the topics strictly forbidden in interracial conversations: "American white women; the Ku Klux Klan; France, and how Negro soldiers fared while there; Frenchwomen; Jack Johnson; the entire northern part of the United States; the Civil War; Abraham Lincoln; U. S. Grant; General Sherman; Catholics; the Pope; Jews; the Republican party; slavery; social equality; Communism; Socialism; the 13th, 14th, and 15th Amendments to the Constitution; or any topic calling for positive knowledge or manly self-assertion on the part of the Negro." He learned also of the depths of abasement to which blacks could plunge while accommodating themselves to the mores of the South. While Wright and a white man were riding one day in an elevator in the building where they both worked, Shorty, the corpulent black elevator operator, asked the white man for money to buy lunch. Although intelligent and widely read, Shorty played the traditional role of an oafish Sambo before whites. When the white man hesitated to comply with Shorty's request, Shorty clownishly offered to be kicked in exchange for the money. Gladly accepting the offer, the white man dropped a coin to the floor, and as Shorty stooped to retrieve it, "bared his teeth and swung his foot into Shorty's rump with all the strength of his body." The white man's conversation with Shorty had been sprinkled with gross racial insults. Appalled and disgusted by this obscene ritual, Wright reproached Shorty. " 'Listen, nigger,' he said to [Wright], 'my ass is tough and quarters is scarce.' "[14]

In the summer of 1926 Wright himself was maneuvered into a position of pandering to the sadistic ego of the white man. Mr. Olin, Wright's foreman at the optical company, approached him one day with the story that Harrison, a black of Wright's age who worked at another optical company nearby, held a grudge against Wright that he planned to satisfy by using a knife. Olin had told the same story of Wright to Harrison, gleefully awaiting the mayhem expected to ensue. Nervously and distrustfully meeting, Wright and Harrison each disavowed hostility and intent to harm the other.

[14] *Black Boy*, pp. 202, 199, 200.

Disappointed that blood had not been spilled, Olin and the other white men involved in the game finally decided to arrange a boxing match between the two with a purse of five dollars for each combatant. Urged on by Harrison as well as by the whites, Wright reluctantly agreed. Afterward, he realized his own abasement: "I felt that I had done something unclean, something for which I could never properly atone."[15]

He had more on his mind at this time, however, than racial prejudice and its effects; his intellectual development was beginning in earnest. Back in Mississippi eleven years before, his imagination had been stirred by the tale told by the female boarder in his grandmother's house. He had read avidly if indiscriminately in cheap fiction from an early age. He harbored ambitions of becoming a writer. He was now simmering, and H. L. Mencken brought him to a boil.

While working at the optical shop, Wright was accustomed to arrive early in order to read the newspaper in the downstairs bank lobby, where the black porter was an acquaintance. In this way he would save the five cents the paper cost. On the morning of 28 May 1927 he read an editorial attack on H. L. Mencken "concluding with one, hot, short sentence: Mencken is a fool." Wright's curiosity was irrepressibly aroused: "I wondered what on earth this Mencken had done to call down upon him the scorn of the South. . . . Were there, then, people other than Negroes who criticized the South? . . . Knowing no more of Mencken than I did at that moment, I felt a vague sympathy for him. Had not the South, which had assigned me the role of a non-man, cast at him its hardest words?"[16]

The editorial in question, entitled "Another Mencken Absurdity," was indeed a vigorous attack on Mencken, particularly on his *Baltimore Sun* editorial of 23 May 1927 on the great Mississippi flood of that year. Since no intelligent human beings lived on the 9,000 square miles covered by the floodwaters, Mencken had suggested, it was difficult to arouse the sympathy of people in other sections of the country. The Memphis editorialist leaped to the de-

[15] Ibid., pp. 204-6, 212, 213.
[16] Ibid., p. 214.

fense of the South and replied in kind to Mencken's invective, or at least as near to kind as his more limited rhetoric would permit:

> Henry L. Mencken never made himself more ridiculous.... Substituting for facts the wild creations of his own imagination, and blundering on in a reckless way to illogical conclusions, Mencken proves his ignorance ... more convincingly than in any of his previous harangues.... If failure to use what intelligence one has, to talk foolishly without knowledge, has any relation to a moron, Mr. Mencken has not proved himself so far above the level of those whom he scorns.... For his story contains neither truth nor sense.... he ... displayed naught but the extreme arrogance of ignorance....

The final sentence of the editorial was longer than Wright remembered, if just as hot: "As time goes on and more editorials of the type of 'The Mississippi Flood' appear the suspicion grows that H. L. Mencken is either a charlatan or a narrow-minded fool — and that what he writes is largely bilge."[17]

What is at first glance striking about Wright's response to this editorial is that it was automatic. If Mencken had been attacked by a white southern newspaper, he must have merit. The logic of the stereotype works both ways in a racist society. In fact, however, the editorial criticized in passing the Ku Klux Klan and religious fundamentalists. Indeed, it even at one point suggested that the flood victims should have an equal share of pity regardless of race: "Mr. Mencken says that sympathy is lacking because there were no human victims. Where has he been reading his flood news? He does not believe, we hope, that black brethren are less to be pitied than white. But the number of negroes known to have been drowned is large and the number of whites, though considerable, is not known at present."[18] But Wright's instinctive preference for Mencken over the *Memphis Commercial Appeal* was not so mistaken after all. If the newspaper condemned the Klan, mob rule, and lynching in other editorials of the time, it on the other hand gave extensive coverage to news of racial conflict and black crime. It also carried on its front page an offensive cartoon series by J. P.

[17] *Memphis Commercial Appeal,* 28 May 1927, p. 6.
[18] Ibid.

Alley entitled "Hambone Meditations," presenting a cruel carica-
ture of a lower-class black speaking in very broad dialect. Wright
knew where the newspaper's heart lay, however much it might
politely denounce lynchers through motives of genteel respectability
or civic pride.[19]

Determined to learn more about a target of white southern wrath,
Wright still faced the considerable problem of laying his hands on
books by so subversive an author. Barred by race from using the
"public" Cossit Library, he had to find a white person with a library card willing to help him. The only possible candidate seemed
to be an Irish Catholic employee of the optical shop who was de-
spised by his white fellow workers. This man reluctantly gave him
his card. Wright forged a note over the man's name to present to
the librarian: *"Dear Madam: Will you please let this nigger boy*
— I used the word 'nigger' to make the librarian feel that I could
not possibly be the author of the note — *have some books by H. L.
Mencken?"* Nervous and apprehensive, he entered the library as
he had done before on white men's errands, presented the note,
parried the librarian's questions, and walked out with *A Book of
Prefaces* and one of the volumes of *Prejudices*.[20]

The impact of Mencken on Wright's mind and imagination was
as overwhelming as the story of Bluebeard heard on the front porch
in Jackson years before. While reading *A Book of Prefaces,* Wright
was "jarred and shocked" by the style, impressed by the audacity of
the attack on American institutions and beliefs, and fascinated by
the allusions to the iconoclastic giants of modern literature and
thought:

> But what strange world was this? I concluded the book with the
> conviction that I had somehow overlooked something terribly im-
> portant in life. I had once tried to write, had once reveled in feel-
> ing, had let my crude imagination roam, but the impulse to dream

[19] An editorial two months later denounced separate cases of flogging in
Georgia and Florida, and also denounced robbery in the latter case, where the
superintendent of schools was one of the floggers. The *Commercial Appeal's*
indignation was directed not so much against flogging and robbery as against
the ammunition such incidents gave to traducers of the South like Mencken.
See "Playing into the Hands of Slander," *Memphis Commercial Appeal,* 31 July
1927, sec. 1, p. 6.
[20] *Black Boy,* pp. 215, 216-17.

had been slowly beaten out of me by experience. Now it surged up again and I hungered for books, new ways of looking and seeing. It was not a matter of believing or disbelieving what I read, but of feeling something new, of being affected by something that made the look of the world different.[21]

He promptly began to feed the insatiable hunger that Mencken had aroused, and thus his serious literary education began. In secondhand bookstores he bought books and back issues of *Harper's Magazine, Atlantic Monthly,* and *American Mercury.* After devouring them, he resold them and bought more. He continued his trips to the library with forged notes. He read Sinclair Lewis and recognized his employer as a Babbitt type. He read Edgar Lee Masters, Sherwood Anderson,[22] Joseph Conrad,[23] and Charles Dickens, but he was repelled by the latter's sentimentality.[24] And significant for the course of his later career, he read Dreiser, perhaps his favorite novelist at the time: "I read Dreiser's *Jennie Gerhardt* and *Sister Carrie* and they revived in me a vivid sense of my mother's suffering; I was overwhelmed. I grew silent, wondering about the life around me. It would have been impossible for me to have told anyone what I derived from these novels, for it was nothing less than a sense of life itself. All my life had shaped me for the realism, the naturalism of the modern novel, and I could not read enough of them."[25]

But if his reading intensified his sense of life, it also increased his estrangement from his immediate environment. Most of the black people he knew were not readers, and whites were suspicious of those who were. To avoid the scrutiny of whites, he concealed books he took to work by wrapping them in newspapers. When on one occasion his package was opened, he was warned, " 'You'll addle your brains if you don't watch out.' " Thus the liberation that Wright

[21] Ibid., pp. 217, 218.

[22] Ibid., pp. 198, 218-19, 227.

[23] Peter Lennon, "One of Uncle Tom's Children," *Manchester Guardian,* 8 December 1960, p. 8.

[24] Roy Wilder, "Wright, Negro Ex-Field Hand, Looks Ahead to New Triumphs," *New York Herald Tribune,* 17 August 1941, sec. 6, p. 4.

[25] *Black Boy,* p. 219. In a 1941 interview he called Dreiser "the greatest writer this country had ever produced. His 'Jennie Gerhardt' is the greatest novel." Wilder, "Wright, Negro Ex-Field Hand, Looks Ahead to New Triumphs."

experienced was of an agonizingly ambivalent kind. A new vision of the possibilities of life had come, but with it an even clearer view of the restrictions of his present situation.[26]

By winter Wright had saved enough money to send for his mother and brother. With them he established a household for the first time since the grim days in West Helena. He even began to eat regular meals. His brother found work, and they immediately began to save and plan for the trip north to Chicago. When Aunt Maggie visited them, her second husband having deserted her, it was decided that she and Richard would go first, to be followed when financially possible by his mother and brother. Taking leave from his employer with warnings not to fall into Lake Michigan and not to speak to white girls ringing in his ears, he once again boarded a northbound train: "With ever watchful eyes and bearing scars, visible and invisible, I headed North, full of a hazy notion that life could be lived with dignity, that the personalities of others should not be violated, that men should be able to confront other men without fear or shame, and that if men were lucky in their living on earth they might win some redeeming meaning for their having struggled and suffered here beneath the stars."[27]

When Wright and his Aunt Maggie arrived in the Black Belt on the South Side of Chicago late in 1927, they first stayed with another aunt, Cleo, before finding a flat to house his mother and brother.[28] Wright took a job as porter in a Jewish delicatessen located in a white neighborhood. The proprietors, named Hoffman, were relatively unprejudiced, but that very fact caused uncertainty in Wright's mind about his relation to them. When in the spring of 1928 he decided to take a civil service examination for a position as postal clerk, he lied about his absence from work because he feared that his employer would resent his desire to improve his situation. Sensing his lie, Mr. Hoffman questioned Wright about it. As he was later to show in the behavior of Bigger Thomas, Wright discovered that white sympathy and pity could be as psychologically

[26] *Black Boy*, pp. 220, 198, 219.
[27] Ibid., pp. 223, 224, 225, 228.
[28] Richard Wright, "American Hunger," *Mademoiselle*, XXI (September 1945), 164, 300.

intolerable as overt prejudice to a young, unprepared black man:
"It dawned upon me that they were trying to treat me as an equal,
which made it even more impossible for me ever to tell them that I
had lied, why I had lied. I felt that if I confessed I would give them
a moral advantage over me that would be unbearable. . . . Working
with them from day to day and knowing that they knew I had lied
from fear crushed me. I knew that they pitied me and pitied the
fear in me. I resolved to quit and risk hunger rather than stay with
them."[29]

A week later he found work as dishwasher in a newly opened café
in the Patricia Hotel on Fullerton Street on the North Side, some
five miles from his rooms. The long round-trip by streetcar and
the lonely nights gave him time to continue his voracious reading
— Gertrude Stein, Stephen Crane, Dostoevsky, Proust, as well as
psychological and sociological works.[30] His work in the café brought
him for the first time into close contact with white girls of his own
age. He was impressed by their friendly, nonchalant manner, but
he also recognized the ignorance and superficiality of their lives.
During the year that he worked in this café, he was also impressed
by Tillie, the Finnish cook, whose strange habit of spitting into the
food she was preparing he happened to observe one morning. After
she was discharged, he remembered the clothing store in Jackson
from which he himself had been fired, and he "wondered if a Negro
who did not smile and grin was as morally loathsome to whites as
a cook who spat into the food."[31]

In the summer of 1929 Wright was called to fill a vacancy as
substitute postal clerk, one of the highest positions to which a black
man could then reasonably aspire. By that time his mother and
brother had joined him and Aunt Maggie in Chicago.[32] With a
decent job and the family united, good fortune at last seemed at
hand. But any elation that he may have felt was soon stifled. Aunt

[29] "Early Days in Chicago," pp. 306, 310-11, 312, 313.
[30] "American Hunger," pp. 165, 301. See also Embree, *13 against the Odds*,
p. 36. In "American Hunger" Wright does not mention the delicatessen job,
but speaks of the dishwashing job as being taken a week after his arrival in the
city. Several sentences appear in identical form in both "American Hunger"
and "Early Days in Chicago."
[31] "Early Days in Chicago," pp. 313-17, 320.
[32] Ibid., p. 320. See also Embree, *13 against the Odds*, pp. 38-39.

Cleo, who had lived in Chicago for a number of years,[33] fell ill and died of a cardiac disease. Soon afterward his brother began to suffer from stomach ulcers, and his sickly mother had another relapse. On top of these difficulties, the effects of the Depression were immediately felt in Chicago, causing Wright to be laid off his job at the post office. As he roamed the streets searching for work, he found himself one of a swelling army of unemployed on the South Side.[34]

Through a distant cousin, however, Wright was able to obtain a position as an insurance agent and worked for about a year in that capacity. He had qualms of conscience about preying upon the desire of the poor and ignorant of the South Side, denied a decent life, for a decent burial. These qualms became acute when he became party to a swindle of one of his clients, but the economic exigencies of himself and his family prevailed. The chief fringe benefit of this job was that it made him thoroughly familiar with black life in Chicago, thus making possible *Lawd Today* and *Native Son*. He visited hundreds of slum flats to collect weekly premiums. Often he had casual sex relations with his clients, and "a long, tortured affair with one girl by paying her ten-cent premium each week." Illiterate and ignorant, she made only one request — that he take her to a circus. The relationship ended, however, before a circus came to town to relieve momentarily her drab existence.[35]

As the Depression deepened in 1931, he went on relief, feeling as he sat in the office waiting with dozens of others to make application a sense of collective desperation. In the city parks he began to pause to listen to radical speakers. In December of that year he was called back to the post office for seasonal work. He talked to white co-workers about "world happenings, the vast armies of unemployed, the rising tide of radical action."[36] The seeds of a decade of devotion to the Communist party were being sown in the fertile soil of his lifelong deprivation.

Little indication of either Depression unrest or radical action is found, however, in Wright's second published story, "Superstition,"

---

[33] *Black Boy*, p. 76.
[34] "Early Days in Chicago," pp. 320-21.
[35] Ibid., pp. 321-22, 323-25.
[36] Ibid., pp. 327, 329.

which appeared in the spring of 1931 in a Chicago magazine for blacks. On the contrary, the story concerns a middle-class northern black who observes in a southern black family — "primitive folk," as they are called, although they too are middle-class — the operation of the fearful superstition that at a family reunion one member of the family is destined to die. Twice this superstition becomes a self-fulfilling prophecy because of "the fearful hearts of a primitive folk . . . bowing abjectly to the terror of an unknown created by their own imaginations." Thus the story reveals the estrangement Wright felt from his southern past and the terror that was to be such a persistent emotion in his fiction. As literature, "Superstition" is an unqualified failure, with stereotyped characters, contrived action, and stilted diction. The daughter of the Lancaster family who is the first victim of the superstition, for example, is straight out of Edgar Allan Poe:

> She appeared to be in her early twenties. Her narrow face, pale and emaciated, attracted me. Her hair was brushed backwards and revealed a broad, bulging forehead below which, shining in contrast to her pallid features, were a pair of dark sunken eyes. They seemed lit with a strange light. She seemed feverish and nervous, as if preyed upon by a secret illness. The most unusual thing about her was a timid and perpetual smile, a smile that seemed melancholy and slightly cynical. A peculiar air of resignation pervaded her whole being.[37]

Clearly the author of this short story had not yet found either his style or his proper subject matter.

After Wright's temporary work in the post office expired in January 1932, the relief system placed him in a medical research institute in Michael Reese Hospital to work as an orderly at thirteen dollars a week. Here he toiled for more than a year mopping floors, cleaning the cages of experimental animals, and holding the animals during injections. The experience was a cruel parody of his boyhood dream of a career in medical research. In the hospital he was subjected to a particularly onerous form of Jim Crow treat-

---

[37] "Superstition," *Abbott's Monthly*, II (April 1931), 73, 47. For a full account of Wright's use of Poe in this story and elsewhere, see Michel Fabre, "Black Cat and White Cat: Richard Wright's Debt to Edgar Allan Poe," *Poe Studies*, IV (June 1971), 17-19.

ment, being confined to the basement corridors when not performing a specific task so as not to mingle with white patients, visitors, or staff. It was here, perhaps, that the image of the black as an invisible man, a subterranean dweller, first occurred to Wright: "The hospital kept us four Negroes as though we were close kin to the animals we tended, huddled together down in the underworld corridors of the hospital, separated by a vast psychological distance from the significant processes of the rest of the hospital — just as America had kept us locked in the dark underworld of American life for three hundred years — and we had made our own code of ethics, values, loyalty."[38] A decade later he was to write "The Man Who Lived Underground," one of the most impressive of his tales, and after another decade one of his younger friends, Ralph Ellison, expanded and developed the metaphor still further in *Invisible Man*.

But Wright's close relationship to his three black co-workers did not engender any sense of camaraderie. These three, one Wright's age and two "elderly," were almost totally brutalized. Bill, the young one, was an alcoholic with a simple formula for solving racial problems: " 'Let the government give every man a gun and five bullets, then let us all start over again. Make it just like it was in the beginning. The ones who come out on top, white or black, let them rule.' " The two older men quarreled constantly. On one occasion in the winter of 1932 their enmity exploded in a violent brawl in which one was armed with a knife and the other with an ice pick. As they struggled, they knocked over tiers of cages freeing experimental animals within. Fearful of losing their jobs, they ceased fighting to join Wright and Bill in "the impossible task of sorting the cancerous rats and mice, the diabetic dogs, the Aschheim-Zondek rabbits, and the Wassermann guinea pigs" and returning them to their proper cages. Nothing was ever said to the four orderlies, and the course of medical research continued without apparent disruption. Wright thought of reporting the accident, but the discriminatory treatment he had received in the hospital

[38] "Early Days in Chicago," pp. 330, 342. An earlier, somewhat different version of this part of "Early Days in Chicago" dealing with his hospital experiences is "What You Don't Know Won't Hurt You," *Harper's Magazine,* CLXXXVI (December 1942), 58-61.

and his unwillingness to risk losing his job overcame his altruistic impulse.[39] He found himself once again in the familiar pattern of alienation. Excluded from the white world because of race, he was estranged from the black world because he had somehow managed to retain his sensitivity and protect it from brutalization. Now reading such writers as T. S. Eliot, Ezra Pound, Joseph Wood Krutch, and Aldous Huxley,[40] he could hardly communicate with his drunken, brawling companions. He remained an outsider.

But Wright's alienation was soon to be alleviated, though not permanently, by his membership in the Communist party. Out of work again in 1933, he became an assistant precinct captain in the Republican primary election upon the promise of a job. When the promise was not kept, he served in the same capacity for the Democratic party, but again no job was forthcoming.[41] This personal experience with the major parties only served to accelerate his movement leftward.

Sometime in the latter part of 1933 Wright attended a party with some of his white friends from the post office. A number of them, he learned, had joined the Communist party. One had written a story accepted for publication by the *Anvil*, Jack Conroy's little magazine of proletarian fiction, and he spoke glowingly of his affiliation with the John Reed Club. Knowing of Wright's literary ambitions, his friend invited him to attend meetings of the club. Skeptical of the motives of all whites, Wright nevertheless one Saturday night in the fall of 1933 walked up a dingy stairway in the Loop to attend a meeting of the Chicago John Reed Club "in the capacity of an amused spectator."[42] He went to scoff, but this was the beginning of a strong attachment to the cause the club served.

The John Reed clubs had been organized at a national conference held in Chicago 29-30 May 1932. Closely controlled by the Communist party, the clubs were designed to serve as one of its cultural instruments. The express purpose, in the language adopted at the organizing conference, was:

[39] "Early Days in Chicago," pp. 331, 337-38, 339, 341-42.
[40] Wilder, "Wright, Negro Ex-Field Hand, Looks Ahead to New Triumphs."
[41] "Wright, Richard," *Current Biography, 1940,* ed. Maxine Block (New York, 1940), p. 886.
[42] "I Tried to Be a Communist" (August 1944), p. 61.

"(a) To make the Club a functioning center of proletarian culture; to clarify and elaborate the point of view of proletarian as opposed to bourgeois culture; to extend the influence of the Club and the revolutionary working class movement.

"(b) To create and publish art and literature of a proletarian character; to make familiar in this country the art and literature of the world proletariat, and particularly that of the Soviet Union; to develop the critique of bourgeois and working class culture; to develop organizational techniques for establishing and consolidating contacts of the Clubs with potentially sympathetic elements; to assist in developing (through cooperation with the Workers Cultural Federation and other revolutionary organizations) worker-writers and worker-artists; to engage in and give widest publicity to working class struggles; to render technical assistance to the organized revolutionary movement."

To achieve these ends, the clubs proposed to engage in agitational and propagandistic writing, art, and activities, including

publication of pamphlets, sponsoring of national contests for proletarian stories, plays, songs, drawings, etc., distribution of literature, exhibiting revolutionary drawings and paintings, holding public lectures and debates, establishing JRC art schools and schools for worker-correspondents, active participation in strikes and demonstrations, making of posters and contributing of literature to working class organizations, giving of chalk talks, dramatic skits and other entertainment at workers' meetings, and active assistance to campaigns (Scottsboro, Mooney, Berkman) involving special issues.

Formal party membership was not a condition for joining a club, but one was required to endorse the preamble, which recognized "the irreconcilable struggle between workers and capitalists as two contending classes" and which insisted that "the interests of all writers and artists should be identified with the interests of the working class."[43]

The language seems cold and utilitarian, but the welcome that Wright received at the club was warmly courteous and uncondescending. After operating for more than a year, the club recognized

[43] Oakley Johnson, "The John Reed Club Convention," *New Masses,* VIII (July 1932), 15.

the need for more black members.[44] Thus Wright was encouraged to sit in on an editorial meeting of *Left Front*, the organ of the club. He was given back issues of *New Masses* and *International Literature* to take home. For all his defensive skepticism about white motives, he could detect no insincerity in the behavior of his new friends. "The members," he recalled of the club after he had left the party, "were fervent, democratic, restless, eager, self-sacrificing." Even more revelatory was the impact of the magazines he was given to read. Sitting up until dawn reading them, he "was amazed to find that there did exist in this world an organized search for the truth of the lives of the oppressed and the isolated." He knew that to this search he could make a contribution from his own bitter experience as a black person, an experience that he was beginning to learn was similar to the experience of exploited classes around the globe. If a unity of suffering existed between black and white, could not unity be achieved between them in revolutionary activity to correct that suffering? His evening at the club had suggested that it could, and the pages of the radical magazines provided confirmation. As dawn neared, he "wrote a wild, crude poem in free verse" to express this new vision.[45] This poem must have been "I Have Seen Black Hands," the last section of which speaks hopefully of black and white uniting to fight:

> I am black and I have seen black hands
> Raised in fists of revolt, side by side
>     with the white fists of white workers,
> And some day — and it is only this which
>     sustains me —
> Some day there shall be millions and millions
>     of them,
> On some red day in a burst of fists on a new
>     horizon![46]

"I Have Seen Black Hands" was published in the 26 June 1934 issue of *New Masses*, but poems were published earlier that year in

[44] "The Midwest John Reed Conference," *Left Front*, I (September-October 1933), 11.

[45] "I Tried to Be a Communist" (August 1944), p. 63.

[46] *New Masses*, XI (26 June 1934), 16.

*Left Front* and the *Anvil.* Thus, except for the adolescent "The Voodoo of Hell's Half-Acre" and "Superstition," Wright's first published work was poetry. Curiously, during the last months of his life, in the fourteenth year of his expatriation in Paris, he again turned to poetry, though at this time haiku, a far cry from his agitprop verse of the middle thirties.

For the most part, one must accept Wright's own adjective, "crude," in describing his proletarian poetry. Through this poetry he hoped to humanize Communist propaganda, to effect a rapprochement between Communist intellectuals and the masses, to interpret each to the other: "The Communists, I felt, had oversimplified the experience of those whom they sought to lead. In their efforts to recruit masses, they had missed the meaning of the lives of the masses, had conceived of people in too abstract a manner. I would try to put some of that meaning back. I would tell Communists how common people felt, and I would tell common people of the self-sacrifice of Communists who strove for unity among them."[47] But often the revolutionary hope is grafted to the trunk of black experience in a much too arbitrary fashion. In "I Have Seen Black Hands," for example, the final section quoted above is immediately preceded at the end of the third section by a description of lynchings:

> And the black hands fought and scratched and
>       held back but a thousand white hands
>       took them and tied them,
> And the black hands lifted palms in mute and
>       futile supplication to the sodden faces
>       of mobs wild in the revelries of sadism,
> And the black hands strained and clawed and
>       struggled in vain at the noose that
>       tightened about the black throat,
> And the black hands waved and beat fearfully
>       at the tall flames that cooked and
>       charred the black flesh...

The transition to black and white fists raised in the Communist salute is abrupt, to say the least. In the first section of the poem,

---

[47] "I Tried to Be a Communist" (August 1944), p. 63.

black childhood and adolescence — subjects with which Wright's touch was always sure — are rendered effectively through synecdoche, the black hands first reaching for "the black nipples at the black breasts of black mothers," then holding "wineballs . . . and sugared cookies in fingers sticky and gummy," then holding marbles and slingshots, then coins, then "rulers . . . and books in palms spotted and smeared with ink," and finally "dice and cards and half-pint flasks and cue sticks and cigars and cigarettes in the pride of new maturity." In the second section, however, as the black hands "jerked up and down at the throbbing machines massing taller and taller the heaps of gold in the banks of the bosses," the poem degenerates into political slogans, as it does in the final section. Part of the problem is that Wright's newly found political conviction had not been successfully assimilated into his stock of experience and his sensibility. Another part is the didactic exigencies of his genre, for in agitprop poetry everything had to be subordinated to the communication of a clear revolutionary message.

Perhaps the most complete failure of the agitprop poems is "I Am a Red Slogan," which begins

> *I AM A RED SLOGAN,*
> *A flaming torch flung to lead the minds of men!*
> *I flaunt my messages from a million banners:*
> *WORKERS OF THE WORLD, UNITE!*
> *I AM A RED SLOGAN,*
> *The axe that whacks to the heart of knotty problems*[48]

This is an embarrassing effort indeed unless one reads it as a deliberate parody of the genre. The sincerity of Wright's adherence to the party at this time,[49] however, precludes that possibility. "Red Leaves of Red Books"[50] is little better. His first two published poems, "Rest for the Weary" and "A Red Love Note," rely on an irony so heavy and obvious as to diminish greatly its effect. In the former, the "panic-stricken guardians of gold" are told that their burdens of wealth and pride will be removed by the "brawny hands" of the

---

[48] *International Literature,* no. 4 (April 1935), p. 35.

[49] Arna Bontemps recalls that "Communism was like a religion to him . . . and he was as grim about it as some other people I have known were about fundamental religious dogma." Letter to the author, 5 April 1965.

[50] *New Masses,* XV (30 April 1935), 6.

workers. "A Red Love Note" is another threat to the exploiters from the proletariat, perhaps somewhat more successful because it sustains the metaphor of a billet-doux to "my dear lovely bloated one" threatening the violent end of bourgeois civilization in amorous slang; the recipient is addressed as "honey," "darling," "sugar-pie," and "dumpling." But here again the irony is heavy.[51] The same is true of "Child of the Dead and Forgotten Gods," in which the innocent and naive liberal is ridiculed — the days of the popular front had not yet arrived — for failing to understand the revolutionary urgency of the moment:

the pounding of police
clubs on the skulls of strikers
and the scream of the riot-siren to dis-
    perse the unemployed
And the noise and clamor of slaughter and
    rapine and greed
drowns out your soft talk of peace and
    brotherhood!

Published in the same issue of the *Anvil* as "Child of the Dead and Forgotten Gods" was "Strength," a pedestrian and highly didactic statement of the futility of individual effort "against the legions of tyranny" contrasted to the inevitable success of collective action.[52]

Less bald is the statement of the revolutionary message in "Everywhere Burning Waters Rise," which attempts to express it through a metaphor of cumulative power and violence. This poem does achieve a sense of developing momentum from the stasis of an arrested economy through the swelling revolutionary impulse to the purgative destruction of the old order. Here too, however, pamphlet slogans intrude. Furthermore, the success of the effort to achieve geographical scope in the first seven lines is immediately vitiated by the artificial and self-conscious conceits that follow: "tenemented mountains of hunger," "ghetto swamps of suffering," "breadlined forests of despair," and "peonized plains of hopelessness." The poet is trying to show the human suffering resulting from the economic stagnation indicated in the preceding lines while maintaining the

[51] *Left Front,* I (January-February 1934), 3.
[52] *Anvil,* no. 5 (March-April 1934), pp. 30, 20.

sense of spatial amplitude, but the metaphorical conjunction of urban ("breadlined"), geographical ("forests"), and abstract ("despair") elements is much too contrived. These quasi-metaphysical conceits are not integrated into the essentially Whitmanesque tone of the entire poem. The sudden transformation of the flood into "waters of fire" is likewise unhappy; the change is effected "strangely" indeed.[53]

If poetically unsuccessful, however, the combined fire-water imagery is biographically explicable. Fire and flood were the images of violence most deeply embedded in Wright's imagination. The opening pages of *Black Boy* relate the incident of his setting his house afire at the age of four. The fire motif recurs often in his work, e.g., the fateful furnace of *Native Son* and the catastrophic inferno of the blazing dancehall in *The Long Dream*.[54] Living in the Mississippi valley, often in towns along the river, during his childhood and youth, he had long been conscious of the destructive power of floods. In his last year in the South he had witnessed from the central vantage point of Memphis the terrible devastation of the great flood of 1927. Two of his most successful short stories, "Down by the Riverside" and "Silt," deal directly with floods. Furthermore, the biblical associations of "Fire and Cloud" — to use the title of another of his short stories — had been thoroughly assimilated in his youth. It is understandable, then, why he would use flood imagery in "Everywhere Burning Waters Rise" to represent the accumulation of revolutionary resentment among the dispossessed, and why he would shift to more vivid fire imagery to depict the apocalyptic fury of revolutionary violence and destruction.

Destructive violence occurs over and over in Wright's early poetry and remains a dominant motif throughout his entire writing career. At times the violence is masochistic, as in "Rise and Live," where the downtrodden are incited to a suicidal rebellion: "Let's feel in our flesh the rip of their steel! / Let's feel in our throats the burn of their gas!"[55] More often the violence is aggressive. In "Every-

---

[53] *Left Front*, I (May-June 1934), 9.

[54] In his review of *The Long Dream*, Henry F. Winslow comments briefly but perceptively on this fire motif. See "Nightmare Experiences," *Crisis*, LXVI (February 1959), 122. For a fuller treatment, see Dan McCall, *The Example of Richard Wright* (New York, 1969), pp. 175-78.

[55] *Midland Left*, no. 2 (February 1935), p. 14.

where Burning Waters Rise" the last two lines seem distinctly an afterthought; the violent destruction of the old order gripped the poet's imagination more forcefully than the construction of a new world possibly could. In "A Red Love Note" no mention is made of a new world, but rather of "a red clap of thunder rising from the very depths of hell" to destroy the old.[56] The same is true of "Strength," where the revolution is once more depicted as a natural force: "a raging hurricane vast and powerful, / wrenching and dredging by the roots the rotting husks of the trees of greed."[57]

The fiery violence of Wright's most successful early poem, "Between the World and Me," is not an almost impersonal force resembling a natural phenomenon but an all too malevolently human mob action, particularized in its depiction of a sadistic lynching.[58] Almost intolerable in its savage intensity, the violence in this poem is nevertheless strictly controlled by the emotional movement shared by the speaker and the audience. Through a kind of shock therapy, both the "I" of the poem and the reader are brought to an identification with the lynch victim. At the beginning of the poem the speaker comes by chance upon the scene of a lynching. Shocked by the sight, he nevertheless remains calm enough to notice with accuracy each of the grisly concrete details, including "peanut shells," which suggest the festive spirit of the lynch mob, and "a whore's lipstick," which suggests, to one familiar with southern mores, the ostensible motive of the lynching.[59] The catalog of details culminates in line 10: "And through the morning air the sun poured yellow surprise into the eye sockets of a stony skull. . . ." Here the skull is passive, receiving the sunlight. Shocked fascination

[56] *Left Front,* I (January-February 1934), 3.

[57] *Anvil,* no. 5 (March-April 1934), p. 20.

[58] *Partisan Review,* II (July-August 1935), 18-19. The intensity with which Wright viewed lynching as a central symbol of American race relations is revealed explicitly in his poem "Obsession," *Midland Left,* no. 2 (February 1935), p. 14.

[59] One is reminded of Wright's account in *Black Boy* of the 1924 lynching of Bob Greenley (The name is fictitious, the real name being Robinson, the brother of Wright's friend C. T. Robinson. See Webb, *Richard Wright,* p. 64.) for being discovered with a white prostitute. The presence at a lynching of the white woman whose black lover was the lynch victim was not uncommon. To save face such a woman often cried rape and incited the mob to action. Erskine Caldwell gives extended treatment to such a situation in his novel *Trouble in July,* which Wright reviewed in "Lynching Bee," *New Republic,* CII (11 March 1940), 351-52.

now gives way to fear, then to a reenactment of the lynching so powerfully immediate as to become more real than vicarious. The observer of the scene now becomes the victim in the actual event, and the observed details, previously static or dead, leap luridly to life: "The gin-flask passed from mouth to mouth; cigars and cigarettes glowed, the whore smeared the lipstick red upon her lips," and the lynching takes place again. In the last line of the poem the image of line 10 is repeated, but with a significant difference: "my face a stony skull staring in yellow surprise at the sun. . . ." The sadistic-masochistic frenzy of the description of the lynching in the preceding lines might have seemed too wildly sensational without this return at the very end of the poem to a kind of calm. On the other hand, since the observer — and the reader — have become the victim, detachment and passivity are no longer possible, not even in death. For this reason the skull does not now passively receive the sunlight but becomes, in a sense, active, "staring in yellow surprise at the sun. . . ." "Between the World and Me," then, is an intensely felt and potently realized poem in which the theme of human solidarity in suffering goes far beyond the excessive subjectivity of another lynching poem, "Obsession," or the Marxist sloganeering of some of the other early poems.

Wright was not incapable of a lighter touch. "Spread Your Sunrise!"[60] is an exuberant mixture of comic exaggeration in the American folk tradition, Whitmanesque geographical sweep, and modern American slang. The vision in the poem is of "a bushy-haired giant-child" striding from Russia across Europe and the Atlantic into America:

> Hoooly Chriiist!
> What *is* that he's got in his hands?
> By George, in one he's holding a bucketful
>     of sunrise,
> And in the other he's swishing a long tall
>     broom,
> And Jeeesus, the fool's splashing crimson
>     everywhere,
> Just painting the whole world red!

[60] *New Masses*, XVI (2 July 1935), 26.

At times a cliché-ridden and incongruous seriousness intrudes into the poem, as when the giant figure is called "a man-child of the Revolution: / Seed of fiery workers' loins, / Fruit of October's swollen womb!" but the dominant effect is of an editorial cartoon by William Gropper or Hugo Gellert with the unaccustomed added ingredient of a boisterous humor. This ingredient is unfortunately missing from "Transcontinental,"[61] a long, ambitious poem indebted to Louis Aragon, in which the progress of the revolution across North America is expressed through the metaphor of an automobile journey. The conception is arresting, but Wright's execution of it is heavy and labored. "Hearst Headline Blues"[62] contains humor but of a grim and sardonic kind, similar in tone to that of "A Red Love Note" and "Rest for the Weary." The poem, in five rhymed quatrains, consists entirely of Hearst-type headlines revealing the social unrest and official hypocrisy of Depression America. The final two stanzas are typical:

> "Woman Dynamites Jail to Free Her Lover"
> "Starvation Claims Mother and Tot"
> "Roosevelt Says the Worst Is Over"
> "Longshoremen Picket; Two Are Shot"

> "Father Butchers Son With Axe"
> "Many Gold Voices to Be Heard on Air"
> "Attorney Dodd Uncovers Facts"
> "The Right Reverend O'Connell Urges Prayer"

The last two poems published during Wright's Chicago period are "Old Habit and New Love"[63] and "We of the Streets."[64] The first uses rather confused imagery to attempt with indifferent success to show the new love of revolutionary creativity growing out of the old habit of industrial drudgery. The theme of the second is the quality of the collective consciousness of the urban masses, but the poem's statement of this theme seems too self-conscious. Wright's poetic idiom is uncertain in these two ambitious poems, but they do show

---

[61] *International Literature,* no. 1 (January 1936), pp. 52-57.
[62] *New Masses,* XIX (12 May 1936), 14.
[63] *New Masses,* XXI (15 December 1936), 29.
[64] *New Masses,* XXIII (13 April 1937), 14.

him moving away from the facile oversimplifications of the agitprop formula.

None of the poems discussed thus far is racial in idiom. "I Have Seen Black Hands" deals with racial experience but in a nonracial way. "Hearst Headline Blues" is not really a blues at all except in the loosest popular sense. Three of Wright's poems, however, deal with racial experience in a racial idiom. Among his poems they come closest to satisfying the critical precepts expressed in his essay "Blueprint for Negro Writing," where he prescribes the use of black folk material within the context of an advanced, i.e., Marxist, social understanding and a militant class-consciousness.[65] "Ah Feels It in Mah Bones,"[66] written entirely in dialect, presents the effects of the Depression on a young lower-class black, who is transformed from a thoughtless hedonist devoted to wenching and gambling into an incipient revolutionary. The dialect rings true throughout, often achieving a vivid, highly poetic folk locution: "An' long-lopin' mah old proud sweet stuff like a greyhound pup!" The didactic message of revolutionary awareness is artfully implicit; slogans are absent from this poem. "Ah Feels It in Mah Bones," however, does not entirely avoid the danger inherent in all black dialect poems — serving to confirm white prejudices and stereotypes. A "razor-totin' " dice-shooter, the white readers of *International Literature* must have felt, would be a questionable candidate for party membership even after he had reformed. Stereotyping of some degree would seem virtually inevitable in dialect poetry, and this poem does not escape it. "Ah Feels It in Mah Bones" does suggest, in any case, that if its author had cared to cultivate this genre, he would probably have attained a skill equal to that of its most able practitioners — Paul Laurence Dunbar, James Weldon Johnson, Sterling Brown, and Langston Hughes.

The last-named collaborated with Wright on "Red Clay Blues,"[67] which was recorded, Hughes recalled,[68] by Josh White. Alone Wright wrote another blues song, "King Joe," recorded by Paul

[65] *New Challenge*, II (Fall 1937), 53-65.
[66] *International Literature*, no. 4 (April 1935), p. 80.
[67] *New Masses*, XXXII (1 August 1939), 14.
[68] Letter to Michel Fabre, 25 April 1963. I have not been able to locate this recording.

Robeson with the Count Basie Orchestra.[69] Wright's interest in the blues continued for the rest of his life. In 1941, the same year as "King Joe," he wrote "Notes on Jim Crow Blues" as a jacket liner for a phonograph record album by Josh White.[70] During the years in Paris he often listened to his large collection of blues and jazz recordings.[71] One of his last essays was a foreword to a study of folk blues by a British scholar.[72] The difficulty of dealing with blues songs as printed poems is that perhaps more than most other folk music, they are inseparable from their performance. "Red Clay Blues," a song expressing the city migrant's nostalgia for the physical environment of his rural past and also his resentment against the tenant system, was probably fairly well rendered by Josh White, a skillful performer tasteful in his popularization of folk music. The recording of "King Joe," however, is a dismal and unqualified failure. Robeson's bass voice, so richly resonant in singing spirituals, is painfully lugubrious, and the incongruously sophisticated music of Count Basie is disastrously slow. The total effect is ludicrous. To judge effectively this blues song about the prowess of Joe Louis, one would need to hear it from the lips of such an authentic blues-singer as Leadbelly or Lightnin' Hopkins.

Wright's apprenticeship did not lead to a later major achievement in poetry, but it did bring him much-needed recognition and encouragement. It also gave him experience in dealing with subjects, themes, and metaphors, especially those involving racial conflict, that he was to exploit more fully in his prose. And it produced one poem of unmistakable merit, "Between the World and Me."

The young proletarian poet's activity in the Chicago John Reed Club quickly increased. Early in 1934 he was elected executive secretary of the group, and in March of that year he spoke to the John

[69] *New Letters,* XXXVIII (Winter 1971), 42-45. The recording, on an Okeh label, may be found in the James Weldon Johnson Memorial Collection of the Yale University Library.

[70] *Southern Exposure,* Keynote Recordings 107. This album may be found in the James Weldon Johnson Memorial Collection of the Yale University Library.

[71] Smith, "Black Boy in France," p. 34.

[72] Paul Oliver, *Blues Fell This Morning* (New York, 1961).

Reed Club of Indianapolis.[73] Soon afterward he joined the Communist party.[74] The party provided an intellectual framework and an emotional home for Wright during the next decade; indeed it influenced his thinking for the rest of his life, even after he had wholly renounced it. Equally important in its impact on his writing was his increasingly conscious study of black people as individuals and as a social group. If Marxist principles provided a methodology for interpretation, black experience provided subject matter for the young writer. At the beginning of the Depression, his work as an insurance agent had taken Wright into hundreds of Black Belt flats. He had been assigned by the relief system to sweep streets in early 1934, but this work soon stopped. After a period of inactivity he was assigned to work in the South Side Boys' Club, where he took advantage of the opportunity to study closely the Bigger Thomas type by taking notes of speech patterns and psychological reactions to the oppressive environment. Among black Communists, too, he collected material for his writing, especially that concerning their experiences in the South, which would be used in the stories of *Uncle Tom's Children*.[75]

No sooner did Wright become immersed in the activities of the John Reed Club, however, than those activities ceased. At a conference of leftist writers of the Midwest in the early summer of 1934, he vainly sought a literary rather than a strictly political emphasis. Much against his wishes, *Left Front* ceased publication in June with the fourth issue. Later in the summer a national John Reed Club congress met in Chicago. Again despite Wright's arguments to the contrary, the Communist party announced its decision to dissolve the clubs. The exigencies of the development of a popular front required that the needs of militant young writers be subordi-

[73] "Midwest Club News," *Left Front*, I (May-June 1934), 21.

[74] "I Tried to Be a Communist" (August 1944), pp. 63-64. Elsewhere Wright states that his membership in the party began in 1932. *Black Power* (New York, 1954), p. xi. If one accepts Wright's assertion in "I Tried to Be a Communist" that his affiliation with the John Reed Club and *Left Front* preceded party membership — and there seems to be no reason to doubt it — 1932 cannot be the year that he joined the party, for the first issue of *Left Front* did not appear until June 1933. Although one cannot be precise, the most reasonable conclusion is that Wright received his party card in the spring of 1934.

[75] "I Tried to Be a Communist" (August 1944), pp. 66-68.

nated to a policy that would attract more famous and more in-fluential fellow travelers.[76]

Despite these disappointments, Wright's activities on behalf of the party did not cease. His poems and articles continued to appear in the party press, and he could be counted on to sign statements approved by the party. Indeed his period of most intense party activity was to be in 1937 in New York as a correspondent for the *Daily Worker*. His devotion to Marxist principles was unflagging. For these reasons, one must consider as exaggerated his account in "I Tried to Be a Communist" of his alienation from the party. On the other hand, it seems clear that he chafed under party discipline. To provide an organization that would replace the John Reed clubs and greatly expand their function, a call was issued early in 1935 for an American Writers' Congress. Wright was one of the sixty-four early signers.[77]

The American Writers' Congress opened in New York on 26 April 1935 for three days of papers and discussions. Though many non-Communist writers attended and participated in the proceedings, the congress was controlled by the Communist party. Eager to achieve a united front of intellectuals under party guidance, Communist spokesmen welcomed various factions of the left. Even those writers holding party membership, Earl Browder assured the congress, surrendered neither their time to party hackwork nor their artistic autonomy: ". . . the first demand of the Party upon its writer-members is that they shall be good writers, constantly better writers, for only so can they really serve the Party. We do not want to take good writers and make bad strike leaders of them."[78] An appeal of this kind to established writers served

[76] Ibid., pp. 68-69.

[77] "Call for an American Writers' Congress," *New Masses*, XIV (22 January 1935), 20. Other signers included Nelson Algren, Maxwell Bodenheim, Kenneth Burke, Erskine Caldwell, Robert Cantwell, Jack Conroy, Malcolm Cowley, Edward Dahlberg, Theodore Dreiser, James T. Farrell, Waldo Frank, Joseph Freeman, Mike Gold, Horace Gregory, Granville Hicks, Langston Hughes, Joshua Kunitz, John Howard Lawson, Grace Lumpkin, Joseph North, Isidore Schneider, Edwin Seaver, Lincoln Steffens, Genevieve Taggard, Alexander Trachtenberg, and Nathanael West.

[78] "Communism and Literature," *American Writers' Congress*, ed. Henry Hart (New York, 1935), p. 68.

party strategy, but it did not, Wright thought, serve the interests of apprentice revolutionary writers, who needed the encouragement and opportunity to publish that the John Reed clubs could give. Hitchhiking to New York, he contemplated the problems of the young writers on the left. But upon arrival, the inescapable problem of color prejudice intruded on these thoughts. Only with considerable difficulty was he able to find a white Communist willing to put him up for the night. Even in the midst of the Communist party, he bitterly recognized, there was racial discrimination: "I went to the sidewalk, sat on a bench, took out pencil and paper, and tried to jot down notes for the argument I wanted to make in defense of the John Reed Clubs. But the problem of the clubs did not seem important. What did seem important was: Could a Negro ever live halfway like a human being in this goddamn country?" After attending the first day's sessions of the congress, he visited Harlem for the first time. Refused a room at a Harlem hotel for whites only, he found lodgings at the 135th Street YMCA.[79]

Despite his state of outrage induced by these racial insults, he collected himself sufficiently to argue at one of the sessions of the congress in favor of retaining the John Reed clubs. When the vote was taken, only Wright voted against dissolving the clubs.[80] The summary of the discussion in *American Writers' Congress* does not mention the John Reed clubs specifically, but it does quote Wright on the isolation of the black writer: "Some of the more obvious results are lack of contact with other writers, a lack of personal culture, a tendency toward escape mechanisms of ingenious, insidious kinds. Other results of his isolation are the monotony of subject matter and becoming the victim of a sort of traditional Negro character. . . . Some of them [young black writers] are unaware of the vast field of experimental fiction that is being carried on in the little magazines."[81] If, as Wright asserts in "I Tried to Be a Communist," the party frowned on his opposition to its policy in this instance,[82] its anger was not sufficient to prevent his being elected, along with

[79] "I Tried to Be a Communist" (August 1944), pp. 69-70.
[80] Ibid., p. 70.
[81] Hart, ed., *American Writers' Congress*, pp. 178-79.
[82] "I Tried to Be a Communist" (August 1944), p. 70.

thirty-eight others, to the national council of the League of American Writers on 28 April, the last day of the congress.[83] The league replaced the John Reed clubs, and whatever his misgivings, Wright was to remain a faithful member of the league until his break with the party itself.

According to his account in "I Tried to Be a Communist," Wright attempted to reduce his political activity after the congress, but he was subjected to attacks from Chicago party leaders as a "petty bourgeois degenerate," a "bastard intellectual," and an "incipient Trotskyite." Apparently the party wished to welcome famous authors of varying political persuasions to such a front group as the League of American Writers, but it was not willing to tolerate deviation on the part of its own younger writers. In spite of Earl Browder's speech at the congress, during the fall of 1935 the party imposed heavy nonliterary duties on Wright's time, such as organizational work concerning the high cost of living, housing, and other black problems. Wright especially resented this work because he was busy with a novel, probably *Lawd Today*. Because of his writing he refused late in the same year a proffered trip to Switzerland and the Soviet Union as a Communist youth delegate, much to the surprise of party officials. Working during the day at the South Side Boys' Club and writing at night were too exhausting to permit him to engage in extensive party activity. To escape party discipline with its incessant demands on his time, he even took the drastic step of requesting that his name be dropped from party rolls, carefully specifying, however, that no ideological disagreement was at issue. Though this request was refused, Wright was harassed by party members in various ways during his remaining year and a half in Chicago.[84]

[83] Hart, ed., *American Writers' Congress*, p. 188. In keeping with united front policy, non-Communists such as Van Wyck Brooks, Robert Herrick, Sidney Howard, Robert Morss Lovett, and Lewis Mumford were elected to the national council along with such party stalwarts as Nelson Algren, Harry Carlisle, Eugene Clay, Jack Conroy, Joshua Kunitz, Moishe Nadir, and others. The same was true of the smaller executive committee, and Waldo Frank, a non-party member, was chosen secretary of the league. On both governing bodies, however, party people held clear majorities.

[84] "I Tried to Be a Communist" (September 1944), pp. 48, 50, 51.

During this period he found other young black writers whose companionship filled the gap left by the demise of the John Reed Club. In February of 1936 he attended in Chicago the first National Negro Congress, which at that time was not yet under Communist control.[85] Here he met the poet Frank Marshall Davis, who was to become a close friend.[86] In the fall of that year Wright introduced himself to another black writer, the playwright Theodore Ward, with whose cooperation Wright shortly afterward formed a discussion group of black writers, most of whom were associated with the Federal Writers' Project. The group met at the Abraham Lincoln Center on Sunday afternoons to read manuscripts and discuss problems of their craft.[87] In addition to Wright, Ward, and Davis, this group included the poets Arna Bontemps and Margaret Walker. The latter, who had just graduated from Northwestern University, was attracted to Wright and hoped to marry him. Some of the stories that were to appear in *Uncle Tom's Children* were read and discussed by this group, which had no affiliation with the Communist party although its members were generally on the left.[88]

In March of 1936 the relief system transferred Wright from the South Side Boys' Club to the Chicago Negro division of the Federal Theatre of the Works Progress Administration. His assigned function was to handle publicity for the company, but he immediately became interested in the potentialities of authentic black drama, potentialities hardly realized, he thought, in the current production, an adaptation of *Everyman*. Through friends in the WPA, he arranged for a transfer of the white female director and for her replacement by Charles DeSheim. He suggested to DeSheim that the group produce Paul Green's *Hymn to the Rising Sun*. His plans were frustrated, however, by the black actors of the group, who considered the play indecent, ceased its rehearsal, and forced both DeSheim and Wright to seek transfers elsewhere, the latter by threat

[85] Wright reported on this convention in "Two Million Black Voices," *New Masses*, XVIII (25 February 1936), 15.

[86] Letter from Frank Marshall Davis to the author, 24 October 1964.

[87] Letter from Theodore Ward to the author, 8 July 1965. See also Dorothy West, "Dear Reader," *Challenge*, II (Spring 1937), 41.

[88] Letter from Frank Marshall Davis to the author, 24 October 1964. See also Wright, "Negro Writers Launch Literary Quarterly."

of physical violence. Wright later learned that this harassment had been instigated by Communists.[89]

After working briefly as publicity agent for the white Federal Theatre in Chicago, Wright was again transferred, this time to the Federal Writers' Project, where he worked on Chicago theatrical records, Illinois history, and other tasks.[90] He writes that here his persecution by Communists continued, culminating in his physical ejection from the May Day parade of 1937. Later he recalled: "I remembered the stories I had written, the stories in which I had assigned a role of honor and glory to the Communist Party, and I was glad that they were down in black and white, were finished. For I knew in my heart that I should never be able to write that way again, should never be able to feel with that simple sharpness about life, should never again express such passionate hope, should never again make so total a commitment of faith."[91] Actually Wright seems here to be making retroactive a later loss of faith in Communism, for he did remain in the party and did continue to present Communists favorably in his writing.

With the pressure of party duties relieved, Wright now had more time for his writing. His first real success in fiction was "Big Boy Leaves Home," which was published on 2 November 1936 in *The New Caravan*, an anthology edited by Alfred Kreymborg, Lewis

[89] "I Tried to Be a Communist" (September 1944), pp. 52-53, 55. Theodore Ward adds that the black actors demanded that DeSheim, who was white, be replaced by a black director. Letter to the author, 8 July 1965. A different version of this episode is given by Hallie Flanagan, the head of the Federal Theatre, in *Arena* (New York, 1940), pp. 136-37: "After performing in a deeply religious *Everyman,* the Negroes were ready to open with Mr. Green's play, which they felt to be equally serious drama. On the opening night, while the audience milled around the lobby, the administrator explained to newspapermen that the play was 'of such a moral character that I can't even discuss it with a member of the press.' The closing of this play caused the resignation of the company's director, Mr. DeSheim, and such demoralization and timidity on the part of the Negro group that it was months before we finally got them to face another audience." See also Webb, *Richard Wright,* pp. 111-13.

[90] Embree, *13 against the Odds,* p. 40. In "I Tried to Be a Communist" (September 1944), p. 55, Wright states that he worked on guidebooks, but John T. Frederick, who became state director of the Illinois Writers' Project after Wright left for New York, states: "I am positive that Wright did not write any part of the *Illinois Guide.* If he had done writing for the project, it is my impression that it had been taken from the files before I arrived." Letter to the author, 8 April 1965.

[91] "I Tried to Be a Communist" (September 1944), pp. 55-56.

Mumford, and Paul Rosenfeld. In addition to the prestige of publishing under such auspices, the story brought the young writer two concrete practical benefits — enough money to have some needed dental work performed[92] and a higher ranking in the Writers' Project, for he was now classified as "professional writer, temporarily out of work," and made acting supervisor of essays.[93]

It is well that he experienced this taste of success, for in the following spring his dedication to a literary career was severely tested. As he was preparing to leave for New York with a bundle of manuscripts to seek publishers, he received notification of his nearly perfect score on his third civil service examination and an offer of a permanent postal clerkship at the then attractive salary of $2,100.[94] The decision was a crucial one between security, extremely dear to a person of his background, and the hazards of an uncertain writing career: "With that money I could marry, settle down, and vote the Republican ticket."[95] He chose literature.

Moving to New York in May 1937, in time for the second American Writers' Congress the following month, Wright took a room in the Douglas Hotel on St. Nicholas Avenue in northwest Harlem.[96] Later he moved to 136th Street in the heart of Harlem.[97] His first year in New York was to be a busy one, but he no longer had to sweep streets or scrub away rat feces. Instead, all his activities now involved writing of some kind — for *New Challenge,* for the *Daily Worker* and *New Masses,* for the New York City Writers' Project, and for his first published book, *Uncle Tom's Children.*

*New Challenge* was a continuation of Dorothy West's little magazine, *Challenge,* with a more radical emphasis and also the organ of a new group of young black writers in New York and Chicago. The first issue of *Challenge* had appeared in March 1934. Its pur-

---

[92] Wilder, "Wright, Negro Ex-Field Hand, Looks Ahead to New Triumphs."
[93] Embree, *13 against the Odds,* p. 40.
[94] Ibid., pp. 40-41.
[95] Wilder, "Wright, Negro Ex-Field Hand, Looks Ahead to New Triumphs."
[96] Letter from Langston Hughes to Michel Fabre, 25 April 1963.
[97] Change-of-address notice from Wright to Langston Hughes, 13 April 1938, deposited in the James Weldon Johnson Memorial Collection of the Yale University Library. At this time Wright was moving from 230 West 136th Street to 175 Carlton Avenue, Brooklyn, where he took a room in the home of Herbert and Jane Newton, good friends from Chicago active in party work.

pose was to revive the creative spirit of the Harlem Renaissance, which had not survived the onset of the Depression. At first there was no discernible political orientation. In the fourth issue (January 1936), however, the pressure of the rise of proletarian literature was being felt: "Somebody asked me why *Challenge* was for the most part so pale pink. We said because the few red articles we did receive were not literature. We care a lot about style." But the editor was eager to print stylistically competent social protest material, for she could not shut her eyes to conditions in Harlem: "We would like to print more articles and stories of protest. We have daily contact with the underprivileged. We know their suffering and soul weariness. They have only the meagre bread and meat of the dole, and that will not feed their failing spirits."[98] By the time of the 1937 spring issue, Miss West had become willing to compromise her stylistic standards if necessary to encourage young writers: "Certainly we prefer a progressive magazine. Certainly we prefer manuscripts from new Negro writers; or, rather, we are happiest when the greater balance of the magazine is devoted to the young Negro. But we have no intention of dictating style, choice of subject, or content. We could defeat the purpose of the magazine, mainly to foster developing talents, if we rejected these early gropings toward style, social consciousness and adulthood." Since her desire was "for the young Negro to grow to complete awareness of his heritage, his position as a member of a minority group, and his duty to take some active part in social reform," she was pleased by the Chicago group of which Wright was a member, and she promised it a forum in her next issue of *Challenge*.[99] The next issue turned out to be *New Challenge*, and Wright and Marian Minus, another Chicagoan, shared editorial duties with Miss West.

The shift in editorial emphasis in this little magazine provides in capsule form an instructive example of the general change in Afro-American writing from the exotic bohemianism of the Harlem Renaissance to the social consciousness of Wright and other WPA writers. Indeed, as Arna Bontemps has pointed out,[100] one may

98 Dorothy West, "Dear Reader," *Challenge*, I (January 1936), 38.
99 "Dear Reader" (Spring 1937), pp. 40-41.
100 "Famous WPA Authors," *Negro Digest*, VIII (June 1950), 43-47.

speak of a WPA school that included Bontemps himself, who was a veteran of the Harlem Renaissance, Wright, Margaret Walker, the early Frank Yerby, Willard Motley, Robert Hayden, Frank Marshall Davis, Theodore Ward, William Attaway, and others. In the case of many writers not actually on the Writers' Project, such as Langston Hughes, the same development is seen.

What were the duties and opportunities of the newest of the New Negro writers? To this question Wright addressed himself briefly in his *Daily Worker* article announcing *New Challenge* and at length in "Blueprint for Negro Writing," which appeared in the first issue of the magazine. The latter essay begins by rejecting the Harlem Renaissance writers because they pandered to a white audience rather than directing themselves to the needs of black people. In so doing, according to Wright, they ignored the collective consciousness embodied in black folklore and thus abdicated their social responsibility in favor of literary posturing and clowning, which, however clever and ornamental, were essentially sterile both culturally and artistically.[101]

But Wright was not calling for a mere photographic representation of black folkways in the manner of, say, Zora Neale Hurston, a novelist who turned her anthropological training to the purposes of fiction. Instead, he urged the assimilation of black folklore into a sophisticated sensibility guided by a Marxist analysis of society and steeped in modern literature (Eliot, Stein, Joyce, Proust, Hemingway, Anderson, Gorky, Barbusse, Nexø, and London are mentioned in the essay). A writer who met these qualifications would both accept black nationalism and transcend it, would both express the meaning of the black man's past experience in America and formulate his future role: "He is being called upon to do no less than create values by which his race is to struggle, live and die."[102] Such a messianic function could operate only within the framework of a fluid social situation in which capitalism was dying and the new order was being born.

Wright's Marxist perspective on literature in "Blueprint for Negro Writing" is by no means crude, however. He is fully aware

---

[101] "Blueprint for Negro Writing," pp. 53-56.
[102] Ibid., p. 59.

of the dangers of programmatic Marxist didacticism: "Yet, for the Negro writer, Marxism is but the starting point. No theory of life can take the place of life. After Marxism has laid bare the skeleton of society, there remains the task of the writer to plant flesh upon those bones out of his will to live." More specifically, he resists any limitations on the writer's choice of technique or his apprehension of reality: "Negro life may be approached from a thousand angles with no limit to technical and stylistic freedom. . . . If the sensory vehicle of imaginative writing is required to carry too great a load of didactic material, the artistic sense is submerged."[103] In some respects, indeed, the essay may be considered an implicit criticism of his earliest poetry. By 1937, then, Wright could no longer be considered an artist-in-uniform either in his critical theory or, as we shall see, in his fiction.

Suffering a common fate of little magazines, *New Challenge* ceased publication with its first issue. But before its demise, Wright as one of its editors made a signal contribution to American literature by encouraging Ralph Ellison to turn from music to literature as the chief outlet of his creative energy. Having read with interest one of Wright's poems, presumably "We of the Streets," Ellison met him soon after his arrival in New York. Evidently impressed by the younger man, Wright first asked him to review E. Waters Turpin's novel *These Low Grounds* for *New Challenge* and then to write a short story.[104] In addition to encouragement and example, Wright offered him literary guidance, particularly concerning fictional technique: "Fortunately for me, Wright, then on the verge of his first success, was eager to talk with a beginner and I was able to save valuable time in searching out those works in which writing was discussed as a craft. He guided me to Henry James' prefaces, to Conrad, to Joseph Warren Beach and to the letters of Dostoievsky."[105] Ellison has protested, rather too strongly, against claims that his work was deeply influenced by Wright. One may readily con-

---

[103] Ibid., pp. 60, 62, 63.

[104] Ralph Ellison, "The Art of Fiction VIII," *Paris Review*, III (Spring 1955), 56-57. See also Ellison, "That Same Pain, That Same Pleasure: An Interview," *Shadow and Act* (New York, 1964), pp. 14-16.

[105] Ralph Ellison, "Hidden Name and Complex Fate: A Writer's Experience in the United States," *Shadow and Act*, p. 161.

cede that during the long gestation of *Invisible Man* other in-
fluences were doubtlessly exerted, but it seems clear that Langston
Hughes, who introduced the two, was close to the truth when he
said that "for [Ellison] Wright became a sort of literary god for a
time."[106]

In addition to his editorial duties on *New Challenge* and his own
writing, Wright was kept busy during the latter part of 1937 as a
Communist journalist. At the beginning of August he became chief
Harlem correspondent for the *Daily Worker*. During the next five
months he contributed forty signed articles to the party newspaper,
and most of the briefer, unsigned dispatches from the Harlem
bureau were perhaps also from his hand. Of the forty signed articles, ten deal with hardships of life in Harlem, eight with more
general aspects of the black struggle, six with party affairs, six with
political campaigns and elections, six with foreign affairs (Spain,
China, and Latin America), three with black theater and art, and
one with labor news. For the most part, this writing is routine party
reporting with the usual propagandistic slant. Much of it must have
seemed a waste of time and effort to a young writer who rightfully
thought that he was destined for less perishable work. Doing such a
piece as "Harlem Women Hit Boost in Milk Price," he must have
recalled the earlier importunate intrusions on his time by trivial
party activities in Chicago.[107]

On the other hand, his *Daily Worker* reporting served to widen
his acquaintance with life in Harlem, as his insurance work had
given him greater understanding of Chicago's South Side, and thus
helped to prepare him for his section on Harlem in *New York*

[106] Letter to Michel Fabre, 25 April 1963. Ellison's hypersensitivity to the
contention that he was influenced by Wright is revealed in his interesting ex-
change with Irving Howe. See Howe, "Black Boys and Native Sons," *Dissent*,
X (Autumn 1963), 353-68, and "A Reply to Ralph Ellison," *New Leader*,
XLVII (3 February 1964), 12-14, and Ellison, "The World and the Jug,"
*New Leader*, XLVI (9 December 1963), 22-26, and "A Rejoinder," *New
Leader*, XLVII (3 February 1964), 15-22.

[107] Of those earlier intrusions, Wright was to write, "I was in the midst of
writing a novel and he was calling me from it to tabulate the price of groceries."
"I Tried to Be a Communist" (September 1944), p. 50. As Frank Marshall
Davis has observed, "The Party blindly did not encourage and make use of
his talents; instead he was sent to pass out leaflets and do the work which could
have been performed just as effectively by the members without artistic po-
tentials." Letter to the author, 24 October 1964.

*Panorama*. It also served to continue his education on American racial matters in general. Occasionally it seems to have contributed specifically to his fiction. For example, the epigraph of *Uncle Tom's Children* was probably suggested by a comment of Edward Strong, executive secretary of the Southern Negro Youth Congress, in an interview with Wright: "In many sections of the South the days of Uncle Tom are over. Among the younger generation of Negroes there is a saying that Uncle Tom is dead. Young Negroes are taking their destiny into their own hands."[108] Similarly, Boris Max's questioning of Henry Dalton about his real estate policies in the last part of *Native Son* draws directly from Wright's coverage of a hearing conducted by the New York State Temporary Commission on Conditions among Urban Negroes.[109] Finally, his reporting for the *Daily Worker* brought his name repeatedly before the Communist public, which was to be a receptive audience for his early books.

The liberal audience, too, was to encounter Wright's name before the appearance of his first book. "Big Boy Leaves Home" had appeared late in 1936, and a year later he wrote a review for the *New Republic*.[110] Much of his energy after arriving in New York was consumed by his work on the Federal Writers' Project of New York City. In August his powerful essay "The Ethics of Living Jim Crow," the germ of *Black Boy*, was published in *American Stuff*, an anthology of creative writing by members of the Writers' Project from across the country. His main responsibility, however, was work on the Harlem sections of *New York Panorama* and *New York City Guide*, two volumes in the American Guide Series, the major achievement of the Federal Writers' Project. The latter is a detailed, factual work, but *New York Panorama* offered some opportunity for interpretation. Wright's portion of this book is chapter 5, "Portrait of Harlem." Actually the chapter is more comprehensive than its title suggests, for it deals with blacks in New York generally and begins with a historical sketch of the race's three centuries in

[108] Richard Wright, "Negro Youth on March, Says Leader," *Daily Worker,* 7 October 1937, p. 3.
[109] "Gouging, Landlord Discrimination against Negroes Bared at Hearing," *Daily Worker,* 15 December 1937, p. 6. Cf. *Native Son* (New York, 1940), pp. 276-79.
[110] "A Sharecropper's Story," *New Republic,* XCIII (1 December 1937), 109.

the city. Virtually all aspects of contemporary life are treated: housing, employment, business, restaurants, religion, political and social movements and organizations, the effect of New Deal relief measures, literature, art, theater, music, dance, sports, reading, and education. Though restrained and edited to fit the communal nature of a Writers' Project publication, "Portrait of Harlem" exposes frankly the facts of racial prejudice and discrimination. The concluding paragraph implicitly renounces both the myth of the happy black man and reformist New Deal optimism and delivers a foreboding prophecy: "The question of what will ultimately happen to the Negro in New York is bound up with the question of what will happen to the Negro in America. It has been said that the Negro embodies the 'romance of American life'; if that is true, the romance is one whose glamor is overlaid with shadows of tragic premonition."[111]

[111] *New York Panorama,* p. 151.

# Lawd Today and Uncle Tom's Children

# THREE

Romance and glamour, Wright knew, were precisely the qualities most conspicuously absent from black life in America, and thus those most necessary for guilt-ridden whites to invent. This truth so guardedly stated at the end of "Portrait of Harlem" is central in Wright's first two works of fiction, *Lawd Today* and *Uncle Tom's Children,* the former depicting the brutalization of black life in the urban North and the latter the terror of direct white oppression in the rural South.

Though published posthumously in 1963, *Lawd Today* is Wright's first novel, begun probably in 1934 or 1935 and finished in 1937. As has been noted earlier,[1] Wright was working on a novel in the fall of 1935. Since the setting of *Lawd Today* is Chicago early in 1937, indicated by topical references,[2] the composition of the book obviously extended into that year. It also seems clear that the novel was completed before *Uncle Tom's Children* and certainly before *Native Son*. Aside from artistic weaknesses indicating an apprentice work, evidence suggesting that it could not have been

---

[1] See above, p. 65. In an autobiographical note written to accompany "Big Boy Leaves Home" in 1936, Wright said, "At present I'm busy with a novel." *The New Caravan,* ed. Alfred Kreymborg, Lewis Mumford, and Paul Rosenfeld (New York, 1936), p. 663.

[2] "You know . . . it looks like we black folks is just about to be shutout. We done got two outs on us in the ninth inning. Old Haile Selassie and Joe Louis *both* done struck out!" *Lawd Today,* p. 52. Louis lost to Max Schmeling on 19 June 1936, and the last Ethiopian resistance to Italian occupation crumbled early in 1937.

written later is provided by the fact that Wright's works in progress were well publicized after he achieved fame. Furthermore, a fellow proletarian novelist from Chicago, Albert Halper, has stated that before the publication of *Native Son* Wright had written an unpublished novel "about the Chicago Post Office where he had been employed as a night-shift sorter."[3]

It is useful to approach *Lawd Today* with "Blueprint for Negro Writing" clearly in mind, for the essay seems a clear statement of the novel's intention, if not its achievement. This intention was to bring a sharpened class and social consciousness to black people, utilizing the rich tradition of black folklore but at the same time attempting to transcend the black nationalism, imposed by a segregated society, out of which this folklore grew. For a novel with such a purpose, *Lawd Today* is remarkably free from overt propagandizing; certainly this is the case when one compares it to other radical novels of the time, including Wright's own *Native Son*. For the most part, Wright was content in his first novel to let the implications of his protagonist's blighted and futile existence speak for themselves.

The simple but neat structure of *Lawd Today* was implicit in Wright's choice of a subject — one sordid but typical day in the life of Jake Jackson, a Chicago postal clerk who hates his job, his wife, his race, and himself, from the time he awakes until he sinks into a drunken sleep some twenty hours later, bleeding from cuts suffered in a vicious brawl with his wife. In the interim, Jake in Part One, "Commonplace," bathes, dresses, eats breakfast, quarrels with and beats his wife, looks over his mail, leaves his house to visit a policy parlor, gets a haircut at "Doc Higgins' Tonsorial Palace," plays bridge with three fellow postal workers, watches a street vendor selling quack medicine, eats lunch, witnesses a black nationalist parade, and rides to work on the elevated train. Part Two, "Squirrel Cage," relates Jake's dismal workday at the post office. As it begins, Jake faces the board of review, which is on the point of firing him because of his wife's complaint of his brutality, but he is saved by a telephone call from the politically influential barber,

---

[3] Albert Halper, ed., *This Is Chicago* (New York, 1952), p. 130. See also Halper's memoir, *Good-bye, Union Square* (Chicago, 1970), pp. 231-39.

Doc Higgins.[4] Jake endures the dull routine of the physically and emotionally enervating postal work only with the aid of escapist daydreams and conversations. The final part of the novel, "Rats' Alley," deals with the misadventures of Jake and his friends in a South Side brothel, where he is robbed and beaten. Regaining consciousness in an alley with his friends, Jake stops in a beer tavern before stumbling home to a violent fight with his wife.

This day, the reader infers, is a typical one in Jake's life, but it is also a particular day — 12 February 1937. *Lawd Today* not only presents the frustrations and misery of an individual black man, but also turns to the larger forces that have shaped — or warped — his life and that he so thoroughly misunderstands. Wright uses three main devices to achieve this additional dimension. The first is the newspapers that Jake reads at breakfast and in the taxi on the way to the brothel. His comments on the news reports reveal his assimilation of some of the most deleterious values of white American society, such as empty Republican clichés, money worship, and even racism directed against "Jews, Dagos, Hunkies, and Mexicans."[5] Indeed, Jake here sounds like nothing so much as a black George F. Babbitt. Jake's conversations with his friends, particularly Doc Higgins and the three fellow postal clerks, also lead outward from Jake's private hell to the social forces that created it. Finally, the most successful device for achieving this dual focus is the recurrent use of snatches from a radio broadcast celebrating Lincoln's birthday and the northern victory in the Civil War. Here the irony is more complex, for the point is not merely Jake's bored reaction to the broadcast and the contrast between the importance of the events it relates and the triviality of Jake's life, but also the tragic failure of America to fulfill the promise of the idealism of Lincoln and Garrison, a failure that made possible such a life as Jake's, so that the tones of the radio speaker are inevitably pompous and hollow.

Irony is indeed the pervasive mood of *Lawd Today*, but the method is an unsparing naturalism. The dreary monotony of work in the post office, for example, is recorded in minute detail. In classic naturalistic tradition, moreover, individual lives are deter-

---

[4] Doc Higgins is patterned after the real B. Doc Huggins, a South Side barber and ward leader. See Webb, *Richard Wright,* pp. 101-2.

[5] *Lawd Today,* p. 31.

mined by biological as well as socioeconomic forces. The exigencies of food, drink, and sex, particularly the last, influence Jake and his friends as much as racial and economic discrimination.

Jake's frustration is thus both social and personal. In the dream from which he is awakened by the Lincoln Day radio broadcast at the beginning of the novel, he is climbing an endless stairway, called on by the voice of his boss. This dream clearly represents the futile treadmill of his life, for as a Chicago black in the Depression he can hardly hope to rise higher than his position as a postal clerk, but it also has a Freudian significance[6] immediately reinforced by the erotic dream that follows it as he drowses before being fully awakened by the arrival of the milkman, whose innocent chat with Lil, Jake's wife, arouses his jealousy. Sexual frustration, indeed, is a central theme of *Lawd Today*. Lil is incapable of sexual relations as a result of the abortion that Jake forced upon her. Jake is recurrently titillated by erotic daydreams and by passing women. On one occasion he lasciviously gazes at pornographic photographs. Even in the brothel Jake is aroused and titillated but unfulfilled, for the fight takes place as he prepares to pay the prostitute for her impending services but discovers that his pocket has been picked. Of Jake's three friends, Bob is incapacitated by venereal disease, and the tubercular Slim's voracious sexual appetite signifies his inability to achieve real sexual fulfillment.

It must be conceded, however, that Wright is not successful in relating Jake's sexual frustration to the economic and social implications of his existence. The very difficult rapprochement of Freud and Marx is not achieved in *Lawd Today*.

Nor does Wright manage to weave his interest in urban black folklore closely enough into the fabric of his tale of Jake's day. Often the reader is uncomfortably aware of the abrupt shifts of emphasis from Jake to black life in general, as in the descriptions of the policy parlor, the street vendor of a bottled panacea, and the black nationalist parade. The conversations of Jake and his three friends, in which the identities of the separate speakers tend to blur,

---

[6] "Steep inclines, ladders, and stairs, and going up or down them, are symbolic representations of the sexual act." Sigmund Freud, *The Interpretation of Dreams*, in *The Basic Writings of Sigmund Freud*, trans. and ed. A. A. Brill (New York, 1938), p. 372.

form a kind of communal choric chant of black people, but their relevance to Jake's individual situation is often quite tangential. The point is not that the often tediously detailed descriptions of such matters are unrelated to the thematic concerns of *Lawd To-day;* on the contrary, the circulars Jake finds in his mailbox advertise policy-diviners and patent medicines for sexual impotence and alcoholism, thus indicating that sex, drink, and gambling are the opiates of black people, and the description of the obese street vendor is a satirical vignette of the American petit bourgeois capitalist similar in spirit and detail to one of William Gropper's *New Masses* caricatures: "A *red* tie with a horseshoe stickpin nestled between the wings of a soiled collar, and each jerk of his neck set up a shower of *white* and *blue* sparks. His lips were plump and loose, and his little red eyes were all but drowned in the oily fat of his cheeks. A round potbelly rose and bulged over a wide belt like an inflated balloon. . . ."[7] The point is rather that the sociological themes of the novel are not fully integrated into the story of Jake's ordeal, but often seem to be included for their intrinsic interest, which is great (who would wish to dispense with the magnificently obscene comedy of the bout at "the dozens" between Jake and Al), or for their doctrinal import.

This failure in the fusion of the novel's materials accounts in part for the relaxed effect of the narrative, though of course this quality of aimlessness results also from the meaningless routine of Jake's life. Most strikingly absent from *Lawd Today* when compared to the rest of Wright's early fiction is the extraordinary tension of the first two parts of *Native Son* and the concentrated intensity of the stories in *Uncle Tom's Children.*

*Lawd Today* is not a story of crises in the lives of the black proletariat, but the story of an ordinary day in the life of Jake Jackson, a *lumpen-proletarier* with unfulfillable bourgeois illusions. Despite its moments of tedium, its failure to integrate its dual focus on Jake and on his environment, and its weaknesses of proportion, *Lawd Today* offers much vivid writing, as in the physical description of Jake awakening or in the wildly sensual atmosphere of the brothel. Above all, the novel conveys an undeniably real impression of ordi-

---

[7] *Lawd Today*, p. 83. Italics mine.

nary black life in the Chicago of the thirties. The quality of this life is not enveloped in unrelieved gloom; Jake has moments of rough but genuine camaraderie with his friends and even moments when he senses the attraction of a different level of life, as when a branch of the Chicago Public Library arouses his mild curiosity. Jake also enjoys the early hint of spring when he steps from his house in the morning. But he awoke that morning with lacerated nerves, a sour taste in his mouth, and a queasy stomach. As the day wears on, the weather turns bad, and as the novel ends, Jake sleeps, drunken and bleeding, and his wife, also bleeding, wishes she were dead, while "outside an icy wind swept around the corner of the building, whining and moaning like an idiot in a deep black pit."[8] The cyclic nature of Jake's day — and his life — is clear enough. Characteristically, Wright presents in *Lawd Today* an emotionally crippled protagonist living a blighted life. Characteristically also, Wright does not permit the reader to evade his wrathful indictment of the society responsible for creating a Jake Jackson.

Issued by a small publishing house more than a quarter-century after its composition, *Lawd Today* was little noticed in the United States, despite the great topical interest in books concerning black people. Only a handful of American reviews appeared. Granville Hicks and Lewis Gannett both regarded it as clearly an apprentice work, though Hicks found in it redeeming naturalistic virtues of honesty and power.[9] One reviewer praised its characterizations but found its environmental determinism anachronistic.[10] A Catholic

---

[8] Ibid., p. 189. Wright used this vivid simile again in *Native Son*, p. 200: "Outside in the cold night the wind moaned and died down, like an idiot in an icy black pit."

[9] Granville Hicks, "Dreiser to Farrell to Wright," *Saturday Review*, XLVI (30 March 1963), 37-38; Lewis Gannett, "*Lawd Today*. By Richard Wright," *New York Herald Tribune Books*, 5 May 1963, p. 10. The extent to which Wright had been forgotten in his native land is well illustrated by Gannett's review. After saying that the novel was written in 1936, Gannett asserted erroneously that this was "in the floundering years after Wright had left the Communist Party...." Gannett should have remembered the chronology of Wright's career more accurately, for he himself had reviewed *Uncle Tom's Children* (twice), *Native Son*, *12 Million Black Voices*, *Black Boy*, and *Black Power*.

[10] Louise Giles, "Wright, Richard. Lawd Today," *Library Journal*, LXXX-VIII (1 April 1963), 1549.

reviewer was impressed by Wright's "undeviating honesty" but, predictably if inconsistently, deprecated his "excessive realism."[11] *Time* magazine was perhaps most impressed by the novel, though it called Wright artistically "as crude and humorlessly 'sincere' as his Depression-period white twin, James Farrell." Comparing Wright to James Baldwin, the review acknowledged the debt the younger man owed his predecessor. It concluded sanguinely: "No more books can be written in which the fate of the U.S. Negro is as nasty, brutish, short and hard as it was only yesterday for Jake Jackson. But *Lawd Today* is a thing to remember."[12] The most damning American notice came from black critic Nick Aaron Ford, who, deeply shocked by the novel's unflattering portrayal of blacks, expressed doubts that the work was Wright's own.[13]

Ironically, the most penetrating review of *Lawd Today* was English, not American. The *Times Literary Supplement* spoke trenchantly of the artistic defects of the book, but it seemed unaware of the work's early date, and it was less than reliable in its estimate of what it called Wright's "dubious sociological presumptions." Chief of these was that society is responsible for its Jake Jacksons: "In memorable works like *Native Son* and *Black Boy,* Richard Wright took the lid off social sewers of prejudice and exploitation; in this posthumous novel he has taken the lid off the sewer of a human mind. If Jake is a victim of social abuse, he is so only by implication; but by graphic demonstration he is himself an arrogant and thoughtless animal, and nothing in the novel convinces the reader that this is a fault of society."[14] *Time,* on the other hand, was pleased by the fact that "Jake is no left-wing stereotype of a good man. He and society match each other in crude nastiness."[15] It is absurd, however, to suppose that he is a match for those social forces that produced him, and it is artistically unreasonable to urge that Wright

11 Doris Grumbach, "Fiction Shelf," *Critic*, XXI (June-July 1963), 82.
12 "Native Sons," *Time*, LXXXI (5 April 1963), 106. The *Time* reviewer had no more success than Lewis Gannett in getting his facts straight, for he asserted that Baldwin first met Wright in Paris. Actually the two met in Brooklyn in the winter of 1944-45. See James Baldwin, *Nobody Knows My Name: More Notes of a Native Son* (New York, 1961), p. 191.
13 "The Fire Next Time? A Critical Survey of Belles Lettres by and about Negroes Published in 1963," *Phylon*, XXV (Second Quarter 1964), 129-30.
14 "Martyr or Traitor?" *Times Literary Supplement*, 29 April 1965, p. 324.
15 "Native Sons."

be blatantly explicit in spelling out the causal relationship between those forces and their deformed result. One would have expected the latter objection from a Marxist at the time the novel was written, but hardly from a *Times Literary Supplement* reviewer in 1965 who elsewhere in his review evinces considerable aesthetic sensitivity.

Reviewers of *Lawd Today* wrote with a perspective of Wright's entire career and of the early careers of Ellison and Baldwin, as well as with a knowledge of the changes the twenty-five years from the novel's composition to its publication had wrought in the racial and economic situation of black Americans. It is small wonder that to some the book seemed anachronistic. But when *Uncle Tom's Children* was published in the spring of 1938, the note Wright struck seemed new indeed.

Of the four stories — "novellas" as they are called on the title page — in the first edition of *Uncle Tom's Children,* "Big Boy Leaves Home" was published in *The New Caravan* late in 1936, "Down by the Riverside" was written at about the same time,[16] and one or both of the others were probably also written before Wright left for New York.[17] Because of their arrangement and because of similarities in theme and method, the stories form a unified work of fiction, not merely a collection of disparate tales. Before turning to their collective effect, however, we must examine each of the stories individually.

Like the other stories in *Uncle Tom's Children,* "Big Boy Leaves Home" concerns the terrorized life of blacks in rural Mississippi. Like the other stories also, its focus is mainly within the conscious-

[16] "During the early days of the Chicago Writers' group, he showed me the manuscript of his Down by the Riverside. . . ." Letter from Theodore Ward to the author, 8 July 1965.

[17] See above, pp. 62, 66. Another short story that may have been written before he left Chicago is "Silt," which appeared in *New Masses,* XXIV (24 August 1937), 19-20, and was included as "The Man Who Saw the Flood" in *Eight Men* (1961). "Silt" is an excellent sketch of a black sharecropper who returns to his flood-ravaged farm only to be forced deeper into debt to his white landlord. Wright excluded this story from *Uncle Tom's Children* not, it would appear, because of any literary weakness, but because of its brevity and because its protagonist's acquiescence to his condition was incompatible with the theme of rebellion in the collected stories.

ness of its protagonist, here an adolescent named Big Boy Morrison. Finally, it is similar to the other stories in its emphasis on physical and psychological violence in black-white relations.

As "Big Boy Leaves Home" opens, the title character and three friends, having absented themselves from school, are enjoying an excursion in the countryside. They divert themselves with ribald songs, scuffling, and high-spirited horseplay. The idyllic setting and the exuberant animal spirits of the boys combine to invest the scene with a charming natural innocence (despite, or perhaps with the aid of, their awakening sexuality, which is in any case necessary for the ensuing confrontation with a white woman). After recalling the irascibility of Mr. Harvey, the white owner of the property, the boys hesitate to go swimming in a nearby creek, but nevertheless decide to do so. Stripping, they enter the water and splash about happily. They tire and soon return to the bank to dry in the sun before dressing again.

At this moment a white woman, betrothed to Harvey's son, appears suddenly on the creek bank. After a moment of startled confrontation, the woman hardly more frightened than the boys, she backs away to the tree under which they have left their clothes. When the boys approach her timidly to retrieve their clothes, she begins to scream, and her fiancé arrives with a rifle. In the struggle that follows he kills two of the boys, but is himself shot fatally by Big Boy. Now thoroughly terrified, Big Boy and Bobo, the other survivor, run to their homes.

After hurried and desperate consultation with Big Boy's family and three family friends, a plan of escape from the inevitable lynch mob is reached. Big Boy will hide in one of a number of kilns on a hill until morning, when he will meet a truck-driver, the son of one of his father's friends, conveying cargo to Chicago. Big Boy departs quickly for the hill.

As in much of Wright's fiction, the rhythm of action in "Big Boy Leaves Home" is a crescendo of violence. Approaching one of the kilns, Big Boy comes upon a large rattlesnake slithering out and coiling quickly. He kills it savagely with a stick. Then he crawls in the hole and drifts into a reverie in which he imagines, among other things, himself armed with his father's shotgun heroically selling his life dearly to a lynch mob. This visionary lynch mob is quickly replaced by the arrival of the real thing. As Big Boy crouches in his pit, the mob catches Bobo, to whom the Morrison family has sent a message to meet Big Boy at the kilns to effect a joint escape. In a particularly brutal lynching, Bobo is dismembered and burned alive, while Big Boy looks on from his hole. When the mob begins to disperse, a dog finds Big Boy's hiding place, which nevertheless remains undiscovered by the crowd, hurrying home as rain starts to fall. For the third time in the story, Big Boy must struggle for his life against a "bestial" opponent. In this most violent fight of the three, he manages finally to strangle the dog with his bare hands.

Big Boy passes the night in the rain-soaked pit with the dog's body for company inside and his friend's charred corpse outside. In the morning he meets Will Sanders, the truck-driver, according to plan, and they drive northward — toward Chicago, toward at least comparative "freedom."

This résumé of the story hardly does justice to some of its most interesting qualities, for this apparently simple tale of truancy, murder, lynching, and flight actually achieves its effects with considerable artistic skill. One of these effects is an almost painful intensity, partially inherent in the subject matter but also accentuated by Wright's calculated use of natural setting and point of view. The first device is fairly simple. As the boys come "out of the woods into cleared pasture," they lie with "their shoulders . . . flat to the earth . . . their faces square to the sun." As they sing, they begin "pounding bare heels in the grass."[18] Clearly they are, however briefly, enjoying a harmonious relationship with their natural environment. When they begin swimming, the warmth of the sun gives way to the chill water, now that the disaster is impending. Similarly, as the lynching takes place near the end of the story, "The sky sagged low, heavy with clouds. Wind was rising." The moment before the dog discovers Big Boy, "cold water chilled his ankles. He could hear raindrops steadily hissing."[19] Thus changes in the physical environment accompany, heighten, and correspond to changes in the narrative line, particularly at critical moments. It should be added that

[18] Richard Wright, *Uncle Tom's Children: Four Novellas* (New York, 1938), pp. 3, 5, 6.
[19] Ibid., pp. 61, 64-65.

Wright effects this discreetly and unobtrusively, well within the boundaries of realism; nowhere is there a hint of the pathetic fallacy.

The use of point of view to heighten intensity is somewhat more complex. In the first two sections of the story, the narrative focus is upon all four boys and then upon them and the two whites. The point of view is clearly third person. In the third section, the interest begins to center on Big Boy, though here his family and his father's friends also share it. In the climactic fourth section, the reader's attention is appropriately concentrated wholly on Big Boy during his ordeal. Indeed, the point of view makes the actual shift to first person during his reveries in the kiln. The reader witnesses the lynching from Big Boy's peculiar vantage point and, as it were, through his eyes, not from a neutral vantage point as in the fight between the boys and Jim Harvey. In the brief concluding section, the denouement of Big Boy's escape with Will, the strict concentration of the fourth section is appropriately relaxed somewhat. Thus the intensity of this story is heightened by a careful manipulation of natural setting and point of view.

The theme of "Big Boy Leaves Home" is a familiar one in American literature: the initiation of a youth into violence and his escape from it. Big Boy, indeed, may be considered a kind of postpubescent black Huck Finn who must light out for the territory — ironically, in Wright's story, the urban "territory" of Chicago — in order to achieve his freedom. The theme of initiation into violence and escape from it is one Wright was obsessed with; it was to recur in the autobiographical *Black Boy*[20] as well as in most of his fiction: *Native Son, The Outsider, The Long Dream,* and several of his short stories. It is, in fact, the major Wrightian theme.

But the theme achieves a special poignance in "Big Boy Leaves Home" through what might be termed a paradisiacal motif. Though something less than a fully and coherently developed symbolic pattern, this motif contributes a kind of emotional resonance to the story. Wright's use of natural setting has been discussed. Here it is only necessary to add that when the boys strip to swim, they are naked in this Edenic setting. As they lie on the bank after their

---

[20] "The Ethics of Living Jim Crow" was reprinted as the preface to the second, enlarged edition of *Uncle Tom's Children*. This important essay is a powerfully compact statement of the theme.

swim, the natural description is particularly peaceful: "A black winged butterfly hovered at the water's edge. A bee droned. From somewhere came the sweet scent of honeysuckles. Dimly they could hear sparrows twittering in the woods. They rolled from side to side, letting sunshine dry their skins and warm their blood. They plucked blades of grass and chewed them."[21] At precisely this moment the woman appears suddenly on this paradisiacal scene. Later, after killing the snake at the kiln, Big Boy "stomped it with his heel, grinding its head into the dirt."[22] In the story, then, there is a pattern of incident reminiscent of Genesis: the Garden, nakedness, the woman, the snake. Into the pastoral innocence of Big Boy's world intrudes violent white racism, driving him from the southern garden toward the uncertain freedom of the North. Like Wright's use of natural setting to reinforce mood, the parallels with Genesis are muted and unobtrusive, but quite effective.

One other device in "Big Boy Leaves Home" deserves mention — the symbolic use of northbound trains. On five separate occasions the whistle of a northbound train is heard. On the first, the response of the boys is to sing "Dis train boun fo Glory." When they hear the second train, its significance is made even more explicit:

"Lawd, Ahm goin Noth some day."
"Me too, man."
"They say colored folks up Noth is got ekual rights."[23]

For Big Boy Morrison, as for Richard Wright at the same age, the north star represents freedom and equality, and at the end of the story Big Boy is traveling toward this dream just as he is fleeing from the southern lynch mob. This theme of flight and quest recurs frequently in Wright's works. *Native Son* and *12 Million Black Voices* were to show that Chicago was not, after all, the haven it appeared to be from rural Mississippi. In his own life Wright found his haven at last in Paris, but even there his restlessness was not fully exorcised.

[21] *Uncle Tom's Children: Four Novellas*, pp. 20-21.
[22] Ibid., p. 49. Cf. Genesis 3:15: "And I will put enmity between thee and the woman, and between thy seed and her seed; it shall bruise thy head, and thou shalt bruise his heel."
[23] *Uncle Tom's Children: Four Novellas*, pp. 6, 20.

For Big Boy, crisis is precipitated out of an ordinary chance incident of daily life, but for the black farmer Mann, protagonist of the second story in *Uncle Tom's Children,* "Down by the Riverside," the situation is critical from the beginning, for the setting is a disastrous Mississippi flood. Mann finds himself and his family trapped in his house by the rising water. Food has been exhausted. Worst of all, his wife, Lulu, is in her fourth day of labor and requires emergency medical attention. Further, the crisis situation of the flood will inevitably intensify the normal persecution of blacks by whites. Mann, then, unlike the innocently irresponsible Big Boy, is burdened with crushing obligations. Again unlike Big Boy, his reaction to his troubles takes the form of confrontation, not escape, but since this confrontation, like Silas's in the following story, is individual rather than collective, it can end only in death.

As "Down by the Riverside" begins, Mann awaits the return of Bob, his brother-in-law, who has been sent to sell the family mule in order to buy a boat. He returns with fifteen dollars, the low price he received for the mule, and a stolen rowboat. Determined to take Lulu to a Red Cross hospital in the stolen boat despite the constantly increasing danger from both the whites and the rising water, Mann sets out against the current with Lulu, his son Peewee, and his mother-in-law, having first sent other family members to high ground in a neighbor's boat. Because of the stolen boat, Mann takes along his pistol.

The trip is a nightmare of physical exertion, natural danger, and human violence. Confused because the flood has concealed familiar landmarks, Mann finds his way with great difficulty, frequently bumping into submerged objects. In a desperate effort to get help for his wife, he rows toward the first lights he sees. Unfortunately his calls are answered by the owner of the stolen boat. Ignoring Mann's appeal for help, the heartless Heartfield starts shooting when he sees the boat. Returning his fire, Mann kills him and then rows away with the screams of Heartfield's wife and son in his ears. At last he encounters two soldiers, the flooded area having been placed under martial law. More impressed by his rowing feat than by his wife's medical emergency, they finally are persuaded to make a telephone call that brings a motorboat to tow Mann to the hospital. Here he is directed to the Jim Crow section, where a doctor examines Lulu and discovers that she is dead.

Mann is not given time to indulge his grief, however, for almost immediately his boat is commandeered, Peewee and Grannie are sent to high ground, and he is conscripted for work on a threatened levee. As he arrives the levee breaks, and he is ordered back to the hospital with another black man, Brinkley, for rescue work. After this has been completed and he is leaving for the hills and possible escape, a colonel gives him a slip of paper with the address of a woman and two children who have telephoned for help. Mann passes the paper to Brinkley, who reads the Heartfield address.

After a perilous trip to the Heartfield house, during which he almost brings himself to seek Brinkley's aid in his predicament, Mann climbs into the second-floor window while his partner remains in the boat. When the Heartfield boy recognizes him, Mann lifts the axe he has brought with him from the hospital, where it had been used in the rescue operations. As he pauses with the uplifted axe, he is thrown suddenly to the floor when the house tilts. In a semi-stupor, he then helps the family into the boat and rides with them to the hills and his doom.

Upon arrival he is not immediately apprehended as he expected to be, but walks past the soldiers and other whites to the tents of the blacks, hoping somehow to escape. As he is drinking coffee, however, soldiers arrive with the Heartfield boy and lead him away. Almost lynched by angry white civilians, he reaches the general's tent and is condemned to death after a summary hearing. As he is being taken out to be executed, he dashes away toward the water. He is shot. When the soldiers reach the body, one of them turns it over with his rifle butt, causing it to roll down the slope to the water — "Down by the Riverside."

The plot of this story has a serious weakness. Mann's two meetings with the Heartfield family seem contrived and implausible. The reader may grant the coincidence of Mann's calling for help from the very family in whose stolen boat he is riding, though it is difficult to understand why the marooned Heartfields did not telephone for aid before the fatal encounter. The coincidence of Mann's being directed to the Heartfield house once again, however, strains credulity to the breaking point, especially when one asks why Mrs. Heartfield did not report the murder of her husband when she finally sought help from the Red Cross hospital. Carelessness in regard to details of the plot is apparent elsewhere in the story. When Elder Murray arrives at the Mann cabin in the first section, "Mann opened the door. It was pitch black outside." A few minutes later when Mann starts on his trip, "Above his head the sky was streaked with faint grey light."[24]

It must be conceded, though, that the casual reader is not likely to notice such contradictions in the swiftly paced narrative. Instead he is caught up in the confused rush and whirl of events and swept along, like Mann, as if in the flood itself. Wright's main means of engaging the reader in this way is his rapid and frequent shifts in point of view from third person to first person and back, as in this paragraph:

> Mann looked, his chin over his shoulder. There were two squares of dim, yellow light. For a moment Mann was puzzled. He plied the oars and steadied the boat. Those lights seemed *too* high up. He could not associate them. But they were on Pikes' Road and they seemed about a hundred yards away. Wondah whut kin tha be? Maybe he could get some help there. He rowed again, his back to the lights; but their soft, yellow glow was in his mind. They helped him, those lights. For awhile he rowed without effort. Where there were lights there were people, and where there were people there was help. Wondah whose house is tha? Is they white folks? Fear dimmed the lights for a moment; but he rowed on and they glowed again, their soft sheen helping him to sweep the oars.[25]

This rapid movement between objective and subjective point of view forces the reader both to understand and to experience the action of the story, to observe and simultaneously to immerse himself in Mann's agony.

The most striking stylistic device employed in "Down by the Riverside" is the careful use and repetition of colors until they acquire symbolic overtones. Throughout his works Wright displays an acute sensitivity to the connotations of white and black, and in

[24] Ibid., pp. 86, 92.
[25] Ibid., pp. 96-97.

this story these two colors, along with the intermediate and likewise racially significant colors of yellow and brown, are especially prominent. They first appear in the description of the floodwaters in the first paragraph:

> Through a dingy pane he saw yellow water swirling around a corner of the barn. A steady drone filled his ears. In the morning the water was a deep brown. In the afternoon it was a clayey yellow. And at night it was black, like a restless tide of liquid tar. It was about six feet deep and still rising; it had risen two feet that day. He squinted at a tiny ridge of white foam where the yellow current struck a side of the barn and veered sharply. For three days he had been watching that tiny ridge of white foam. When it shortened he had hopes of seeing the ground soon; but when it lengthened he knew that the current was flowing strong again.

The sinister implications of the foam's whiteness in this passage are suggested whenever the color recurs in the story. When Bob arrives with a rowboat, the color is insistently repeated:

> Behind him a white rowboat trembled in the current.
> "How yuh come out, Bob?"
> Bob looked up and flashed a white grin.
> "See?" he said, pointing to the white boat.

The hope that Bob brings soon proves illusory, for he tells his relatives that the " 'stingy white ape' " Bowman paid only fifteen dollars for the mule, and that the white boat has been stolen from Heartfield, a white man. Bob attempts to dissuade Mann from rowing the boat into town: " 'Everbody knows his boat when they see it; its white n yuh couldnt git erway wid it. . . . Everwhere Ah looked wuznt nothin but white men wid guns.' " In the encounter with Heartfield the man's white face is emphasized as well as the white boat. During the shooting Mann sees him vividly illuminated by the light of the open door in which he stands: "The man was wearing a white shirt and was playing the yellow flare over the black water."[26] When Mann returns to rescue the Heartfield mother and children, their sinister whiteness is also stressed. The other colors are less consistently used with precise symbolic value, but they frequently do carry racially significant overtones.

[26] Ibid., pp. 73-74, 80, 81, 84, 100.

The use of color is singularly appropriate to the central theme of "Down by the Riverside" — racial persecution and conflict. Racial prejudice emerges constantly in the story when the two races meet or think of each other. Communication between the races is thus difficult or impossible because whites simply will not listen to blacks, preferring instead to consign them automatically to a category of subhuman stereotypes. Calling out to Heartfield for help, Mann says, " 'Mah wifes sick! Shes in birth! Ahm takin her t the hospital! Yuh gotta phone in there?' " Heartfield replies, " 'Nigger, where you steal that boat?' " The soldiers Mann encounters similarly treat him according to their preconceptions of blacks instead of according to the emergency of his actual situation. When he desperately explains his wife's condition to the two soldiers who first stop him, one of them replies, " 'Well, Ill be Goddamned! Nigger, you take the prize! I always heard that a niggerd do anything, but I never thought anybody was fool enough to row a boat against that current...' " After Lulu's death, a colonel quizzes Mann:

"Is that your mother there?"
"Yessuh. Mah ma-in-law."
"Whats wrong with her?"
"She jus ol, Capm. Her gal jus died n she takes it hard."
"When did she die?"
"Jus now, suh."
"Oh, I see... But whats wrong with you? Are you sick?"

And when Mann explains to a soldier who has discovered him sobbing that his wife has just died, the soldier says, " 'Shucks, nigger! You ought to be glad youre not dead in a flood like this.' " Even a relatively sympathetic white nurse can express her sympathy only by muttering, " 'Poor nigger.' "[27]

The moral obtuseness that the southern racial system engenders in whites in their relations with blacks, increased in this story by the situation of crisis, raises the question of how it is to be dealt with by its black victims. One way is simply to accept it with Christian resignation, trusting in God for protection, consolation, and finally salvation. Like "Fire and Cloud" and, in the second, enlarged edition of *Uncle Tom's Children*, "Bright and Morning

[27] Ibid., pp. 98, 99, 107, 118, 122, 113.

Star," the title of "Down by the Riverside" is drawn from a black spiritual, one actually sung early in the story. The religion of southern blacks here and elsewhere in Wright is defeatist and escapist, no matter how consoling. The two main representatives of the religious point of view in "Down by the Riverside" are Grannie and Elder Murray. Grannie chides her son for " 'thinkin sin' " when he avows his temptation to steal from the cheating Bowman, and she almost decides to stay in the cabin and drown rather than violate her moral scruples by riding in a stolen boat. By evading confrontation with the white oppressor, her religion guarantees her continued subordination. Elder Murray's faith is likewise unrelated to the realities of racial conflict. When Mann takes the reasonable precaution of getting out his pistol for the dangerous trip, Murray's reaction is to say, " 'Brothers n Sistahs, les all kneel n pray.' " As Murray leads the prayer, asking God to " 'soften the hard hearts of them white folks there in town,' " Mann is thinking of the more practical method of exchanging boats with Murray so as not to go into town in a stolen boat. He dismisses the thought, however, realizing that "Hell wanna know why n then Ahll have t tell im Bob stole it. N the Elder ain gonna hep nobody he thinks ain doin right."[28]

Mann himself represents another way of dealing with southern white oppression. He is a pragmatic individualist. His thoughts always center on what he himself can do in a particular situation. And his solitary efforts are heroic. Instead of taking able-bodied Bob along with him on the trip to the hospital, he takes Grannie. He undergoes his ordeal with courage, intelligence, and resourcefulness, but he undergoes it alone. When Brinkley might have saved him, he cannot bring himself to ask for help. Thus Mann's pragmatic skills are fatally limited by his individualism, his penchant for going it alone.

For all his pragmatism, moveover, Mann is not wholly free of his mother-in-law's religious attitudes. He frequently invokes God, though usually only after his own efforts have failed. As he approaches the hills in the boat with Brinkley, Mrs. Heartfield, and her children, "a prayer rose up in him, a silent prayer. Lawd, save me now!" The answer to this prayer is his death. There are some

[28] Ibid., pp. 81, 87, 89.

hints that Mann may be considered a black Christ, a common figure in black writing about lynch victims. As Mann goes to his execution, he has difficulty walking, and the soldiers guarding him have a mocking, Roman callousness. The story ends with a clause that may suggest a Crucifixion image: "one black palm sprawled limply outward and upward, trailing in the brown current..." If Mann is a Christ figure, he is an ironic one, for his death is meaningless. It is more likely that the final clause links Mann's death to another futile death, that of his wife, whose "left arm fell from the table and hung limp"[29] as Mann placed her on it in the hospital. Mann's tragedy is not the Son of man's, for there is no redemptive power in his suffering and death. Nor, indeed, is Mann's tragedy man's, for it is conceived too strictly in racial terms.

"Down by the Riverside," then, demonstrates the failure of both religious faith and pragmatic individualism in coping with white oppression. The answer is not to lay down the sword and shield by the riverside in meek Christian submission; the war is real and must be studied. One cannot wage it alone however. The only viable answer is collective action. Perhaps Mann is correct in thinking that Elder Murray will not aid him, but he does not take the step of asking for his cooperation. Later he reasons that Brinkley would help him: "Ahm black like he is. He oughta be willin t hep me fo he would them..." But again Mann fails to ask for the aid that might be given: "Mann swallowed; then he felt that there would not be any use in his telling; he had waited too long. Even if he spoke now Brinkley would not turn back; they had come too far." When he reaches the camp for blacks in the hills, he once more intends to ask for help but does not do so. The point is most explicitly stated as he is apprehended by the soldiers and led from the midst of the onlooking blacks: "For a split second he was there among those blunt and hazy black faces looking silently and fearfully at the white folks take some poor black man away. Why don they hep me? Yet he knew that they would not and could not help him, even as he in times past had not helped other black men being taken by the white folks to their death..."[30] Black racial solidarity would

[29] Ibid., pp. 151, 166, 111.
[30] Ibid., pp. 141, 156-57.

seem necessary for successful resistance to naked white racial oppression.

The next story in *Uncle Tom's Children* is "Long Black Song," one of two works of fiction written by Wright from the viewpoint of a female protagonist. Sarah is a simple, young, northern Mississippi farmwife, caring for her baby as she awaits her husband's return from his trip to town to sell his cotton crop, shortly after World War I. As the story opens, she is able to pacify her fretful baby only by giving it an old clock, which it proceeds to beat contentedly with a stick. Feeling sharply her loneliness, she thinks of her first lover, Tom, who has been in Europe as a soldier.

Her reverie is interrupted by the sound of an approaching car. The driver is a young white man selling phonographs during the summer to finance his college studies. After showing her an attractive phonograph-clock combination, he seduces her. After their lovemaking he departs, leaving the phonograph-clock on approval at a ten-dollar discount and promising to return the following morning to complete the transaction with her husband.

Later the same night her husband, Silas, returns, having sold his cotton at a good price and having ambitiously bought ten additional acres of land. Elated, he has brought to Sarah not only the piece of red cloth she had requested but also a pair of new shoes. His happiness is soon quenched in a rising tide of jealousy as he discovers first the phonograph, then the white salesman's hat and pencil, and finally the conclusive proof of a damp handkerchief. Enraged, Silas begins to beat her with a rawhide whip, but she manages to escape with her baby into the darkness to spend the rest of the night on a nearby hill.

When she wakes in the morning, she looks down to see her husband standing in front of the house with the whip in his hand. She then hears the approach of the automobile of the salesman and his partner, coming to collect a down payment on the phonograph-clock. Unable to prevent the confrontation, she watches her husband and the salesman argue over the instrument, which Silas smashed the night before. Silas then strikes the man with his whip, struggles with both whites when the second comes to the aid of his partner, and dashes into the house for his rifle. He shoots one of the men, but the other escapes in the car.

When Silas went into the house, Sarah, aware of his intention, began running toward him in a vain effort to stop the fight. Arriving too late, she throws herself at his feet. She attempts to persuade her husband to flee from the ineluctable lynching party, but Silas coldly sends her away, expressing his hatred of whites and his resolution to fight them until death, but recognizing also the equal futility of defiance and acquiescence. As she is leaving, a caravan of automobiles filled with armed whites arrives. She watches as the mob approaches the house shooting, is repulsed briefly by Silas's answering shots, and then sends two men to fire the house. Silas stays inside the blazing house to die, and the story ends as Sarah, seeing the burning walls cave in, turns and runs "blindly across the fields, crying, 'Naw, Gawd!' "[31]

Wright's choice of narrative perspective in this story has important consequences. The action is filtered through Sarah's rather diffuse sensibility. Her personality is a passive one; she reacts rather than acts. In the last half of the story, indeed, she is essentially an observer of the action. The effect on the reader is a reduced sense of immediacy and intensity; he does not suffer with Silas as he does with Big Boy and Mann. From Sarah's perspective on the hill, the encounter of Silas and the salesman seems an encounter of puppets: "They faced each other, the white man standing up and Silas sitting down; like two toy men they faced each other. She saw Silas point the whip to the smashed graphophone. The white man looked down and took a quick step backward. The white man's shoulders were bent and he shook his head from left to right. Then Silas got up and they faced each other again; like two dolls, a white doll and a black doll, they faced each other in the valley below."[32] Sarah is unlike the protagonists of the other stories in *Uncle Tom's Children* in another important respect: she does not participate directly in interracial violence. Indeed, she not only participates in interracial sexual intercourse, but she also has vague notions of interracial amity within a harmonious natural order.

[31] Ibid., p. 217.
[32] Ibid., p. 206.

This harmony, a merging of the rhythm of human life into the rhythms of the natural world, is Sarah's ideal. Her senses have been closely attuned to natural sensations and her emotions to the natural environment: "Yes; there had been all her life the long hope of white bright days and the deep desire of dark black nights. . . . There had been laughter and eating and singing and the long gladness of green cornfields in summer. There had been cooking and sewing and sweeping and the deep dream of sleeping grey skies in winter. Always it had been like that and she had been happy."[33] "White bright days and dark black nights" — the phrase is reiterated throughout the story to represent natural harmony and, finally, to suggest the possible racial harmony in the South yet to be realized.

One important component of Sarah's feeling for harmony with nature is her strong sexual impulse, which is not fully satisfied by Silas, who is older than his wife. Her frustration began when Tom left: "The happiness of those days and nights, of those green cornfields and grey skies had started to go from her when Tom had gone to war."[34] Though a good provider, Silas was distinctly Sarah's second choice sexually. And even Silas has been absent for a week. Sarah, then, is an easy mark for seduction by the young white man. In this way sex, central to the feeling of natural harmony of this earth-mother figure, becomes the trigger for the extreme disharmony of racial conflict.

One of the difficulties between the races is the cultural difference between black rural folk and "modern," urban whites. In point of fact, most whites in Mississippi in 1919 were also rural folk, but Wright makes his white salesman a college student studying science in Chicago, certainly antithetical to Sarah as he intrudes his profit-motivated, clock-regulated values on her natural order. But even before his appearance, the conflict is suggested by the symbol of the clock. Sarah's baby finds pleasure in striking an old broken clock: "Bang! Bang! Bang!" The refrain is repeated no fewer than eleven times in the first section of the story. Blacks need no clock, for their lives are close to the pulse of the earth itself, unlike whites, whose

---

[33] Ibid., p. 175.
[34] Ibid.

mechanical, rational civilization is sterile and artificial. The clock symbol suggests this, but Wright rather laboriously makes the point explicit in a conversation between the salesman and Sarah:

> "But why let her tear your clock up?"
> "It ain no good."
> "You could have it fixed."
> "We ain got no money t be fixin no clocks."
> "Havent you got a clock?"
> "Naw."
> "But how do you keep time?"
> "We git erlong widout time."
> "But how do you know when to get up in the morning?"
> "We jus git up, thas all."
> "But how do you know what time it is when you get up?"
> "We git up wid the sun."
> "And at night, how do you tell when its night?"
> "It gits dark when the sun goes down."
> "Havent you ever had a clock?"
> She laughed and turned her face toward the silent fields.
> "Mistah, we don need no clock."
> "Well, this beats everything! I dont see how in the world any-body can live without time."
> "We jus don need no time, Mistah."

Later they discuss his studies:

> "Whut yuh gonna be?"
> "*Be?* What do you mean?"
> "Whut yuh goin t school fer?"
> "Im studying science."
> "Whuts tha?"
> "Oh, er..." He looked at her. "Its about why things are as they are."
> "Why things is as they *is?*"
> "Well, its something like that."
> "How come yuh wanna study tha?"
> "Oh, you wouldnt understand."
> She sighed.
> "Naw, Ah guess Ah wouldnt."[35]

[35] Ibid., pp. 178, 183.

The symbol of the clock is a complex one. "Bang! Bang! Bang!" suggests also the passing of time, important to the plot because of Silas's impending arrival. The refrain is clearly related, too, to Sarah's libido. When it sounds the second through the sixth times, she thinks longingly of Tom or Silas, and when it sounds the seventh time, she hears the approaching noise of the salesman's automobile. On the penultimate repetition, the sound is quite specifically associated with sex: "She laughed again and mused on the baby, hearing Bang! Bang! Bang! She could hear the white man breathing at her side; she felt his eyes on her face. She looked at him; she saw he was looking at her breasts." The last time is even more overtly sexual: "A liquid metal covered her and she rode on the curve of white bright days and dark black nights and the surge of the long gladness of summer and the ebb of the deep dream of sleep in winter till a high red wave of hotness drowned her in a deluge of silver and blue that boiled her blood and blistered her flesh *bangbangbang*..."[36] When one observes, finally, that the sound may also prefigure the gunshots of the fight between Silas and the white men, the fact that the resources of Wright's prose go beyond a simple, prosaic naturalism becomes apparent.

Sarah's infidelity is the immediate motive for Silas's fury, but more is involved than the cuckold's outrage of sexual jealousy. Silas has long been aware of his wife's love for Tom, and he has reached a modus vivendi with this awareness. What he most resents is white exploitation in general, of which sexual exploitation is only a part: " 'The white folks ain never gimme a chance! They ain never give no black man a chance! There ain nothin in yo whole life yuh kin keep from em! They take yo lan! They take yo freedom! They take yo women! N then they take yo life!' " His outrage is the cumulative outrage of a life of deprivations, of a continual violation of the integrity of his personality. In giving utterance to his sense of indignity, he is the collective voice of his people. The suffering in his individual case is particularly poignant because of his fierce pride in his ability to emulate white success, to play the white man's own game, and in this way to demonstrate his equality. When he tells Sarah that he has bought more land, he adds that he will need to

36 Ibid., pp. 179, 188-89.

take on a hired man to help him: " 'Ain tha the way the white folks do? Ef yuhs gonna git anywheres yuhs gotta do just like they do.' " He had disdained to be a sharecropper. As Sarah recalls while waiting on the hill, "Always he said he was as good as any white man. He had worked hard and saved his money and bought a farm so he could grow his own crops like white men." What is so bitterly intolerable to Silas is that despite this conclusive proof of his equality, it was still not respected by whites; he was still not considered to have rights bound to be honored by white men. Having emulated whites in his struggle for success, he now vows grimly to emulate them in another way: " 'Ahm gonna be hard like they is! So hep me, Gawd, Ah'm gonna be *hard!* When they come fer me Ah'm gonna *be* here!' " When they do arrive, he fulfills his vow, returning their murderous fury in kind until he is killed. He does so with full knowledge of the futility of even this gesture of defiance: " 'It don mean nothin! Yuh die ef yuh fight! Yuh die ef yuh don fight! Either way yuh die n it don mean nothin...' "[37]

Silas expresses his wish that " 'alla them white folks wuz dead! *Dead,* Ah tell yuh! Ah wish Gawd would kill em *all!*' " In contrast to this anguished, nihilistic desire for genocide is Sarah's faith in a harmony of the races in a harmonious natural order. Her Edenic vision is in ironic contrast also to the realities of racial violence that the story presents, but it is deeply felt and movingly stated: "Somehow, men, black men and white men, land and houses, green cornfields and grey skies, gladness and dreams, were all a part of that which made life good. Yes, somehow, they were linked, like the spokes in a spinning wagon wheel. She felt they were. She knew they were. She felt it when she breathed and knew it when she looked."[38] This affirmative sentiment, the one hopeful note in "Long Black Song," is certainly incongruous with Wright's Communist point of view. The fact seems to be, however, that Wright shared the common misgivings of so many American writers about the intrusion of the machine into the American garden.[39] In *Lawd Today, 12 Million Black Voices, Black Boy,* and *The Long Dream,*

[37] Ibid., pp. 211, 192, 203, 211, 212.
[38] Ibid., pp. 210, 213.
[39] See, for example, the description of life in West Helena quoted above, p. 20.

as well as in *Uncle Tom's Children,* Wright's prose grows lyrical, sometimes floridly so, when it depicts southern rural pleasures and scenes. Often, of course, he is merely heightening the contrast with the racial violence that occurs in these settings, but the rural attachment is real. As a black Communist dedicated to a more humane operation of the industrial economy, Wright could have little sympathy with the southern Agrarians, who were taking their stand at this time against industrialism and in favor of social conservatism and paternalistic racism, but he shared to some degree, at least in "Long Black Song," their emotional nostalgia for the pastoral tranquillities of rural life.[40]

The final story in the first edition of *Uncle Tom's Children* is "Fire and Cloud," at once a character study of a black leader facing a crisis and a parable of the need for unified collective action of the southern proletariat, black and white. Dan Taylor is a black preacher and thus, as is frequently the case in the South, a racial leader in his community. As this story of the Depression begins, he is returning to face his hungry people after an unsuccessful attempt to persuade white relief authorities to provide them food. Perhaps, he thinks, a massive demonstration, as Communists in the town have advocated, would force the whites to act. On the other hand, Taylor is extremely reluctant to anger the white power structure. If he fails to act, his people face starvation. Still another difficulty he must contend with is Deacon Smith, "a black Judas" eager to inform on Taylor to the whites in order to secure power for himself. Walking past the fertile fields, Taylor recalls the abundance of his first years of marriage, when he combined preaching and farming. He had thought of himself as a black Moses, but now he must "go

---

[40] In 1955 Wright bought a farm in Normandy, where he spent much of the temperate part of the year writing and raising vegetables, particularly American vegetables not easily available in France. These he would give to friends in Paris, telling one of them that he was essentially a countryman. Interview with O. Rudolph Aggrey, 10 May 1965. See also Harrington, "The Last Days of Richard Wright," p. 85, and Webb, *Richard Wright,* pp. 351-53. Henry F. Winslow has said, "Wright was rural and first focused on the rural realities. . . ." Letter to the author, 12 December 1964. For a fuller treatment of this whole matter, see Keneth Kinnamon, "The Pastoral Impulse in Richard Wright," *Midcontinent American Studies Journal,* X (Spring 1969), 41-47.

and tell his congregation, the folks the Great God Almighty had called him to lead to the Promised Land — he had to tell them that the relief would give them no food."[41]

When Taylor arrives in the black section, he is met by his hot-blooded young son, Jimmy, who tells him that the mayor and two other whites, the deacons of the church, and two Communists are all waiting, in separate rooms and unknown to each other, in his church to see him. The mayor hopes to persuade Taylor to stop the demonstration scheduled for the following day, while bands of white toughs are roaming the streets in automobiles to frighten blacks into staying home. Deacon Smith, Jimmy also informs his father, is carrying on a rumor campaign against him. Entering his church, Taylor is met by still another group, a committee of ten that he had sent to see the mayor. They crowd around him, saying that the mayor repulsed them and pleading for help. Struggling with his problem, Taylor cannot yet reach a decision. Instead he leads them in prayer.

Compelled to prevent the presence of Hadley and Green, the Communists, from becoming known either to the deacons or to the mayor and his companions, Taylor tells his wife, May, to explain to the mayor that he is ill and to the deacons that he is speaking with the mayor. By means of this ruse, he is able to speak first with Hadley, a white man, and Green, a black. The conversation with them reveals further ramifications of his dilemma. The demonstration scheduled for the following morning will be a failure, the Communists insist, unless Taylor gives it his open endorsement. He is reluctant to do so for a number of reasons. He feels a sense of responsibility for his congregation that makes him hesitate to send it marching into police guns. He also has sincere religious compunctions about the methods the Communists propose, as well as reservations concerning the propriety of his involvement as a minister. To defy the white establishment so openly, furthermore, is tantamount in his mind to a kind of civil war. Finally, to alienate his powerful white friends would be to jeopardize his future usefulness as a black leader currying favor from them. Hadley and Green are disappointed in him, much to his discomfiture, for he admires their

[41] *Uncle Tom's Children: Four Novellas,* pp. 228, 227.

dedication. He knows too that his starving people require that something be done. Concluding this conference, he faces the more difficult one with Mayor Bolton, the chief of police, and " 'Mr. Lowe, head of our fine Industrial Squad,' "[42] a Red-baiter.

After some preliminary condescending pleasantries, the mayor, with as much diplomacy as he can muster, gives Taylor to understand that he must dissuade blacks from demonstrating. Taylor, much more diplomatically, presses the plea of his hungry followers for relief. Chief Bruden and Lowe, with no diplomacy whatever, abuse and threaten the minister. The talk resolves nothing. The white men leave Taylor with a final warning against associating with Communists, mentioning Hadley and Green specifically. Taylor now prepares for his last confrontation — with the deacons of his own church. On his way, May applies one more pressure by reiterating an earlier plea not to jeopardize their son's chances in the town by undue militance. For his part, Jimmy had earlier urged increased militance.

The conference with the deacons is verbally dominated by Deacon Smith, who argues vehemently against Taylor and the demonstration. He is not successful in his attempt to discredit Taylor's leadership, though, for desperation has driven the other deacons to the point of demonstration. As they are resolving to march — and as Smith implicitly threatens to inform on them — Jimmy comes in to tell his father that some white men in a car wish to see him outside his church.

These white men abduct Taylor into the countryside, where they tie him to a tree and subject him to a vicious whipping, described with characteristic Wrightian violence. They offer further insult by forcing him to pray under the blows of the lash. When his anger rises to the point of verbal resistance, they beat him with renewed fury until he passes out. Regaining consciousness at two in the morning, he manages to rally enough strength to begin the long walk home. On the way a policeman stops him, but he arrives at last at his church and finds his way to bed.

Jimmy hears his father's entrance and goes to him. When he learns of the beating, he is eager to retaliate, but his father has a

[42] Ibid., p. 256.

more important lesson to impart than blind revenge. This lesson, so painfully learned, is the importance of solidarity: " 'Its the *people*, son! Wes too much erlone this way! Wes los when wes erlone! Wes gotta be wid our folks....' "[43] This lesson has an import so great that his beating and his dismissal from the church by the deacons, who, as Jimmy explains, believe that he has deserted them, pale in comparison. At this point May enters the room and ministers to her husband's wounds.

This task is a common one in the black community that morning, for a battered Deacon Bonds arrives with the news that the terroristic beatings have been general and systematic. The fact is confirmed by the arrival of the mangled congregation as the day dawns. The people are ready to march, with or without Taylor and despite Deacon Smith's animadversions. Taylor speaks to them, renouncing his former style of conciliatory leadership and advocating united action. The march begins and is soon joined by a crowd of poor whites, waiting in a park separating black and white residential areas. The demonstration is so large that the police are afraid to disperse it. The frightened mayor promises food to the hungry people, and Taylor realizes joyfully that " '*Freedom belongs t the strong!*' "[44]

The triumph of "Fire and Cloud" is the story's successful embodiment of social issues in the dilemmas faced by a single individual. The presentation of Taylor's complex ordeal is consistently credible on realistic grounds, but it is charged with ideological significance that enriches rather than, as was too often the case in proletarian fiction, oversimplifies it.

"Fire and Cloud" is particularly appropriate as the concluding story of *Uncle Tom's Children* because Taylor is a fully realized Uncle Tom in the difficult process of self-transcendence. He is an Uncle Tom of the sincere, not the cynical, variety, believing that he can best serve the interests of his people by obsequiously pleading their case to the whites, gaining a bit here and a bit there, never inviting trouble by asking for too much or by forgetting to cringe. As he says candidly to Hadley and Green in an explanation of his

[43] Ibid., p. 301.
[44] Ibid., p. 317.

refusal to permit his name to be used on handbills calling for the demonstration, " 'Ef them white folks knowed Ah wuz callin mah folks in the streets t demonstrate, they wouldnt never gimme a chance t git something fer mah folks ergin....' " And as long as blacks fail to achieve strength through collective action, there is considerable merit in Taylor's argument. On the other hand, collective action would produce substantial collective benefit, not merely a few crumbs from wealthy white bounty. The psychological subservience of the system is deleterious not only to the Uncle Tom himself but to the racial community as a whole. Furthermore, the role of the Uncle Tom almost inevitably leads to self-aggrandizement, no matter how high-minded and sincerely motivated the player of the role. May's plea that her husband think of their son's future is echoed in Mayor Bolton's subtle promise:

> "If you raise that boy right he will be a leader of his people some day, Dan."
> "Thas the one hope of mah life, suh," said Taylor with deep emotion.[45]

In former days Taylor had considered himself specially called by God to lead his people. Whether couched in dynastic or in religious terms, the appeal of power, even the limited power of an Uncle Tom, is strong indeed.

Even in stable times the role is a difficult one at best. In time of crisis it becomes virtually impossible. Taylor plays the role with consummate skill, balancing one faction against another in masterful fashion, but the situation is simply too complex for his abilities. As Deacon Smith observes, harshly but accurately, " 'Yuh wanna stan in wid the white folks! Yuh wanna stan in wid the Reds! Yuh wanna stan in wid the congregation! Yuh wanna stan in wid the Deacon Board! Yuh wanna stan in wid everbody n yuh stan in wid nobody!' " The relative tranquillity of the first years of his ministry cannot be brought back; he must face the present complex crisis as it actually exists. The traditional counsel of the Uncle Tom to his people when whites prove recalcitrant is patience. Deacon Smith, eager to assume the role for its personal rewards, is quick to advo-

---

45 Ibid., pp. 249, 255.

cate this course: " 'N Gawd knows thas all we kin do: wait!' "[46] But when economic crisis reaches the point of actual starvation, such counsel is no longer viable. Taylor's transcendence of the role of Uncle Tom emerges from his growing recognition of the futility of patience and the necessity of action. Implicit in Taylor's inner struggle between accommodation and rebellion is a central theme in Afro-American history: in choosing militance he casts off the robes of a Booker T. Washington and assumes the mantle of a Frederick Douglass or a W. E. B. Du Bois.

Or to state the case in terms of the story itself, he moves from religious resignation to social action. As always in Wright, the futility of religion is emphasized in "Fire and Cloud." In the first section of the story, as Taylor looks at the fertile fields and thinks of his starving congregation, he says, " 'The good Lawds gonna clean up this ol worl some day! Hes gonna make a new Heaven n a new Earth!' " This millennial hope is deflated, however, by the words that quickly follow: " 'Waal, there ain nothin t do but go back n tell em.... Tell em the white folks wont let em eat....' " As between God and the white folks, it is clear where the present power lies. After the prayer he leads for his committee of ten, in which God is again called on for a new heaven and a new earth, one of the committee members puts the immediately relevant question: " 'But, Reveren, whut kin we *do?*' " In similar fashion throughout the story, the religious sentiment is undercut by the present necessity of collective human action. After the ordeal of his beating, Taylor explains to his son the illumination which he has achieved and toward which the entire story has been moving:

> "Its the *people!* Theys the ones whut mus be real t us! Gawds wid the people! N the peoples gotta be real as Gawd t us! We cant hep ourselves er the people when wes erlone. Ah been wrong erbout a lotta things Ah tol yuh, son. Ah tol yuh them things cause Ah thought they wuz right. Ah tol yuh t work hard n climb t the top. Ah tol yuh folks would lissen t yuh then. But they wont, son! All the will, all the strength, all the power, all the numbahs is in the people! Yuh cant live by yoself!"[47]

So Reverend Dan Taylor moves from Washingtonian individual-

---

[46] Ibid., pp. 272-73, 270.
[47] Ibid., pp. 224, 239, 302.

ism and religious resignation to the status quo to a virtual identification of God with collective social action. He does not give up God entirely, of course, for a southern black preacher does not become a full-fledged Marxist revolutionary overnight. But he does shift his religious emphasis to socially viable means and ends. The story's careful use of religious language and allusion, culminating in the hymn of the marching demonstrators, helps to develop and define this shift. Helping also to develop the story's theme is the use of a favorite pattern of imagery in Wright, here related to the religious language — fire. Taylor's beating is repeatedly described in terms of fire. It is a fiery crucible through which he must pass to purge away the vestiges of Uncle Tomism and purify him for his new leadership role: " 'Ah know whut yo life is! Ah done felt it! Its *fire!*' "[48] Having received this sign of the fire, he can merge his personality into the collective will of his people and learn that freedom resides in collective strength.

"Fire and Cloud" is not without faults. The device of the three separate groups waiting to see Taylor is stagy. The union of the poor whites with the marching blacks, however faithful to orthodox party doctrine, is inadequately motivated and essentially unrelated to the basic black themes. For the most part, though, the story is a strikingly successful study of a black leader under multiple and conflicting pressures. At the same time, it achieves the more difficult feat of presenting an ideological lesson in Taylor's struggle in a realistic and artistically satisfying way.

The subject of each of the four stories in *Uncle Tom's Children* is racial conflict issuing in physical violence. In the first three stories, this violence takes the form of homicide of a white by a black and then of a black or blacks by whites. In the fourth, also, two lynchings are mentioned, but they are peripheral to the main action, which involves violence that stops short of homicide. Within this pattern of similarities, however, there are significant differences developed by the arrangement of the stories into a thematic design that gives the volume as a whole a measure of unity and a meaning that transcends the meaning of any of the separate stories, though

[48] Ibid., p. 314.

"Fire and Cloud" comes closest to expressing this general import.

Like so many thousands of his counterparts in actual life, including Wright himself, Big Boy Morrison deals with racial conflict by escaping from it. His murder of Jim Harvey in self-defense is highly fortuitous (though presented in a credible way). Big Boy is responsible only to himself. Hiding from the lynch mob, he is isolated from the black community. His situation, then, is a highly individual one that evokes an individual response. Mann in "Down by the Riverside," on the other hand, is acting on behalf of his family, obviously a larger social unit than the individual. His shooting of Heartfield is partly accidental, but less so than Big Boy's shooting of Harvey. It takes place at a time of abnormal racial tension, and if performed in self-defense like Big Boy's, it is premeditated self-defense, for Mann carried his pistol for just such an eventuality. "Down by the Riverside" represents an advance in social involvement of the protagonist over "Big Boy Leaves Home." Another advance is made by Silas in "Long Black Song." Like Mann, he has the responsibility for his family. Unlike Big Boy's and Mann's, Silas's confrontation with whites is the result of deliberate choice, not of an accident. His is a deliberately calculated resistance to white aggression, but it is still isolated, individual, and so socially meaningless. In "Fire and Cloud" we find the culmination of the movement noted in the first three stories. Reverend Taylor acts finally not for himself or for his family, but for his people as a whole. His resistance is social, not individual, in both ends and means, and it is entirely volitional. For these reasons it is meaningful, not futile, and "Fire and Cloud" concludes *Uncle Tom's Children* with the triumphant assertion that " *'Freedom belongs t the strong!'* " This triumphant truth has been hard won by Taylor in the story and by the writer and reader of the three tragic tales that precede it.[49]

[49] After an interesting examination of Wright's style, with comparisons to Hemingway, Gertrude Stein, Sherwood Anderson, and others, and an analysis of "Long Black Song" and "Bright and Morning Star," Edwin Berry Burgum codifies Wrightian tragedy this way: "A tragedy, then, as a literary form, consists of a conflict in the objective world, through which a contradiction develops, between the external circumstances of the hero's life, which ends in a death imposed by his opponents, and his internal state of feeling, which becomes a sense of fullest living. This contradiction is promoted by his discovery through

The message of *Uncle Tom's Children*, it must be emphasized, emerges from the arrangement and the action of the stories, not from overt propaganda. The work is remarkably free of those homiletic essays placed in the mouths of characters in *Native Son* and *The Outsider*. Instead the dialogue is crisply terse and realistic. Southern black dialect is represented by phonetic spelling, but, for the most part, this device is used with discretion and seldom obfuscates the sense.[50] Wright uses interior monologue freely. Since his characters are usually caught up in a crisis that engages their full attention, this technique concentrates on the present rather than, as in Joyce or Faulkner, on the past. In "Long Black Song" and "Fire and Cloud," however, reminiscence appears in the early parts of the stories. The narrative prose is usually simple and straightforward in syntax and diction, but special effects are skillfully used as needed. As Taylor regains consciousness after his beating in "Fire and Cloud," for example, his acute pain is rendered by an effective hyperbole: "Moonlight pained his eyeballs and the rustle of tree leaves thundered in his ears."[51] Symbolism, too, is used skillfully, as we have seen in the foregoing analyses. The structure of the stories in *Uncle Tom's Children* is relatively simple. The narrative movement is invariably straightforward, following the chronology of the present action with brief flashbacks used only rarely. Perhaps the most impressive quality of Wright's technique is his infallible dramatic sense. Violent conflict, both physical and psychic, between the races is Wright's special subject, and in *Uncle Tom's Children* this subject is presented with an intense dramatic immediacy.

Recognition of the merits of Wright's short stories came quickly. One review of *The New Caravan* singled out Wright's contribution,

---

action of an error of judgment, and ends, through the right use of that discovery, in what is actually the satisfaction of the better integrated personality. . . ." "The Art of Richard Wright's Short Stories," *The Novel and the World's Dilemma* (New York, 1947), p. 259. This essay first appeared in the *Quarterly Review of Literature*, I (Spring 1944), 198-211. Surely, however, "the better integrated personality" is for Wright a by-product of the chief goal — a more equitable society. Burgum strangely ignores "Fire and Cloud" in his discussion of Wright's stories.

[50] One minor stylistic mannerism in *Uncle Tom's Children* is bothersome. Wright almost always omits the apostrophe in contractions, using, for example, "hell" for "he'll."

[51] *Uncle Tom's Children: Four Novellas*, p. 288.

"Big Boy Leaves Home," for special praise.[52] *Uncle Tom's Children* won the $500 first prize in a contest sponsored by Martha Foley's *Story* magazine open to all persons working on the Federal Writers' Project.[53] Wright's manuscript was chosen from some six hundred entries, the best of which were judged by Sinclair Lewis, Harry Scherman, and Lewis Gannett. In an enthusiastic review for the Book Union, a leftist but non-Communist book club of which *Uncle Tom's Children* was the April 1938 selection, Gannett spoke of the process of selection: "I hesitated over the first manuscripts I read. After I came upon *Fire and Cloud,* I had no doubts at all. Here was the voice of a new generation of black America; a hard, fresh voice in which one could still detect something of the melody of the old spirituals. Here, in Richard Wright, was not merely a prize-winner but a new American writer."[54] Most reviews agreed basically with Gannett's estimate. A reviewer for the black popular press boasted that the book gave Wright "a place in the vanguard of American literature. . . . "[55] Scholarly black reviewers were also enthusiastic, but more discriminating. Sterling A. Brown judged the work the best black writing about the South since Jean Toomer's *Cane,* and compared Wright to such white southern writers as Faulkner, Erskine Caldwell, T. S. Stribling, and Paul Green. At the same time, Brown criticized the excessive use of coincidence, and thought "Long Black Song" weak in characterization and structure.[56] Alain Locke predicted "a major literary career" for Wright

[52] Robert Van Gelder, "Books of the Times," *New York Times,* 2 November 1936, p. 19. In one of his perceptive annual reviews of black writing, Alain Locke called the story "the strongest note yet struck by one of our own writers in the staccato protest realism of the rising school of 'proletarian fiction.' " "Jingo, Counter-Jingo and Us — Retrospective Review of the Literature of the Negro: 1937," *Opportunity,* XVI (January 1938), 11.

[53] "Negro Writer Wins Story Contest," *New York Times,* 15 February 1938, p. 14. "Fire and Cloud" was published in *Story,* XII (March 1938), 9-41.

[54] "Uncle Tom's Children by Richard Wright," *Book Union Bulletin,* April 1938, p. 2. Gannett also praised the book highly in another review, "Books and Things," *New York Herald Tribune,* 25 March 1938, p. 17.

[55] Marvel J. Cooke, "Prize Novellas, Brave Stories," *New York Amsterdam News,* 9 April 1938, p. 16.

[56] "The Literary Scene," *Opportunity,* XVI (April 1938), 120-21. In another review addressed to a liberal white audience, Brown wrote that the stories "have power and originality, revealing a people whose struggles and essential dignity have too long been unexpressed." "From the Inside," *Nation,* CXLVI (16 April 1938), 448. Before the publication of *Uncle Tom's Children,* Brown had singled out "Big Boy Leaves Home" for praise in *The Negro in American Fiction* (Washington, 1937), pp. 186-87.

after his demonstration of his ability to use "the novella with the sweep and power of epic tragedy."[57] The only unfavorable review by a black critic was Zora Neale Hurston's. Miss Hurston may well have felt her own preeminence in black fiction threatened by the emergence of Wright; in any case, her review was harsh. Though conceding Wright's "facility" and "beautiful writing," she fastidiously called "all the characters . . . elemental and brutish," and complained oddly that the dialect lacked verisimilitude, the only time that objection was raised to any of Wright's fictional works. Both Brown and Locke recognized the validity of Wright's representation of southern racial violence, but Miss Hurston demurred on this point, charging him with slavish adherence to the party line and concluding her attack with a cattily expressed hope "that Mr. Wright will find in Negro life a vehicle for his talents."[58]

White reviewers of *Uncle Tom's Children* were generally favorable. Radicals among them were of course laudatory, though they did not hesitate to criticize. The *Daily Worker* review was rather surprisingly sensitive to the artistic quality of this former correspondent's book, qualifying its praise by complaining that "it rarely reaches upward toward an intensity of perception and imagery. . . ."[59] One of the most influential Marxist critics, Granville Hicks, rejoiced that "the literature of the left has been immeasurably strengthened" and that "the revolutionary movement has given birth to another first-rate writer."[60] Wright must have particularly valued the praise of James T. Farrell, whom he had met at the American Writers' Congress three years earlier.[61] Though insensitive to Wright's use of symbolism, Farrell praised his realism, his courageous protest, and his skillful use of the vernacular. Farrell concluded his review by calling *Uncle Tom's Children* "a true and

[57] "The Negro: 'New' or Newer — A Retrospective Review of the Literature of the Negro for 1938," *Opportunity,* XVII (January 1939), 8.

[58] "Stories of Conflict," *Saturday Review of Literature,* XVII (2 April 1938), 32. Miss Hurston's own fiction usually emphasizes local color and folklore and avoids racial conflict. It should be added that Wright had written an unfavorable review of Miss Hurston's *Their Eyes Were Watching God* in "Between Laughter and Tears," *New Masses,* XXV (5 October 1937), 22, 25.

[59] Alan Calmer, "Books of the Day," *Daily Worker,* 4 April 1938, p. 7.

[60] "Richard Wright's Prize Novellas," *New Masses,* XXVII (29 March 1938), 23.

[61] Letter from James T. Farrell to Michel Fabre, 22 June 1963.

powerful work by a new American writer. It is a book of bitter truths and bitter tragedies written by an able and sensitive talent. It is not merely a book of promise. It is a genuine literary achievement."[62]

Nonradical reviewers were also pleased. Malcolm Cowley found the stories "both heartening, as evidence of a vigorous new talent, and terrifying as the expression of . . . racial hatred. . . ."[63] Other reviewers were also impressed by Wright's talent, but defensive toward his attack on racism. One would expect this attitude on the part of such a southern critic as Allen Maxwell,[64] but it also appeared in reviews in the *New York Times* Charles Poore admired Wright's "descriptive power" and his "amazing ability to make you see searingly melodramatic episodes in a memorable way," but deplored the implausibility of "making nearly all the white characters villains."[65] Robert Van Gelder compared Wright's talent to Hemingway's, but was shocked by Wright's "so highly inflammatory" theme. He concluded with the infuriatingly and obtusely complacent assertion that things cannot be so very bad for black people in America, for the fact that *Uncle Tom's Children* won a literary prize was "illustrative of the freedom that minorities enjoy in this country."[66] *Time* magazine was impressed by Wright's "impersonal eloquence in voicing the tragedy of his people."[67] The most ecstatic reviewer, white or black, was Fred T. Marsh. Comparing Wright to Chekhov and nominating *Uncle Tom's Children* for a Pulitzer Prize, he wrote exuberantly: "The novellas are compounded of music and passion; and three of them . . . are as fine long short stories as any of modern times."[68]

This sampling of reviews of *Uncle Tom's Children* indicates the

[62] "Lynch Patterns," *Partisan Review,* IV (May 1938), 58.

[63] "Long Black Song," *New Republic,* XCIV (6 April 1938), 280.

[64] *"Uncle Tom's Children* by Richard Wright," *Southwest Review,* XXIII (April 1938), 362-65.

[65] "Books of the Times," *New York Times,* 2 April 1938, p. 13. Wright must have smiled grimly at the racist implications of the frequent recurrence of the word "amazing" in reviews by whites.

[66] "Four Tragic Tales," *New York Times Book Review,* 3 April 1938, pp. 7, 16.

[67] " 'White Fog,' " *Time,* XXXI (28 March 1938), 64.

[68] "Hope, Despair and Terror," *New York Herald Tribune Books,* 8 May 1938, p. 3.

warmth of the reception for Wright's first published book. Further
recognition was soon to come. A Russian translation got quickly
under way,[69] and upon its release in the fall of 1938, favorable
Soviet reviews appeared in *Pravda* and *Literaturny kritik*.[70] The
final honor of this highly satisfactory year was the award of another
prize, $200 to "Fire and Cloud" for second place in the O. Henry
short-story contest.[71] As important as such recognition was for the
ego of a young black writer, the money the prizes and the book provided was equally important, for it would permit him to leave the
Writers' Project and devote more time to work on a novel.[72]

The first fruit of his newly acquired leisure, however, was another
story, "Bright and Morning Star," first published in the *New Masses*
of 10 May 1938 and then included, along with "The Ethics of
Living Jim Crow," in an enlarged edition of *Uncle Tom's Children,*
published in 1940 after the success of *Native Son*. Like "Long Black
Song," "Bright and Morning Star" has a female protagonist, but
the governing passion of Sue is maternal, not sensual, love. A mid-
dle-aged rural black widow living within sight of the searchlight
of the Memphis airport, Sue takes in laundry to support herself
and her two sons, Sug and Johnny-Boy, who are dedicated Communist party organizers working with the sharecroppers, black and
white, of the area. As the story begins, however, Sug has been in
jail for several weeks, and Sue is anxiously awaiting the return of
Johnny-Boy, who is out in the stormy night notifying people of a

[69] "Honored," *New York Amsterdam News,* 30 July 1938, sec. 2, p. 3. This
announcement also stated, "Mr. Wright has made arrangements with Langston
Hughes . . . to dramatize some of the stories . . . ," but nothing came of this
project.

[70] See Deming Brown, *Soviet Attitudes toward American Writing* (Princeton, N.J., 1962), p. 128.

[71] "Wright Wins a New Prize," *New York Amsterdam News,* 12 November
1938, p. 15. One of the judges, Harry Hansen, called Wright "an artist of high
intelligence and great earnestness." Harry Hansen, ed., *O. Henry Memorial
Award Prize Stories of 1938* (New York, 1938), p. ix. The other judges were
Irita Van Doren, Fred T. Marsh, and Edward Weeks.

[72] As he told reporters, " 'I'll be able to write for a while without worrying
about where money for rent and food is coming from.' " "In the News Columns
— Richard Wright," *Opportunity,* XVI (March 1938), 70. Constance Webb
states in *Richard Wright,* p. 166, however, that cautious prudence won out and
"he decided to continue working for the Federal Writers' Project. . . ."

party meeting. Her ironing is interrupted by the arrival of Reva, a white girl in love with Johnny-Boy, who warns that her father's house, where the meeting for the following night is scheduled, is being watched by the sheriff's men. In order to prevent the disclosure of the identities of party members, it is necessary to notify them of the meeting's cancellation. When Johnny-Boy arrives soon after Reva's departure, his mother feeds him before telling him the bad news. He goes out into the rain again to warn his comrades of the danger.

Sue is awakened by the arrival of the sheriff and his rowdy posse. When she defiantly refuses to give them any information, the sheriff beats her brutally before leaving to continue the search for Johnny-Boy. Coming to after an indeterminate time, she sees Booker, a new white recruit to the party, leaning over her. After ministering to her, he tells her that Johnny-Boy was caught before he could carry out his task. Despite her misgivings about his reliability, she finally yields to his persuasion and identifies her son's comrades, whom he says he intends to warn now that Johnny-Boy cannot do so. Anxious about her son's safety and Booker's trustworthiness, Sue sits by the stove until she is roused from her moping by the return of Reva, who brings chilling news from her father that Booker is an informer. Full of pity for the exhausted girl, Sue puts her to bed without telling her of Johnny-Boy's capture or Booker's fatal knowledge. As the girl sleeps, Sue formulates a plan. Taking a winding-sheet for her son, as the sheriff had threateningly suggested, she wraps it around a gun and sets out by a shortcut for Foley's Woods, where her son is held, hoping to arrive ahead of Booker and kill him before he can speak. When she arrives at the scene, the sheriff orders her to make her son talk, promising to release him if he does, but she refuses, even though she is forced to watch him tortured. When Booker arrives, she shoots him. The enraged mob then kills Johnny-Boy and his heroic mother.

"Bright and Morning Star" attempts to make even more explicit the theme of "Fire and Cloud," itself a thematic culmination of the previous stories in *Uncle Tom's Children*. In "Bright and Morning Star" there is again a movement in an individual from a belief in a consolatory Christianity to a militant collectivism. For Sue the transition takes place over a longer period of time and is more complete than that of Reverend Taylor, who made only an initial step toward Communism. For her the change takes place under the tutelage of her sons, like Jimmy in "Fire and Cloud," more militant than the older generation. From the "wondrous vision" of the Savior, Sue turns to the "new and terrible vision" of Sug and Johnny-Boy: "And day by day her sons had ripped from her startled eyes her old vision; and image by image had given her a new one, different, but great and strong enough to fling her into the light of another grace. The wrongs and sufferings of black men had taken the place of Him nailed to the Cross; the meager beginnings of the party had become another Resurrection; and the hate of those who would destroy her new faith had quickened in her a hunger to feel how deeply her new strength went." She does not divest herself utterly of the trappings of the old faith; snatches of hymns come unbidden to her lips, and she thinks of her new faith in the images of the old. But she does meet superbly the test for which she hungered, achieving with her son at the end of the story Communist martyrdom and even a kind of canonization: "Focused and pointed she was, buried in the depths of her star, swallowed in its peace and strength; and not feeling her flesh growing cold, cold as the rain that fell from the invisible sky upon the doomed living and the dead that never dies."[73]

In so overtly Communist a story about southern sharecroppers attempting to organize as "Bright and Morning Star," it was obligatory for Wright to show black and white uniting to fight. In doing so, however, he encountered difficulties that the story does not successfully resolve, either ideologically or artistically. Sue feels a visceral distrust of white people. Johnny-Boy, on the other hand, rises above racial feeling to a clear-minded economic perception, as a good Marxist should: " 'Ah cant see white n Ah cant see black,' he said. 'Ah sees rich men n Ah sees po men.' " Mother and son often argued over this point; "always she would be pitting her feelings against the hard necessity of his thinking, and always she would lose."

This disagreement reflects the growing political awareness of the

[73] "Bright and Morning Star," *New Masses,* XXVII (10 May 1938), 98, 124.

younger generation. The difficulty is that the events of the story prove her right and her son wrong. It is Booker, a white man, who betrays his comrades, as Sue had feared. To support Johnny-Boy's point of view, Wright introduces — rather extraneously — Reva, whose love for the young black man suggests the new mood of the southern proletariat. Reva, however, is not successfully realized. As a character she seems as pale as her white skin and blond hair. Far more believable are the casually brutal sheriff and his gang, who help themselves to Sue's jam, cornbread, and greens before beating her. When she regains consciousness after her beating, she sees "a vast white blur . . . suspended directly above her. . . . Gradually the blur resolved itself into a huge white face that slowly filled her vision."[74] This frightful apparition recalls the identical one in "The Ethics of Living Jim Crow," where it also represents the white terror.[75] "Bright and Morning Star" does not resolve the question of trust or distrust of whites. Intellectual conviction and political necessity argue for the former, but experience, the logic of emotions, and the actual events of the story seem to justify Sue's ingrained suspicions. The ambivalence in the story suggests the similar ambivalence in the author's own mind and experience, which was to be expressed also in the third part of *Native Son*.

There is confusion too in Wright's use of symbols. Three principal symbols are used: the yellow beacon light, the "white mountain," and the star of the title. The first is used with contradictory implications. At the beginning of the story it is ominous: "it would hover a second like a gleaming sword above her head." Later it is called a "yellow blade of light." Elsewhere it is quite the opposite of a sword of Damocles: "If in the early days of her life the white mountain had driven her back from the earth, then in her last days Reva's love was drawing her toward it, like the beacon that swung through the night outside." The white mountain clearly and consistently represents white oppression, but the metaphor is sometimes sadly — or comically — mixed: "But as she had grown older, a cold white mountain, the white folks and their laws, had swum

---

[74] Ibid., pp. 117, 116, 118.

[75] See above, pp. 28, 29. Wright returned obsessively to this image in *Native Son* (see below, pp. 128, 135) and "The Man Who Lived Underground," *Cross-Section*, ed. Edwin Seaver (New York, 1944), p. 59.

into her vision and shattered her songs and their spell of peace."[76] The star symbol is more successful. In the hymn it of course represents Christ. Then it becomes the general struggle for Communism, "a strange star for a new freedom," and finally it is the specific act of heroism in which Sue dies. All three symbols, it must be said, are used awkwardly, obtrusively, self-consciously.

"Bright and Morning Star," then, is not a good story. It is gripping in a melodramatic way, but the excitement is not sustained by an artistic and thematic integrity comparable to that of the other stories in *Uncle Tom's Children*. Even the prose itself is at times tainted. The concluding lines of the story quoted above, for example, may seem impressive until one realizes how reminiscent they are in rhythm and imagery of the closing passage of Joyce's "The Dead." Despite its defects, however, "Bright and Morning Star" received critical honors. It was reprinted in *The Best Short Stories 1939*, a volume dedicated to Wright and Jesse Stuart, and in *50 Best American Short Stories*, where it was called "his best short story."[77] It has since been reprinted in three collections of black writing and in one general anthology of American literature.[78]

The publication and favorable reception of *Uncle Tom's Children* were the central facts of Wright's life in 1938. This success improved his already good status with the Communist party, though he could never get along with James W. Ford.[79] Freed from the routine *Daily Worker* journalism of the previous year, he continued to contribute to the Communist press. *New Masses* in March printed Wright's review of a story of the Spanish Civil War, and in July he wrote an interesting article on Harlem's jubilant reaction

[76] "Bright and Morning Star," pp. 97, 98, 99, 116, 98. The "white mountain" appears again in *Native Son*. See below, p. 136.

[77] Edward J. O'Brien, ed., *50 Best American Short Stories* (Boston, 1939), p. 868.

[78] Sterling A. Brown, Arthur P. Davis, and Ulysses Lee, eds., *The Negro Caravan* (New York, 1941); John Henrik Clarke, ed., *American Negro Short Stories* (New York, 1966); Houston A. Baker, ed., *Black Literature in America* (New York, 1971); and John Herbert Nelson and Oscar Cargill, eds., *Contemporary Trends: American Literature since 1900* (New York, 1949). It was also reprinted in the special Richard Wright issue of *Negro Digest*, XVIII (December 1968), 53-77.

[79] See Webb, *Richard Wright*, pp. 136-37, 153-54.

to Joe Louis's victory over Max Schmeling in a return match.[80] In
June at a reception in his honor at the International Workers' center in Harlem, his appointment to the editorial board of *New
Masses* was announced.[81] In October, Granville Hicks introduced
him to a leftist literary tea in Boston.[82] His devotion to the party
passed the test of the Moscow purge trials, which gave pause to
many Communist literary intellectuals.[83] The successful young
Communist writer was to achieve even greater fame with his first
published novel, *Native Son*.

[80] "Adventure and Love in Loyalist Spain," *New Masses*, XXVI (8 March
1938), 25-26, and "High Tide in Harlem," *New Masses*, XXVIII (5 July
1938), 18-20.
[81] "Richard Wright Given Literary Post for Work," *New York Amsterdam
News*, 25 June 1938, p. 6.
[82] Granville Hicks, *Part of the Truth* (New York, 1965), p. 164; letter from
Granville Hicks to the author, 3 December 1965.
[83] Richard Wright et al., "Statement of American Intellectuals," *International Literature*, no. 7 (1938), p. 104. This statement styles the trials as "the
efforts of the Soviet Union to free itself from insidious internal dangers, principal menace to peace and democracy." It should not be thought, however,
that only the names of inconsequential party hacks appeared with Wright's
on this statement. Other signers included, among many, Nelson Algren, Harold
Clurman, Jack Conroy, Dashiel Hammett, Lillian Hellman, Langston Hughes,
Rolph Humphries, Paul de Kruif, Jay Leyda, Dorothy Parker, Irwin Shaw,
Max Weber, and Frances Winwar.

# FOUR

Shortly after the publication of the first edition of *Uncle Tom's Children,* Wright moved from Harlem to Brooklyn, where he took a room at 175 Carlton Avenue in the home of Jane Newton, an old friend from Chicago whose intelligence and literary taste he respected.[1] Here, in 1938, he began to write *Native Son.* He had completed enough of the manuscript by early in 1939 to win, on the strength of it and *Uncle Tom's Children,* a Guggenheim Fellowship.[2] The award of $2,500 supported him for a year until the novel was published by Harper's on 1 March 1940 and issued as a Book-of-the-Month Club selection. With *Native Son,* Richard Wright became one of the important figures of twentieth-century American fiction.

During his literary apprenticeship, Wright had read carefully the critical doctrine as well as the imaginative works of some of the masters of early modern fiction.[3] One of these was Henry James.

[1] Change-of-address notice from Richard Wright to Langston Hughes, 13 April 1938, deposited in the James Weldon Johnson Memorial Collection of the Yale University Library. Information concerning Jane Newton in letter from Theodore Ward to the author, 8 July 1965.

[2] In his review of the novel, Charles Poore states that "the Guggenheim awards committee read 'Native Son' in manuscript." "Books of the Times," *New York Times,* 1 March 1940, p. 19. See also "Guggenheim Fund Names 69 Fellows," *New York Times,* 27 March 1939, p. 21, and Richard Wright, *How "Bigger" Was Born* (New York, 1940), p. 34. The latter essay was first published in an abridged version in the *Saturday Review of Literature,* XXII (1 June 1940), 3-4, 17-20.

[3] See above, p. 71.

But the young black author must have disagreed sharply with "The Art of Fiction," for in the fiction of social protest, of which *Native Son* is an outstanding example, the donnée has an interest almost equal to that of the artistic treatment. If the reader is concerned with the relation of literature to society, he must not be content merely to grant the novelist his materials and concentrate on his fictional technique; he must examine carefully the factual substance on which the novelist's imagination operates. If this task is preliminary to literary criticism in the strict sense, it is necessary if that criticism is not to be impressionistic or narrowly aesthetic. In his fiction Wright usually drew from personal experience and observation, the condition of the society about him, and his theoretic concerns. In *Native Son* these elements may be identified, respectively, as certain episodes in Wright's life in Mississippi, the social conditions of black Chicago and the Nixon trial, and Communist ideology.

Charles I. Glicksberg is surely speaking hyperbolically when he asserts of the relation between author and protagonist that "Richard Wright is Bigger Thomas — one part of him anyway. Bigger Thomas is what Richard Wright, had circumstances worked out differently, might have become."[4] Nevertheless, there is some truth in the assertion, and not merely in the general sense, according to the  formulation of James Baldwin, that "no American Negro exists who does not have his private Bigger Thomas living in the skull."[5] The general similarities between Wright at the age of twenty and the fictional character are obvious enough: both are Mississippi-born blacks who migrated to Chicago; both live with their mothers in the worst slums of the Black Belt; both are motivated by fear and hatred; both are rebellious by temperament; both could explode into violence.

More specific likenesses were recovered from Wright's subconscious by Dr. Frederic Wertham, the eminent psychiatrist. When Wright worked for the Bibbs family in Jackson, his duties included

---

[4] "The Furies in Negro Fiction," *Western Review,* XIII (Winter 1949), 110.
[5] "Many Thousands Gone," *Partisan Review,* XVIII (November-December 1951), 678, reprinted in James Baldwin, *Notes of a Native Son* (Boston, 1955), pp. 24-25.

chopping wood, carrying coal, and tending the fire. The Bibbses' pretty young daughter was generally kind to him within the limits of southern custom, but when on one occasion he chanced upon her in her bedroom while she was dressing, "she reprimanded him and told him to knock before entering a room." The diffident and fearful young black handyman, the amiable white girl, the sexually significant situation — these elements, transmuted, found their way into *Native Son* in the relation between Bigger and Mary Dalton. The name Dalton itself may bear an unconscious symbolic import. In the Chicago hospital where he worked, Wright learned of that variety of color blindness called Daltonism.[6] In their fashion, the wealthy Daltons in the novel strive toward color blindness, though they fall tragically short of achieving it.

Essentially Bigger Thomas is a conscious composite portrait of a number of individual blacks Wright had observed over the years. In that remarkable exercise in self-examination, *How "Bigger" Was Born,* Wright sketched five such Bigger prototypes he had known in the South. All of them were rebellious defiers of the Jim Crow order, and all of them suffered for their insurgency: "They were shot, hanged, maimed, lynched, and generally hounded until they were either dead or their spirits broken." In Chicago, especially when Wright worked at the South Side Boys' Club, he observed other examples of the Bigger Thomas type — fearful, restless, moody, frustrated, alienated, violent youths struggling for survival in the urban jungle.[7]

The slum conditions of the South Side so vividly portrayed in *Native Son* had been the daily reality of a decade of Wright's life. He had lived in cramped and dirty flats with his aunt, mother, and brother, and had visited scores of similar dwellings while working

[6] Waldemar Kaempffert, "Science in Review: An Author's Mind Plumbed for the Unconscious Factor in the Creation of a Novel," *New York Times,* 24 September 1944, sec. 4, p. 11. This article asserts that the Bibbs girl loaned Wright money for his graduation suit, but *Black Boy,* p. 156, says that Mrs. Bibbs did so. Dr. Wertham explains his experiment with Wright in "An Unconscious Determinant in *Native Son*," *Journal of Clinical Psychopathology and Psychotherapy,* VI (July 1944), 111-15, and more briefly in "The Dreams That Heal," his introduction to *The World Within: Fiction Illuminating Neuroses of Our Time,* ed. Mary Louise Aswell (New York, 1947), p. xxi.

[7] *How "Bigger" Was Born,* pp. 6, 28-29. See also Wright's pamphlet *The Negro and Parkway Community House* (Chicago, 1941).

as an insurance agent. The details of the Chicago environment in the novel have a verisimilitude that is almost photographic. The Ernie's Kitchen Shack of the novel, located at Forty-seventh Street and Indiana Avenue, for example, is a slight disguise for an actual restaurant called The Chicken Shack, 4647 Indiana Avenue, of which one Ernie Henderson was owner.[8] Similar documentary accuracy is observed throughout the book.

Aside from his wide personal experience, moreover, Wright was becoming increasingly more interested in sociology at the time he was writing *Native Son*. The caseworker for the Wright family in Chicago was Mary Wirth, the wife of Louis Wirth of the University of Chicago, who was in the process of conducting an enormous research project on the urban ecology of the city. Wright read extensively in sociological literature, conferred with Wirth, examined the files of his project, and met Horace R. Cayton, Wirth's black research associate, who was himself to become a distinguished sociologist and a warm friend of the novelist.[9] Sociological concepts, quite as much as Marxist theories, are apparent in the novel, especially in the final part.

As if to confirm Wright's notions about the Bigger type and society's attitude toward him, when the writer "was halfway through the first draft of *Native Son* a case paralleling Bigger's flared forth in the newspapers of Chicago."[10] This case involved Robert Nixon and Earl Hicks, two young blacks with backgrounds similar to that of Bigger. According to the first of a long series of highly sensational articles in the *Chicago Tribune,* on 27 May 1938 Mrs. Florence Johnson "was beaten to death with a brick by a colored sex criminal . . . in her apartment."[11] Nixon and Hicks were arrested soon after and charged with the crime. Though no evidence of rape was

[8] Advertisement for The Chicken Shack, *Chicago Defender,* 8 January 1938, p. 3.

[9] Horace R. Cayton, *Long Old Road* (New York, 1965), pp. 247-48. Cayton gives further details in a symposium on Wright included in *Anger, and Beyond: The Negro Writer in the United States,* ed. Herbert Hill (New York, 1966), pp. 196-97. Having written the finest fictional portrayal of the South Side, Wright was the inevitable choice of Cayton and St. Clair Drake to write the introduction to their classic sociological treatise on the area, *Black Metropolis* (1945).

[10] *How "Bigger" Was Born,* pp. 30-31.

[11] "Sift Mass of Clews for Sex Killer," *Chicago Daily Tribune,* 28 May 1938, p. 1.

adduced, the *Tribune* from the beginning called the murder a sex crime and exploited fully this apparently quite false accusation.[12] Nixon was chosen for special attack, perhaps because he was darker and less ostensibly remorseful than Hicks. He was repeatedly referred to as "brick moron," "rapist slayer," "jungle beast," "sex moron," and the like. His race was constantly emphasized. The casual reader of *Native Son* might consider the newspaper article that Bigger reads in his cell early in Book Three greatly exaggerated in its racism;[13] actually it is an adaptation of a piece in the *Tribune*. Although Nixon came from "a pretty little town in the old south — Tallulah, La.," the *Tribune* reporter wrote, "there is nothing pretty about Robert Nixon. He has none of the charm of speech or manner that is characteristic of so many southern darkies." The reporter proceeded to explain:

> That charm is a mark of civilization, and so far as manner and appearance go, civilization has left Nixon practically untouched. His hunched shoulders and long, sinewy arms that dangle almost to his knees; his out-thrust head and catlike tread all suggest the animal.
>
> He is very black — almost pure Negro. His physical characteristics suggest an earlier link in the species.
>
> Mississippi river steamboat mates, who hire and fire roustabouts by the hundreds, would classify Nixon as a jungle Negro. They would hire him only if they were sorely in need of rousters. And they would keep close watch on him. This type is known to be ferocious and relentless in a fight. Though docile enough under ordinary circumstances, they are easily aroused. And when this happens the veneer of civilization disappears. . . .

[12] David H. Orro, a black reporter, wrote that police stated Nixon and Hicks were "bent upon committing a sex crime," but that "authorities were unable to state whether the woman had been sexually attacked." " 'Somebody Did It,' So 2 Youths Who 'Might Have Done It' Are Arrested," *Chicago Defender*, 28 May 1938, p. 24. The date as printed is an error; this is actually the issue of 4 June 1938.

[13] Hubert Creekmore, white novelist from Mississippi, charged that "the press is shown as chiefly concerned with unsubtle inspiration of hatred and intolerance. The manner and content of these newspapers exceed belief. Again Mr. Wright makes them present incidents and ideas which reflect his own mind rather than an editor's mind or the public mind." "Social Factors in *Native Son*," *University of Kansas City Review*, VIII (Winter 1941), 140.

As he talked yesterday Nixon's dull eyes lighted only when he spoke of food. They feed him well at the detective bureau, he said. He likes cocoanut pie and strawberry pop. It was after a generous meal of these refreshments that he confessed two of his most shocking murders. . . . These killings were accomplished with a ferocity suggestive of Poe's "Murders in the Rue Morgue" — the work of a giant ape.

Again the comparison was drawn between Nixon and the jungle man. Last week when he was taken . . . to demonstrate how he had slain Mrs. Florence Johnson, mother of two small children, a crowd gathered and there were cries of: "Lynch him! Kill him!"

Nixon backed against a wall and bared his teeth. He showed no fear, just as he has shown no remorse.

The article concluded by quoting from a letter from the Louisiana sheriff of Nixon's home parish: "It has been demonstrated here that nothing can be done with Robert Nixon. Only death can cure him."[14]

This remedy was applied almost exactly a year after the murder of Mrs. Johnson. During this year the case became something of a local cause célèbre. The Chicago police quickly accused Nixon of a number of other murders, and the Los Angeles police did the same.[15] Early in the case the International Labor Defense became interested, providing white attorney Joseph Roth to aid black lawyers in representing Nixon and Hicks.[16] Public emotion ran high, stimulated by the lurid treatment given the case by the *Tribune*. A week after the crime the Illinois House of Representatives "approved a bill sponsored by State's Attorney Thomas J. Courtney of Cook county to curb moronic attacks." In debate on this bill Nixon was mentioned prominently.[17] A complicated series of confessions and repudiations, charges of police brutality, and dramatic outbursts of

[14] Charles Leavelle, "Brick Slayer Is Likened to Jungle Beast," *Chicago Sunday Tribune,* 5 June 1938, sec. 1, p. 6. Cf. *Native Son,* pp. 238-40.

[15] "Science Traps Moron in 5 Murders," *Chicago Daily Tribune,* 3 June 1938, p. 1.

[16] "Robert Nixon Attacked by Irate Hubby," *Chicago Defender,* 11 June 1938, p. 6.

[17] "Pass Courtney Moron Bill in Heated Debate," *Chicago Daily Tribune,* 8 June 1938, p. 1.

violence[18] preceded the trial, which began in late July under Judge John C. Lewe after attorneys for the youths won a change of venue because of the prejudiced atmosphere.[19] The trial itself, despite some apparently contradictory evidence, was very brief, lasting just over a week, with the jury reaching a first-ballot verdict of guilty after only one hour of deliberation. The death sentence was imposed on Nixon.[20] By this time, however, leaders of the Chicago black community were thoroughly aroused. The National Negro Congress, which had been providing legal representation for the two youths, continued its efforts on their behalf, including the sponsorship of a fund-raising dance.[21] Prominent Chicago black clergymen joined the struggle to save Nixon.[22] With the aid of such support, together with some irregularities in the evidence presented by the state, Nixon was able to win several stays of execution, but his struggle ceased in the Cook County electric chair three minutes after midnight on 16 June 1939.[23]

By the time Nixon was finally executed, Wright had completed *Native Son*. He did not need to wait the outcome of the legal appeals and maneuvers to know the "Fate" (his title for Book Three of the novel) of Robert Nixon or of his fictional counterpart, Bigger

---

[18] When police took Nixon and Hicks to the scene of the crime, a hostile, lynch-minded mob required police control. Then "a dramatic incident occurred just as the police were about to leave with their prisoners. Elmer Johnson, the bereaved husband ... drove up with his two children, and his brother-in-law, John Whitton ... Johnson said nothing, but Whitton clenched his fists and shouted, 'I'd like to get at them.' Police hurried the prisoners away." "2 Accuse Each Other in Brick Killing," *Chicago Daily Tribune*, 30 May 1938, p. 2. Perhaps Elmer Johnson was merely waiting for a better opportunity, for at the inquest he attacked the handcuffed Nixon savagely before police intervened. Shortly after this attack, Nixon attempted to retaliate. Johnson explained his intention to a reporter: "I hoped to hit him hard enough so his head would fly back and his skull would be cracked against the wall." "Beats Slayer of Wife; Own Life Menaced," *Chicago Daily Tribune*, 8 June 1938, p. 3. See also "Robert Nixon Attacked by Irate Hubby." Cf. the incident in *Native Son*, p. 265, in which Bigger is attacked at the inquest.

[19] "Brick Slayers' Trial Assigned to Judge Lewe," *Chicago Daily Tribune*, 19 July 1938, p. 6.

[20] "Guilty of Brick Murder; Gets Death in Chair," *Chicago Daily Tribune*, 5 August 1938, p. 2.

[21] "Dance Profits to Aid Nixon, Hicks," *Chicago Defender*, 20 August 1938, p. 5.

[22] "Nixon Plea to Be Given to Governor," *Chicago Defender*, 15 October 1938, p. 6.

[23] "Nixon Dies in Chair," *Chicago Defender*, 17 June 1939, pp. 1-2.

Thomas. In any event, Wright's use of the Nixon case was that of a novelist, not that of a historian or journalist. He adapted whatever seemed useful to his fictional purpose, changing details as he wished. He followed the facts of the Nixon case fairly closely in his account of the newspaper treatment of Bigger Thomas. The inquest and trial scenes also resemble in certain respects their factual prototypes. Among the more significant distortions of Nixon material are those relating to Wright's polemic purpose as a Communist writer.

In the Nixon case the role of the International Labor Defense and its representative, attorney Joseph Roth, was small and initiatory; it was soon replaced by the National Negro Congress. In *Native Son,* however, Wright magnifies the role of this organization (changing its name slightly to "Labor Defenders") and its radical Jewish attorney, Boris Max, who is made Bigger's sole lawyer. Another change illustrates even more vividly Wright's shift of emphasis in transforming fact to fiction. One of the murders to which Chicago police elicited confessions, later repudiated, from Nixon was that of a Mrs. Florence Thompson Castle a year before the murder of Mrs. Johnson. According to a newspaper report, in his account of this crime Nixon "told of picking up a lipstick belonging to Mrs. Castle and scrawling on the dresser mirror these words: 'Black Legion.' "[24] When Bigger in the novel wishes to divert suspicion to an extremist group, he selects leftists rather than fascists, signing the kidnap note to the Daltons in such a way as to implicate the Communist party.[25]

As a fervent party member, Wright maintained a thoroughly Communist point of view in *Native Son.* The courtroom arguments of Max in the final section, of course, are patently leftist. He equates racial and class prejudice, both being based on economic exploitation.[26] He repeats the basic party concept of the time regarding the collective status of black people in America: "Taken collectively, they are not simply twelve million people; in reality they constitute a separate nation, stunted, stripped, and held captive *within* this nation, devoid of political, social, economic, and property rights."[27]

[24] "Brick Moron Tells of Killing 2 Women," *Chicago Sunday Tribune,* 29 May 1938, p. 5.
[25] *Native Son,* p. 151.
[26] Ibid., pp. 326-27.
[27] Ibid., p. 333.

He discerns in Bigger a revolutionary potentiality.[28] Not all of Max's courtroom speech reflects Communist doctrine so directly, but none of it is inconsistent with the party line on racial matters.

Communist material is obvious enough in the final section of the novel, but it is often implicit elsewhere. Early in Book One, to cite a single example, while Bigger and his friend Gus are loafing on the street, they amuse themselves by "playing white," assuming roles of the white power structure. The youths are themselves nonpolitical, but the white activities Wright has them imitate are precisely those which he and other Communists view as typical of the American capitalist society: warfare, high finance, and political racism.[29] Prejudice against Communists is frequently depicted in the novel, and party members Jan Erlone[30] and Max are idealized portraits of selfless, noble, dedicated strivers toward the new social order.

These are the main elements that went into the composition of Native Son. Much of the powerful sense of immediacy felt by the reader of the novel derives from the genesis of the work in the author's personal experience and observation. Communist ideology provided him with an intellectual instrument with which to render meaningful the personal and social materials of the novel. The nice balance of subjective and objective elements prevents Native Son from being either a purely personal scream of pain, on the one hand, or a mere ideological tract on the other. It is a work of art as well as an expression of protest, and an examination of the way in which Wright organized his narrative, presented his characters, and employed symbols to enrich his meanings will reveal a high degree of artistic seriousness.

The structure of Native Son is a simple one, indicated in its broad outline by the titles Wright gave to the three parts of the novel — "Fear," "Flight," and "Fate." It is Bigger's fear that precipitates the chain of events leading to his inevitable fate. In a sense, the narrative action can be considered the externalization of Bigger's psy-

---

[28] Ibid., pp. 337-38.
[29] Ibid., pp. 15-17.
[30] Wright's model for this character was Jan Wittenber, a white friend who was active in the Chicago John Reed Club and who served as secretary of the Illinois State International Labor Defense. See also Webb, *Richard Wright*, p. 403.

chic instability, itself the result of his racial status. Living with his mother and younger brother and sister in a sordid, one-room "kitchenette" apartment in a South Side slum during the Depression, Bigger recognizes his own propensity for violence very early in Book One: "He knew that the moment he allowed himself to feel to its fulness how they lived, the shame and misery of their lives, he would be swept out of himself with fear and despair.... He knew that the moment he allowed what his life meant to enter fully into his consciousness, he would either kill himself or someone else." Shortly afterward when he is talking to Gus, he expresses this same sense of foreboding: " 'Sometimes I feel like something awful's going to happen to me.... Naw; it ain't like something going to happen to me. It's.... It's like I was going to do something I can't help....' "[31] This feeling of inevitability not only affirms the determinism of Wright's naturalistic and Marxist vision, but also increases the coherence and tension of the novel.

The chief device employed to create a sense of fate is a careful foreshadowing of subsequent events. In the opening scene in the Thomas flat, Bigger kills a terrified black rat that ceases its flight and turns desperately on its antagonists when all avenues of escape are closed. This scene prefigures Bigger's own fate. When Bigger takes his girl friend, Bessie Mears, to the deserted building where she is to wait for the ransom money, "something with dry whispering feet flitted across his path, emitting as the rush of its flight died a thin, piping wail of lonely *fear*." Another rat appears when they enter another building as they flee from Bigger's fate. Bigger encounters still another one as he is searching for a vacant apartment in which to hide. The final "rat," of course, is Bigger himself, who likewise fights his pursuers when further flight is hopeless. Rats contribute to the naturalistic verisimilitude of the South Side setting, but more important, they forecast Bigger's fate and help tighten the coherence of the work. When Bigger attends the movies with Jack, he sees a film entitled *The Gay Woman*, which depicts the life of the leisure class. The thoughts stimulated in Bigger by this film foreshadow, rather too accurately for plausibility, what is to happen a

[31] *Native Son*, pp. 9, 17, 19.

few hours later: "Maybe Mr. Dalton was a millionaire. Maybe he had a daughter who was a hot kind of girl; maybe she spent lots of money; maybe she'd like to come to the South Side and see the sights sometimes. Or maybe she had a secret sweetheart and only he would know about it because he would have to drive her around; maybe she would give him money not to tell." Still another example of the same device is Bigger's response to Bessie's first suspicion that something has happened to Mary Dalton: "He stiffened with fear. He felt suddenly that he wanted something in his hand, something solid and heavy: his gun, a knife, a *brick*."[32] It is with a brick, of course, that he later bashes in Bessie's head.

In addition to such prefiguring of subsequent events, Wright increases the cohesion of the novel by repetition of key phrases. One of Bigger's most typical reactions to adverse circumstances is a desire to "blot out" whatever offends him: "He wanted to wave his hand and blot out the white man who was making him feel like this."[33] The phrase "blot out" occurs at least eight times in the novel. When moments of extreme fear drive him to the point of violence, he sees or recalls a real (Mrs. Dalton) or imaginary "white blur"[34] approaching him. Such repetition helps to relate one event or scene to another through the medium of Bigger's sensibility, and thus concentrates and unifies the effect of the action on the reader.

This concentrated emotional tension also inheres in the rapid movement of events in the short time span of the first part of the plot. Books One and Two take place in a period of some sixty hours, from the battle with the rat in the Thomas flat on Saturday morning to the capture of Bigger late Monday night. The reader's attention, furthermore, focuses constantly on the developing action; there are no flashbacks to interrupt the relentless forward momentum of the narrative.

The first two parts of *Native Son*, then, form a tight fictional structure created by the rapid pace of the narrative, a brief time

[32] Ibid., pp. 155, 29, 123. Italics mine. It should be recalled here that the weapon used to murder Mrs. Johnson in the Nixon case was a brick.

[33] Ibid., p. 41. Cf. pp. 60, 85, 115, 119, 138, 251, 281, 282.

[34] Ibid., p. 73. Cf. pp. 74, 77, 78, 94, 200, 315.

span, the focus on Bigger's actions and reactions, the repetition of key phrases, and the foreshadowing of subsequent events in the plot. The tension relaxes and the pace slows in Book Three as the center of emphasis shifts somewhat from Bigger the individual to Bigger the social symbol. In contrast to his earlier frenzy, Bigger is now passive, withdrawn, almost catatonic. The action of Book Three, Bigger's imprisonment and trial, is analytical, verbal, and psychological, not dramatic, physical, and psychological as in Books One and Two. Kenneth Burke used the terms "imagistic" and "conceptual" in describing the novel before and after Bigger's capture.[35] The central question of Book Three is whether Bigger can be reached by anyone, whether he can derive some meaning from his nightmarish experiences. To the extent that he is representative of black people in America, this question of the meaning of his individual "fate" relates to the polemic intent of the novel as a whole, which is concerned with the collective racial situation and destiny of American blacks. If the account of Bigger's imprisonment and trial seems pallid after the earlier action, the reader should remember that Wright's intention was not merely to write gripping melodrama but to confront in his fiction the meaning, as well as to express the agony, of black experience in America. To do so he found it necessary to speak through Boris Max, a more sophisticated mouthpiece than Bigger could possibly be. To the objection that the meaning of the novel should have been embodied in the main action, one may reply that it is; the final section, though perhaps too static and essayistic, recapitulates explicitly the implicit meaning of Books One and Two.

"But always, from the start to the finish," Wright explains in *How "Bigger" Was Born*, "it was Bigger's story, Bigger's fear, Bigger's flight, and Bigger's fate that I tried to depict. I wrote with the conviction in mind . . . that the main burden of all serious fiction consists almost wholly of character-destiny and the items, social, political, and personal, of that character-destiny."[36] To a quite remarkable degree, *Native Son* is Bigger's book; it is difficult to recall

---

[35] *A Grammar of Motives* (New York, 1945), p. 339.
[36] *How "Bigger" Was Born*, pp. 35-36.

another modern American novel that focuses so sharply on the mind and emotions of its protagonist and that at the same time analyzes so carefully the "social, political, and personal" soil out of which they grew.

The emotional complex of Bigger's personality comprises fear, shame, and hatred as its primary elements. His name, suggesting "nigger" or "big nigger,"[37] indicates the origin of his fear, which is created by racial oppression from a white world so vast and powerful that he is helpless before it. His consciousness of his fear creates a sense of shame at his own inadequacy, equated by whites with his racial status. The combination of this fear and shame produces hatred, both self-hatred and hatred for the inequities of his life and the whites responsible for those inequities and his consequent humiliation. Unable to cope with his dilemma in any rational way, he can respond only by withdrawal or by aggression, by brooding or by violence: "These were the rhythms of his life: indifference and violence; periods of abstract brooding and periods of intense desire; moments of silence and moments of anger. . . ."[38]

Bigger's emotional pattern precludes any viable human relationship. He is profoundly alone. His father was killed in racial strife when Bigger was a small child. Toward his remaining family, Mrs. Thomas, Vera, and Buddy, he feels hatred "because he knew that they were suffering and that he was powerless to help them."[39] His conflict with his mother is intensified because of her nagging and because her religious resignation contrasts sharply with his own rebellious instincts. With Vera he is constantly bickering. Only his younger brother, Buddy, can evoke some feeling of tenderness, but even he is not entirely exempt from Bigger's surge of murderous fear and rage when he finds Mary's money that Bigger has dropped on the floor of the Thomas flat.

Nor does Bigger find friendship or love with his companions or his mistress. With Gus he can articulate his bitter frustration in a

[37] Leslie Fiedler thinks that Bigger Thomas "is identified by his very name as a reaction to Uncle Tom. . . ." *Waiting for the End* (New York, 1964), pp. 106-7. It should be noted, though, that Wright had known a person named Biggy Thomas in Jackson. See Wright, *Letters to Joe C. Brown*, pp. 10, 11.

[38] *Native Son*, p. 24. My analysis at this point is indebted to Cayton, "A Psychological Approach to Race Relations."

[39] *Native Son*, p. 9.

racist society, but he can also a few hours later vent that frustration on this "friend" with furious violence. Bessie is, as Max points out at the trial, merely a means of sexual release. Her life, as well as Bigger's, is too blighted for their relationship to develop any further dimension. When it seems necessary, Bigger crushes her skull and disposes of her body, as if it were nothing more than an object, by throwing it down an air shaft. Such are his relations with other blacks.

His relations with whites are of course even more distant and fearful. He at least partially understands other blacks, however alienated from them, but white people are strange as well as threatening, and at the same time enticing. They represent to Bigger a world both fascinating and forbidden, a world of power and wealth but also of cruelty and danger. Bigger and his companions have committed numerous crimes against blacks, but robbing a white delicatessen is quite a different matter: "They had the feeling that the robbing of Blum's would be a violation of ultimate taboo; it would be trespassing into territory where the full wrath of an alien white world would be turned loose upon them; in short, it would be a symbolic challenge of the white world's rule over them; a challenge which they yearned to make, but were afraid to." At the Dalton house Bigger replies to his white interlocutors in monosyllables; communication across the racial barrier is almost impossible. Bigger's reactions to whites, it should be emphasized, are determined more by the total configuration of his crippled personality than by the specific circumstances of his encounters with them or by their actual attitudes toward him. He is so conditioned by the racial situation that he cannot respond to individual whites as separate persons, but only as abstract embodiments of white power — "that white looming mountain of hate."[40] In Book One of *Native Son* white people are kind to Bigger. Mr. and Mrs. Dalton hope to improve the economic condition of Bigger and his family. Mary and Jan offer him, however awkwardly, egalitarian friendship and political enlightenment. Even the Daltons' Irish maid, Peggy, gives him good food, kindness, and, in her own way, understanding.[41] But

[40] Ibid., pp. 12, 306. "Looming" occurs over and over in *Native Son* and other works by Wright to describe the threatening white presence.
[41] " 'My folks in the old country feel about England like the colored folks

to all of these well-meant advances Bigger responds with his familiar emotional pattern of fear, shame, and hatred, just as he does later to the overt hostility of whites like Britten and Buckley. Eventually Jan and Boris Max are able to elicit from Bigger some dawning sense of his solidarity with oppressed whites. Their personal goodwill is so persistent, too, that it finally begins to melt Bigger's hostility. But their success in these efforts in Book Three has seemed to many readers, including this one, rather too contrived.

In order to achieve such an intense realization of Bigger's character, Wright has written, it was necessary to restrict point of view in the novel "to what Bigger saw and felt, to the limits of his feeling and thoughts, even when I was conveying *more* than that to the reader."[42] Wright was not entirely consistent in carrying out this limitation, which does not take the form of first-person narrative, but it does account for an important difference in the characterization of other persons in the novel. The depiction of blacks, whom Bigger understands, is sharp and realistic. The depiction of whites, whom Bigger cannot fathom, is deliberately vague and one-dimensional, for his perception of them is imperfect: they are all, in a sense, "white blurs" to his vision.

The members of Bigger's family are vividly particularized. Mrs. Thomas toils and worries to keep her family together, but in her submissiveness and blind, compensatory piety she is quite unable to understand Bigger's rebellious spirit. Vera is a nervous and self-conscious adolescent. Buddy sides with his elder brother, but he is still too young to muster enough courage to rebel, like Bigger, against his mother's values. Bessie too is a thoroughly convincing character. Her monotonous days of toil in the kitchens of white people are relieved only by the few hours of alcohol and sex that she seizes when she can. The aimlessness of her life makes her helpless before the hard concentration of Bigger's purpose:

---

feel about this country. So I know something about colored people.' " Ibid., p. 49. It is possible that this passage looks forward to Max's emphasis in Book Three on the solidarity of the oppressed, but it seems more likely that Wright, like James Baldwin in his famous meeting with Attorney General Robert Kennedy in 1963, is here grimly aware of the qualitative difference between black and Irish suffering.

[42] *How "Bigger" Was Born*, p. 36.

"Bigger, please! Don't do this to me! *Please!* All I do is work,
work like a dog! From morning till night. I ain't got no happiness.
I ain't never had none. I ain't got nothing and you do this to me.
After how good I been to you. Now you just spoil my whole life.
I've done everything for you I know how and you do this to me.
*Please,* Bigger...." She turned her head away and stared at the
floor. "Lord, don't let this happen to me! I just work! I ain't had
no happiness, no nothing. I just work. I'm black and I work and
don't bother nobody...."[43]

Her plea is a valid one, but it does not move either Bigger or the
Lord.

Even the minor black characters in *Native Son* are sketched vividly. Gus, G.H., and Jack are primarily foils to Bigger, but the
quality of their life is imparted to the reader with economic preci-
sion. The corpulent poolroom-owner, Doc, "who held a half-
smoked, unlit cigar in his mouth and leaned on the front counter,"[44]
is roused from boredom to lazy mirth by Bigger's sadistic assault on
Gus, but then flies into a rage when Bigger cuts the felt cloth on a
pool table. Reverend Hammond, pitiable in the helpless sincerity of
his religious convictions, is also memorable, as is the crazed university student in Bigger's cellblock.

The white characters in *Native Son*, on the other hand, are vague
stereotypes, for our sense of them is filtered through Bigger's sensibility. Mr. Dalton is a South Side slumlord who fails to recognize
the inconsistency and futility of his philanthropic activities on behalf
of blacks. The blind Mrs. Dalton is so vague as a person, in her
flowing white clothes and accompanied by her white cat, that she
operates almost wholly as a symbol. Mary Dalton is sophomoric in
her parlor radicalism. Her thoughtless efforts toward camaraderie
with Bigger induce terror rather than trust. Such overt racists as
Britten, the Daltons' private detective, and State's Attorney Buckley,
of course, are simply typical spokesmen for the pervasive white
hatred that is responsible for Bigger's plight. Bigger sees both of
these men as official representatives of the dominant white society,
instinctively recognizing their hostility. The reader, too, sees them
solely in this role.

[43] *Native Son,* p. 153.
[44] Ibid., p. 19.

The case of two other white characters, Jan Erlone and Boris Max, is somewhat different. Wright obviously wished to present these Communists favorably. If Jan's goodwill is expressed in a bumbling and insensitive manner in his initial approach to Bigger, he more than compensates for this mistake by his heroic support of Bigger after Mary's death. Jan's nobility, indeed, is too pure to be entirely credible. The point is not that Jan's attitude is unmotivated, for such a devout Communist would be fully capable of suppressing personal grief for a higher ideological cause. The difficulty is rather that we are given hardly a glimpse of the inner conflict, so fraught with opportunities for emotional dishonesty, that would issue in such a decision as Jan's. The reason, again, is that we know Jan primarily through Bigger, but whereas white foolishness or malice may be so presented, white sacrificial love — given the general emotional tone of the novel — cannot be. The accord and fraternity which Jan and Bigger achieve is not emotionally convincing, though it may be ideologically necessary. Insofar as attorney Max is a person in the novel, he serves as a kindly father surrogate to Bigger. Clearly his main function, however, is that of authorial mouthpiece. But as shown below, even as sympathetic and knowledgeable a white man as Max at last shrinks from the final truth about Bigger Thomas.

Characterization in *Native Son*, then, is sharply vivid for the black characters, vague and one-dimensional for the rather stereotyped whites. The reason for this difference, which is an artistic achievement rather than a liability, is the restriction of point of view mainly to Bigger. One may argue, of course, that Wright was simply incapable of the imaginative projection necessary for the creation of rounded white characters, but that is to ignore the necessary concentration on Bigger's sensibility. Furthermore, in such later works as *The Outsider, Savage Holiday,* and *The Long Dream,* Wright was to show his ability to present convincing white characters in fiction.

Characterization, action, and overt statement convey most of the meaning of *Native Son,* but Wright's naturalism is by no means so thorough as to preclude the use of symbols to enrich that meaning. The opening scene of the rat at bay, as has been noted, foreshadows symbolically Bigger's own destiny. His aspirations, fed by an American social system that both stimulates them and denies the opportunities for their fulfillment, soar to the heavens. Early in the novel Bigger gazes longingly at a skywriting airplane:

> "Looks like a little bird," Bigger breathed with childlike wonder.
> "Them white boys sure can fly," Gus said. . . .
> "I could fly one of them things if I had a chance," Bigger mumbled reflectively, as though talking to himself. . . .
> "If you wasn't black and if you had some money and if they'd let you go to that aviation school, you *could* fly a plane," Gus said.[45]

Instead, white society consigns him to the hell of the Dalton basement to maintain the glowing, searing, fiery furnace. Like Big Boy in his kiln, like the protagonist of "The Man Who Lived Underground," and like Wright himself in the subterranean corridors of the Chicago hospital where he once worked, Bigger is an underground man. The nearest he comes to the heights, ironically, is his ascent of the water tank on the tenement roof, but the white mob quickly brings him down.

The color white in *Native Son,* as is often the case in Wright's fiction, acquires a symbolic dimension. In the first place, the word itself is used with a frequency that goes far beyond the requirements of denotation. In several senses Bigger sees his world in black and white. Mrs. Dalton's whiteness haunts him. Upon first seeing her, he notices that "her face and hair were completely white; she seemed to him like a ghost." Three hours later Bigger goes to the kitchen for a drink of water: "What he saw made him suck his breath in; Mrs. Dalton in flowing white clothes was standing stone-still in the middle of the kitchen floor." He next sees her at the door of her daughter's bedroom: "A white blur was standing by the door, silent, ghostlike."[46] As this "awesome white blur" floats toward the bed, Bigger's fear increases and his fingers press down on the pillow over Mary's face. This same feeling of fear returns to Bigger at each subsequent meeting with Mrs. Dalton. Frequently accompanying Mrs. Dalton is her white cat, which becomes Wright's equivalent to Poe's

45 Ibid., p. 14.
46 Ibid., pp. 40, 52, 73.

black one as a symbol of guilt and fear. As Bigger struggles to force Mary's body into the furnace, "A noise made him whirl; two green burning pools — pools of accusation and guilt — stared at him from a white blur that sat perched upon the edge of the trunk. His mouth opened in a silent scream and his body became hotly paralyzed. It was the white cat and its round green eyes gazed past him at the white face hanging limply from the fiery furnace door."[47] Later when Bigger is in the basement with the reporters, the white cat leaps to his shoulder and perches there like a demon of doom.

Wright's use of Mrs. Dalton and her white cat is rather too self-consciously gothic. More effective is his equation of white power with elemental forces of nature. As Max explains at the trial, blacks vis-à-vis whites in America do not feel " 'that they are facing other men, they feel that they are facing mountains, floods, seas: forces of nature whose size and strength focus the minds and emotions to a degree of tension unusual in the quiet routine of urban life.' " Bigger's image of the alien world is "that white looming mountain of hate."[48] The most persistent symbol of white hostility, however, is snow. Snow clouds are first seen, ominously, when Jan and Mary force the unwilling Bigger to ride in the front seat of the Dalton automobile with them. Later that night as Bigger leaves the Dalton basement, the first flakes are beginning to fall. In Book Two the snow becomes all-pervasive as the blizzard increases its intensity. For Bigger it falls with the relentlessness of his fate: "Around him were silence and night and snow falling, falling as though it had fallen from the beginning of time and would always fall till the end of the world." Book Two ends as Bigger sinks into the ubiquitous, enveloping, suffocating white snow, overwhelmed and mastered by the power of whiteness: "Two men stretched his arms out, as though about to crucify him; they placed a foot on each of his wrists, making them sink deep down in the snow. His eyes closed, slowly, and he was swallowed in darkness."[49]

[47] Ibid., pp. 74, 78-79.
[48] Ibid., pp. 327, 306. For the use of the same image in "Bright and Morning Star," see above, p. 115, and Theodore Ward, "Five Negro Novelists: Revolt and Retreat," *Mainstream,* I (Winter 1947), 108-9.
[49] *Native Son,* pp. 157, 229. Like the end of "Bright and Morning Star,"

The Crucifixion image is emphatic in this final passage of Book Two, and this is not the only place in the novel in which Bigger assumes that role familiar in American literature generally and even more common in Afro-American writing — the Christ figure. In his suffering, Bigger is a black Christ crucified by white America. At the trial Buckley manipulates the sexual phobias of the white judge by speculating that the burning of Mary's body must have been motivated by Bigger's need to destroy the evidence of his bestiality: " 'That treacherous beast must have known that if the marks of his teeth were ever seen on the innocent white flesh of her breasts, he would not have been accorded the high honor of sitting here in this court of law! O suffering Christ, there are no words to tell of a deed so black and awful!' " By appealing to the lynch spirit of the judge, Buckley is actually placing Bigger, "that treacherous beast," in the role of "suffering Christ," as the mob burning the fiery cross had done before. At one point, when his family and companions visit him in his cell, Bigger even feels that his suffering has redemptive power: "Bigger felt a wild and outlandish conviction surge in him: *They ought to be glad!* It was a strange but strong feeling, springing from the very depths of his life. Had he not taken fully upon himself the crime of being black? Had he not done the thing which they dreaded above all others? Then they ought not stand here and pity him, cry over him; but look at him and go home, contented, feeling that their shame was washed away."[50]

There is considerable irony in Wright's use of religious language and symbolism, however, for Bigger rejects totally the consolations of Christianity. When he sneaks into his flat to get his pistol to prepare for robbing Blum's delicatessen, his mother is singing a

the first of these two passages is reminiscent of the final paragraph of Joyce's "The Dead." By my count, snow is mentioned exactly 101 times in the novel, all but three of these in Book Two. See pp. 59, 80, 83, 85, 87, 91, 94, 96, 97, 98 (twice), 102, 103 (twice), 106, 111, 119, 125, 126, 127, 130 (three times), 131 (twice), 140, 146 (twice), 147 (twice), 148, 151, 154 (twice), 155, 156 (twice), 157 (twice), 165 (four times), 168 (twice), 178, 187 (seven times), 188 (four times), 189 (twice), 195, 196, 204, 205 (five times), 206 (twice), 208 (twice), 209, 210, 211, 216 (twice), 217, 218, 219, 221 (three times), 222 (twice), 223, 224 (three times), 225 (three times), 226 (twice), 227, 228 (three times), 229 (three times), and 236.

[50] Ibid., pp. 344, 252.

hymn: *"Lord, I want to be a Christian, / In my heart, in my heart."*
But his mother's religion is wholly ineffective in this world; it does
nothing to forestall his violence. When Bigger is hiding in an empty
apartment, he hears singing from a small church. The mood of
security and resignation that it induces in the worshipers is not without appeal to Bigger, but he cannot accept the surrender, the acquiescence, that religion represents: "Would it not have been better for
him had he lived in that world the music sang of? It would have
been easy to have lived in it, for it was his mother's world, humble,
contrite, believing. It had a center, a core, an axis, a heart which
he needed but could never have unless he laid his head upon a pillow
of humility and gave up his hope of living in the world. And he
would never do that."[51] After his capture he ignores the humble
Reverend Hammond and his wooden crucifix. A more militant
kind of religion is represented by the Ku Klux Klan's fiery cross on
top of the building near the Dalton home. The function of Christianity, Wright is implying, is to serve as an opiate of the black
masses and to lynch those who will not be lulled into oblivion of
their condition. After seeing the flaming cross, Bigger rejects vio-
lently, not merely passively, the wooden crucifix, Reverend Hammond, and later a Catholic priest.

Instead of religious acquiescence, Bigger chooses rebellion as his
way of life. The theme of rebellion is the central meaning of *Native
Son,* which the particulars of Wright's craft — structure, characterization, and symbolism — are designed to express. In his rebellion,
alienation, anguish, and isolation, Bigger is as much an existential
hero as Cross Damon, the protagonist of Wright's next novel, *The
Outsider* (1953).[52] Bigger rebels against religion, against his family,
against his companions and black life in general, and against the
white society that oppresses him. The two most important specific
forms that this rebellion takes are rape and murder, crimes of which
Bigger both is and is not guilty.

[51] Ibid., pp. 30, 215.
[52] For an interesting, if overstated, case for Bigger as existential hero, see
Esther Merle Jackson, "The American Negro and the Image of the Absurd,"
*Phylon,* XXIII (Fourth Quarter 1962), 359-71.

The strongest of all racial taboos, of course, is the sexual. Bigger's feelings toward Mary Dalton are deeply ambivalent, his fear and hatred combining with an attraction to her. She in turn is fascinated by him, by the unknown and, she believes, passional race to which he belongs. Bigger is Othello to Mary's Desdemona, and Buckley is a treacherous Iago.[53] Though Bigger does not actually rape Mary, he is on the point of doing so when Mrs. Dalton appears. When Max questions him on this point, he analyzes his feelings with accuracy:

"Yeah; I reckon it was because I knew I oughtn't've wanted to. I reckon it was because they say we black men do that anyhow. Mr. Max, you know what some white men say we black men do? They say we rape white women when we got the clap and they say we do that because we believe that if we rape white women then we'll get rid of the clap. That's what some white men *say*. They *believe* that. Jesus, Mr. Max, when folks says things like that about you, you whipped before you born. What's the use? Yeah; I reckon I was feeling that way when I was in the room with her. They say we do things like that and they say it to kill us. They draw a line and say for you to stay on your side of the line. They don't care if there's no bread over on your side. They don't care if you die. And then they say things like that about you and when you try to come from behind your line they kill you. They feel they ought to kill you then. Everybody wants to kill you then. Yeah; I reckon I was feeling that way and maybe the reason was because they say it. Maybe that was the reason."

The taboo stimulates the attraction, so that sexual contact with white women becomes a form of defiance, of rebellion against the white creators of the taboo. To enforce the taboo, white society must punish the violators. Buckley recognizes this duty when he shifts the emphasis in his final plea at the trial from murder to rape: " 'He planned to rape, to kill, to collect! He burned the body to get rid of evidence of *rape*! He took the trunk to the station to gain time in which to burn the body and prepare the kidnap note. He killed her because he *raped* her! Mind you, Your Honor, the central crime

---

[53] For further development of the Shakespearean resemblance, see Keneth Kinnamon, "Richard Wright's Use of *Othello* in *Native Son*," *CLA Journal*, XII (June 1969), 358-59.

here is *rape!* Every action points toward that!' "[54] The almost intolerably ironic truth is that although he intends coitus with the unconscious white Mary, he does not perform it; but he does possess the unwilling black Bessie on the cold floor of the abandoned building. Further, his killing of Mary is an accident; his murder of Bessie is deliberate.[55]

Mary's death is an "accident," but at the same time it is not. Like George Hurstwood before the door of the safe and Clyde Griffiths in the rowboat, Bigger Thomas by the bed is in a situation and frame of mind in which the notion of volition becomes highly ambiguous. As Max explains in court, Bigger's entire personality is rebellious to a murderous degree:

> "This Negro boy's entire attitude toward life is a *crime!* The hate and fear which we have inspired in him, woven by our civilization into the very structure of his consciousness, into his blood and bones, into the hourly functioning of his personality, have become the justification of his existence.
>
> "Every time he comes in contact with us, he kills! It is a physiological and psychological reaction, embedded in his being. Every thought he thinks is potential murder. Excluded from, and unassimilated in our society, yet longing to gratify impulses akin to our own but denied the objects and channels evolved through long centuries for their socialized expression, every sunrise and sunset make him guilty of subversive actions. Every movement of his body is an unconscious protest. Every desire, every dream, no matter how intimate or personal, is a plot or a conspiracy. Every hope is a plan for insurrection. Every glance of the eye is a threat. *His very existence is a crime against the state!*"

With the death and cremation of Mary, Bigger has achieved an ultimate level of rebellion. Because of this achievement he is caught

[54] *Native Son,* pp. 297-98, 344-45.

[55] In an early version of the first sexual scene involving Bigger and Bessie, Wright made Bigger think of Mary as he is making love to Bessie: "He placed his hands on her breasts just as he had placed them on Mary's last night and he was thinking of that while he kissed her." The reference to Mary is eliminated in the final version of this passage: "He leaned over her, full of desire, and lowered his head to hers and kissed her." *Native Son,* p. 114. For details concerning the early version of the novel, see Keneth Kinnamon, "Richard Wright Items in the Fales Collection," *Bulletin of the Society for the Libraries of New York University,* no. 66 (Winter 1965).

up in exhilaration, a feeling of elation, freedom, and self-mastery such as he has never known before. For him the act of murder becomes a regenerative force; out of death for Mary comes life for Bigger: "He had murdered and had created a new life for himself." Again Max, speaking for Wright, offers the correct explanation: "It was the first full act of his life; it was the most meaningful, exciting and stirring thing that had ever happened to him. He accepted it because it made him free, gave him the possibility of choice, of action, the opportunity to act and to feel that his actions carried weight."[56]

The difficulty is that such a rebellion is futile, both because of the perversion of human values that it entails and because it brings sure retribution from white society. Bigger's sense of freedom after Mary's death is delusive, for his flight actually draws him closer to his fate. The ultimate truth about Bigger Thomas, a truth from which even Max recoils in horror, emerges at the very end of *Native Son*:

> "I didn't want to kill!" Bigger shouted. "But what I killed for, I *am!* it must've been pretty deep in me to make me kill! I must have felt it awful hard to murder...."
>
> Max lifted his hand to touch Bigger, but did not.
>
> "No; no; no.... Bigger, not that...." Max pleaded despairingly.
>
> "What I killed for must've been good!" Bigger's voice was full of frenzied anguish. "It must have been good! When a man kills, it's for something.... I didn't know I was really alive in this world until I felt things hard enough to kill for 'em.... It's the truth, Mr. Max. I can say it now, 'cause I'm going to die. I know what I'm saying real good and I know how it sounds. But I'm all right. I feel all right when I look at it that way...."[57]

Insofar as Bigger is representative of black people, this is the final social meaning of the novel: white American society has so oppressed the black man that except for the narcosis of religion, the only outlet for his tortured emotions is a futile, murderous, and self-destructive rebellion; Bigger can attain a sense of life only by inflicting death.

Max, however, offers Bigger the vision of a more constructive kind of rebellion — or revolution. He tries to supplant Bigger's racial

[56] *Native Son,* pp. 335-36, 90, 333.
[57] Ibid., p. 358.

consciousness with class consciousness. Here lies the novel's most serious conceptual and artistic weakness. The point is not that Communist or other propaganda is inadmissible or even necessarily detrimental in a serious work of fiction; nor is any question of party control of art involved. If the propaganda is fully assimilated into the imaginative life of the novel, it may indeed prove a positive advantage. But this is not the case in *Native Son*.

The difficulty seems to be that Wright superimposed a consciously held intellectual conviction on a story that otherwise engaged his imagination and experience on the deepest emotional levels. In *How "Bigger" Was Born* Wright makes much of his own recognition that the Bigger Thomas type could be white as well as black. Just as the southern racial system was "but an appendage of a far vaster and in many respects more ruthless and impersonal commodity-profit machine,"[58] so Bigger Thomas was merely a local species of the genus proletariat. Max makes the same point, but Bigger never fully recognizes it. " 'But they hate black folks more than they hate unions,' "[59] Bigger says to his Marxist tutor. Though Wright thinks that he agrees with Max's rebuttal, his heart is really with Bigger's statement. In *How "Bigger" Was Born* he speaks of the "concrete picture" — his sense of his racial experience — and the "abstract linkages"[60] — his Communist theory. The two never completely merge in the novel, just as the understanding between Bigger and Max is never total. Max's speech to the court is an eloquent discourse, but Bigger's bitter comment to Gus at the beginning of the novel is more trenchant, more authentic, and finally more convincing: " 'Goddammit, look! We live here and they live there. We black and they white. They got things and we ain't. They do things and we can't. It's just like living in jail.' "[61]

[58] *How "Bigger" Was Born*, p. 12.
[59] *Native Son*, p. 295.
[60] *How "Bigger" Was Born*, p. 13.
[61] *Native Son*, p. 17. Edward Margolies develops a similar interpretation in *The Art of Richard Wright* (Carbondale, Ill., 1969), p. 113. For different views of the Bigger-Max relationship, see two important recent articles: Donald B. Gibson, "Wright's Invisible Native Son," *American Quarterly*, XXI (1969), 728-38, and Lloyd W. Brown, "Stereotypes in Black and White: The Nature of Perception in Wright's *Native Son*," *Black Academy Review*, I (Fall 1970), 35-44.

In addition to Wright's failure to resolve fully his intellectual (Max) and his emotional (Bigger) understanding of black life, there are other, less important weaknesses in *Native Son* — a certain unevenness in style, the inevitable but still somewhat damaging decrease of tension in Book Three — but these fade before the undeniable total impact of the book. This *power* — the word was used by virtually all reviewers — that one feels in the work is partly inherent in Wright's materials and theme, but it is also created by his careful attention to his craft in the matters of structure, action, characterization, and symbolism. *Native Son* is a major document of the American racial dilemma, but its art makes it also an important American novel.

In the case of a work so centrally concerned with a major social problem as *Native Son,* the matter of its public reception is of special importance. Part of Wright's intention was to make a strong impact on American public opinion about the racial question. The impact of the novel was undeniably great, but at times in ways different from, or even contrary to, those Wright intended. A number of reviewers had special axes to grind, and the book was treated as a social and political as well as a literary event. Diverse criteria of evaluation became inextricably mixed in many reviews. The various patterns of response to *Native Son* may be more clearly seen if some representative reviews are examined in four categories: white American, black American, Communist, and foreign.[62]

*Native Son* was launched with a chorus of critical praise. In her introduction to the novel Dorothy Canfield Fisher compared Wright to Dostoevsky, a comparison frequently made thereafter, and praised his "genuine literary skill."[63] Henry Seidel Canby introduced it enthusiastically to the Book-of-the-Month Club,[64] and Edward Weeks judged it "a performance of great talent — powerful, disturbing,

---

[62] A number of reviews not mentioned in this study are cited in Samuel Sillen, "The Response to 'Native Son,'" *New Masses,* XXXV (23 April 1940), 25-27.

[63] *Native Son,* pp. x, xi.

[64] *"Native Son* by Richard Wright," *Book-of-the-Month Club News,* February 1940, pp. 2-3. See also Canby's editorial "The Right Questions," *Saturday Review of Literature,* XXI (23 March 1940), 8.

unquestionably authentic."[65] This prepublication praise was echoed in many of the early reviews. Charles Poore, who had reviewed *Uncle Tom's Children,* expressed admiration for Wright's "command of the technique and resources of the novel," and extended the favorable comparison from Dostoevsky to Dreiser, Dickens, and Steinbeck.[66] Also familiar with Wright's first book, Lewis Gannett mentioned Steinbeck again and called *Native Son* "a deeply compassionate and understanding novel" as well as "a super-shocker."[67] Milton Rugoff found it "difficult to write temperately of a book which abounds in such excitement, in so much that is harrowing, and in so profound an understanding of human frailty."[68]

Many magazine reviewers were equally laudatory. In the *New Yorker* Clifton Fadiman compared Wright to Dreiser and Steinbeck, praising his "passion and intelligence" that probed "into layers of consciousness where only Dostoevski and a few others have penetrated. . . ."[69] A liberal white southerner flinched from some of the racial implications of the novel, but was impressed by its terror-filled narrative, objectivity, and emotive power.[70] Reviewing Wright again in the *New Republic,* Malcolm Cowley thought *Native Son* better than *Uncle Tom's Children* because the author had more artistic control over his resentment against whites. In contrast to most other reviewers, Cowley deemed the final part of *Native Son* the best.[71] Another liberal reviewer noted some defects in style and characterization, but she thought *Native Son* superior to *The Grapes of Wrath* in its "maturity of thought and feeling."[72]

Some dissenting voices were raised against this predominantly favorable consensus, several of them in the quarterlies. Don Stanford thought the book stylistically weak, but his objection seemed to issue

---

[65] Quoted by Charles Poore, "Books of the Times," 1 March 1940.

[66] Ibid.

[67] "Books and Things," *New York Herald Tribune,* 1 March 1940, p. 17.

[68] "A Feverish Dramatic Intensity," *New York Herald Tribune Books,* 3 March 1940, p. 5.

[69] "A Black 'American Tragedy,' " *New Yorker,* XVI (2 March 1940), 52, 53.

[70] Jonathan Daniels, "Man against the World," *Saturday Review of Literature,* XXI (2 March 1940), 5.

[71] "The Case of Bigger Thomas," *New Republic,* CII (18 March 1940), 382-83.

[72] Margaret Marshall, "Black Native Son," *Nation,* CL (16 March 1940), 367, 368.

more from a priori notions about naturalism than from a close reading of the novel.[73] Wallace Stegner could not accept Bigger as a representative black, and he objected to what he considered behaviorist special pleading.[74] Robert Littell deplored the novel's failure to exploit plot opportunities for surprise and suspense.[75]

The three most severe American attacks on the novel were by — in descending order of cogency — Howard Mumford Jones, David L. Cohn, and Burton Rascoe, all of whom showed considerable insensitivity to the depiction of racial oppression that so impressed most reviewers. Annoyed by the enthusiastic advance publicity given *Native Son*, Jones conceded the excellence of the opening scenes but objected that the dialogue was not well related to the narrative and complained that the characterization was weak, except in the case of Bigger, where it was confused. Wright was also guilty of intellectual confusion in presenting his thesis, which unjustifiably mixed "humanitarianism and determinism." Jones had his own solution to the racial problem — full employment: "The essential wrong done the colored race is not that it [the white race] drives Negroes to murder, but that it does not drive them to work. They are unemployed and stifled. Bigger, however, gets a job."[76] Therefore, the clear implication is, he has little to complain of. Wright may not have seen this review, which appeared in a Boston newspaper, but he could have replied that black people enjoyed relatively full employment before the Emancipation Proclamation, when they were indeed driven to work. Wright did reply to the other two serious American attacks on his novel, those by Cohn and Rascoe.

David L. Cohn, a native of Greenville, Mississippi, and a social historian of the Delta region, called *Native Son* "a blinding and corrosive study in hate." Bigger's hatred for whites, Cohn further asserted, received Wright's advocacy. The lot of the black man in America was improving gradually, but the present disposition of whites would not permit more rapid change. To demand immediate social justice was to upset the delicate balance in race relations

[73] "*The Beloved Returns* and Other Recent Fiction," *Southern Review*, VI (Winter 1941), 619.
[74] "The New Novels," *Virginia Quarterly Review*, XVI (Summer 1940), 462.
[75] "Outstanding Novels," *Yale Review*, XXIX (Summer 1940), x.
[76] "Uneven Effect," *Boston Evening Transcript*, 2 March 1940, sec. 5, p. 1.

achieved "through the exercise of exquisite, intuitive tact": "Hatred, and the preaching of hatred, and incitement to violence can only make a tolerable relationship intolerable." That the relationship was intolerable for blacks, however tolerable for whites, Cohn could not accept. After all, he complacently argued, Jews have been oppressed far longer and far more severely than blacks, and in their plight they had "constructed inexhaustible wells of spiritual resource."[77]

Burton Rascoe's piece in the *American Mercury* was far more vitriolic. Cohn had conceded some literary merit to the book, but Rascoe, comparing it to pulp fiction, could not "conceive of a novel's being worse, in the most important respects, than *Native Son.*" At a luncheon in New York that Rascoe attended, Wright had been feted by whites, thus making him "an embodied refutation of his theme," which Rascoe thought "utterly loathsome." After all, Rascoe wrote in all seriousness, "I can't see that Bigger Thomas had anything more to contend with, in childhood and youth, than I had or than dozens of my friends had."[78] Such infuriating obtuseness, however, was rare in the general white American reception of *Native Son.* Most reviews were favorable, and several were ecstatically so.

Black attitudes toward the novel were governed by two reactions, often combined in the same reader. On one hand, blacks took racial pride in Wright's success and his strong impression on the white world. On the other, many misgivings were voiced that the portrayal of Bigger was so unflinchingly harsh that the book would have the boomerang effect of seeming to confirm white prejudice. From press, platform, and pulpit, comment on *Native Son* poured forth. In a large Chicago church, the minister evinced both typical black reactions: "Mr. Wright has written one of the most powerful novels I have ever read, and I praise God for the ability, imagination, mastery of language, beauty of rhetoric, diction displayed by the writer." But, Reverend Austin insisted, "Had such a book been written when Harriet Beecher Stowe wrote Uncle Tom's Cabin, we would have remained in slavery,"[79] for the sexual theme of *Native Son* tends to

[77] "The Negro Novel: Richard Wright," *Atlantic Monthly,* CLXV (May 1940), 659, 661, 660.
[78] "Negro Novel and White Reviewers," pp. 113, 114, 115.
[79] "Rev. Austin Preaches on Wright's 'Native Son,'" *Chicago Defender,* 15 June 1940, p. 9.

confirm white beliefs that black men are attracted to white women. George R. Dorsey, a sociologist, praised the novel's artistic qualities, but deplored its failure to gain "the reader's sympathy for its leading characters."[80] Some editorialists in influential black newspapers, however, appraised more hopefully the probable social effect of the work in revealing racial injustice to white America.[81]

The most enthusiastic black reviews came from those critics who were impressed equally by the literary merit and the social message of the novel. Wright's protégé Ralph Ellison found in it "an artistry, penetration of thought, and sheer emotional power that places it into the first rank of American fiction."[82] In a review in the official organ of the National Association for the Advancement of Colored People, James W. Ivy, comparing *Native Son* to *Crime and Punishment, An American Tragedy,* and Greek tragedy, called it "a profound and searching analysis of the mind of the American Negro and a penetrating study of the tragic position of the Negro in American life." Ivy concluded: "*Native Son* is undoubtedly the greatest novel written by an American Negro. In fact, it is one of the best American novels, and Mr. Wright is one of the great novelists of this generation."[83] Scholarly Alain Locke was somewhat more restrained, but he praised warmly Wright's "social honesty and artistic integrity."[84] The black reception of the most famous black novel of the time was mixed because of Wright's inflammatory theme and treatment, but the most discerning black reviewers were highly laudatory.

*Native Son* also presented special problems to Communist readers, among whom the debate was equally lively. On the favorable side, Wright was a faithful party member whose book was enjoying a large sale and a generally approving reception by bourgeois reviewers. The party could share in the glory of his achievement, for he was a prime example of the development of the black artist under Communist tutelage. Furthermore, the novel offered an incisive in-

---

[80] "Says 'Native Son' Fails Its Purpose," *Chicago Defender,* 25 May 1940, p. 7.

[81] See "Richard Wright's Native Son," *Chicago Defender,* 16 March 1940, p. 14, and "A Work of Genius," *New York Amsterdam News,* 23 March 1940, p. 14.

[82] "Recent Negro Fiction," *New Masses,* XL (5 August 1941), 22.

[83] " 'Whipped Before You Born,' " *Crisis,* XLVII (April 1940), 122.

[84] "Of Native Sons: Real and Otherwise," *Opportunity,* XIX (January 1941), 4.

dictment of racial oppression in America, which it attempted — correctly, from the party viewpoint — to relate to the class struggle. On the other hand, the portrait of Bigger might be used, as some black commentators were also insisting, to justify the necessity of racial repression. More important, *Native Son* presented in Jan and Mary a Communist and a fellow traveler who were blunderingly insensitive to Bigger's feelings, a point that anti-Communist reviewers were quick to seize upon. There was also a noticeable absence of "progressive" black characters in the novel to balance Bigger's brutalized portrait. These were the issues as most Communist readers saw them. As Horace R. Cayton recalled the matter, Earl Browder himself became involved in the controversy by inviting Wright to see him shortly after the book was published. Although Wright rejected this invitation, Browder finally gave the book his seal of approval: "Things continued in this atmosphere of tension until Browder came into Party headquarters one morning and, throwing a copy of *Native Son* on an official's desk, stated that he saw nothing wrong with it."[85]

Whether or not this anecdote is literally true, the fact is that the *Worker* was remarkably slow in noticing the book. Not until a month after its publication did Mike Gold review it, but when he finally spoke, he was intensely eulogistic, claiming, quite accurately, that "after ten years of fumbling, and experiment, of great visions and uneven fulfilments, our American social realism, our American proletarian literature . . . has finally culminated in two sure classics — Steinbeck's 'Grapes of Wrath' and Richard Wright's 'Native Son.' " As to the "miracle" of Wright's rapid development, Gold was eager to claim credit for the ideology which guided it: "Maybe it is the miracle of complete honesty, of Communist honesty, that fierce morality which burns out all the bunk in a writer. Maybe the way to be a great writer is to love your poor, oppressed folk with the passionate loyalty of Dick Wright." Even in his enthusiasm, however, Gold found it necessary to address himself, if only obliquely,

[85] Cayton, *Long Old Road,* p. 249. Browder himself did not recall asking Wright to see him about *Native Son,* but said that he discouraged party objections to the novel, wishing it to succeed or fail on its own. Interview with the author, 9 March 1966. On the other hand, Adam Clayton Powell, Jr., recalls that when Max Yergan bought Powell's newspaper, *People's Voice,* he dropped the serialization of *Native Son* that Powell had begun because of party discontent with Wright. Interview with the author, 19 November 1968.

to the issue of the characterization of Jan and Mary by refuting Henry Seidel Canby's attack on these "Communist Negrophiles."[86]

Two weeks later Benjamin J. Davis, Jr., wrote an influential review that articulated the reasons for much party discontent with the novel. As the second most important black Communist, a graduate of Amherst College and the Harvard Law School, and Wright's personal friend, Davis was in a strategic position to lecture the author on his ideological shortcomings. After general praise of the novel, Davis objected that "the author overwrites Bigger into a symbol of the whole Negro people," that he distorts the actual racial situation by omitting the progressive majority of blacks, that the masses of white progressives are also ignored, that the few Communists in the book are not typical, and that both Bigger's introspection and parts of Max's courtroom speech are "baffling and mystical."[87] For all of these reasons, *Native Son* falls short as a Communist novel on the racial theme. Whatever his stance vis-à-vis bourgeois critics, Mike Gold, compared to Davis, seemed a champion of artistic autonomy. In two subsequent columns in the *Daily Worker,* Gold replied both to Davis and to numerous letters[88] concerning the novel by rejecting the demand "that our proletarian fictioneers give up all study of complex human nature and write only agitational tracts."[89] Much of the power of *Native Son,* Gold shrewdly pointed out, derives from the "intensive use of the fictional spotlight" on Bigger, a focus that would be blurred if Wright had also "included Negro Communists, militant and intellectual Negroes."[90]

Unlike the *Worker, New Masses* reviewed *Native Son* immediately upon its publication. Like Mike Gold, Samuel Sillen received the novel enthusiastically. Also like Gold, he warned against the reactionary distortions of such critics as Canby. The most impressive

[86] "Change the World: Dick Wright Gives America a Significant Picture in 'Native Son,' " *Sunday Worker,* 31 March 1940, sec. 2, p. 7.

[87] "Richard Wright's 'Native Son' a Notable Achievement," *Sunday Worker,* 14 April 1940, sec. 2, p. 4.

[88] Six of these letters, four siding with Davis and two with Gold, were printed in "Readers Discuss 'Native Son,' " *Daily Worker,* 26 April 1940, p. 7. One of the letters favorable to Gold and Wright was from Herbert Aptheker, then in the process of becoming the foremost Communist historian of black life and today a leading party theoretician.

[89] "Change the World," *Daily Worker,* 17 April 1940, p. 7.

[90] "Change the World," *Daily Worker,* 29 April 1940, p. 7.

aspect of Wright's achievement, Sillen thought, was his "brilliant analysis of the interplay of social and psychological factors in experience," which resulted in an original fusion of "the valid elements in the naturalistic and psychological traditions." This achievement placed him "in the first ranks of American literature in our time."[91] In two later articles, Sillen analyzed and evaluated the response to the novel, both Communist and non-Communist, and invited further discussion from readers of *New Masses*.[92] Among the participants in the continuing debate were Eugene Holmes of Howard University's department of philosophy and Chester B. Himes, later to become a novelist of black protest and Wright's good friend in Paris, both of whom defended the novel, and Joseph H. Cole and Joel Shaw, who commented adversely on Wright's use of Bigger as a representative black.[93] Despite the animadversions of many Communists on doctrinal grounds, the prevailing attitude toward *Native Son*, as best expressed by Gold and Sillen, was favorable. As early as May of 1940, *New Masses* was supporting the novel for a Pulitzer Prize.[94]

Richard Wright's reputation in Europe is beyond the scope of this study, but a few typical reactions to *Native Son* may be cited to conclude this examination of the novel's impact. In the Soviet Union the discussion of *Native Son* followed the same general lines as among American Communists, with the critical balance likewise struck in Wright's favor.[95] The war delayed publication of a French translation until after Wright took up residence in Paris, by which time he had become a literary lion appearing in *Les Temps Modernes* and promoted by Jean-Paul Sartre. In England, however, reactions were immediate and ranged to extremes. With the possible exception of Burton Rascoe's tirade, the English review by Anthony

[91] "Richard Wright's 'Native Son,' " *New Masses*, XXXIV (5 March 1940), 25.

[92] "The Response to 'Native Son' " (see above, n. 62) and "The Meaning of Bigger Thomas," *New Masses*, XXXV (30 April 1940), 26-28.

[93] Samuel Sillen, " 'Native Son': Pros and Cons," *New Masses*, XXXV (21 May 1940), 23-26.

[94] "Pulitzer Awards," *New Masses*, XXXV (14 May 1940), 26. A year later the awards committee was chided for its failure to select *Native Son*, in "The Pulitzer Prizes," *New Masses*, XXXIX (13 May 1941), 21. No award was made in 1941 for the novel.

[95] For an analysis of the Soviet reception of *Native Son*, see Brown, *Soviet Attitudes toward American Writing*, pp. 128-30.

West was the most vicious attack the novel received. Totally unconvinced by Wright's "twaddle" about environmental determinism, West called it "the poisonous guff of Behaviourism" — a word used quite loosely both here and elsewhere in commentary on Wright. Otherwise West found the novel "unimpressive and silly."[96] Rosamond Lehmann, in contrast to West, was completely overwhelmed. Far from being a mere puppet, Bigger seemed to her "a figure of sublime dimensions; one who inspires the kind of love and pity we bestow upon the tragic hero." A "masterpiece," *Native Son* possessed for this critic a "scope and passionate sincerity [that] give it a grandeur, a moral importance at least as great as that of *An American Tragedy*."[97] Between these extremes, the reviewer for the *Times Literary Supplement* expressed carefully qualified admiration for *Native Son*.[98]

The phenomenal sale that *Native Son* enjoyed gave Wright financial security for the first time in his life. His new affluence made possible a trip to Mexico, where despite personal problems resulting from his failing first marriage (with Rose Dhima Meadman, a ballet dancer), he found that "people of all races and colors live in harmony and without racial prejudices or theories of racial superiority."[99] From this vantage point he replied to the attacks on his novel by David L. Cohn and Burton Rascoe.[100] A more important and more comprehensive statement of his intention in the novel is "How 'Bigger' Was Born," which Wright delivered as a speech before and after its appearance in the *Saturday Review of Literature* and which was then published as a separate pamphlet by Harper's.[101] In the

[96] "New Novels," *New Statesman and Nation*, XIX (20 April 1940), 542.

[97] "New Novels," *Spectator*, CLXIV (19 April 1940), 574.

[98] "Criminal or Victim?" *Times Literary Supplement*, 27 April 1940, p. 205.

[99] Richard Wright, "I Bite the Hand That Feeds Me," *Atlantic Monthly*, CLXV (June 1940), 826.

[100] See ibid., pp. 826-28, and "Rascoe-Baiting," *American Mercury*, L (July 1940), 376-77.

[101] For notices of Wright's lectures on *Native Son*, see the following: "Wright Shows New Book," *Chicago Defender*, 24 February 1940, p. 22; "Crowd Hears Noted Author," *New York Amsterdam News*, 16 March 1940, p. 3; " 'Native Son' Author to Relate Birth of 'Bigger,' " *Chicago Defender*, 6 July 1940, p. 6; and Harry Hansen, "The First Reader," *New York World-Telegram*, 9 September 1940, p. 17. The magazine version appeared in June and the enlarged pamphlet version in October.

concluding paragraph of this essay Wright defined the conditions of American life, suggested the possibilities of the black man as a subject for American fiction, and related himself to the American literary tradition:

> I feel that I'm lucky to be alive to write novels today, when the whole world is caught in the pangs of war and change. Early American writers, Henry James and Nathaniel Hawthorne, complained bitterly about the bleakness and flatness of the American scene. But I think that if they were alive, they'd feel at home in modern America. True, we have no great church in America; our national traditions are still of such a sort that we are not wont to brag of them; and we have no army that's above the level of mercenary fighters; we have no group acceptable to the whole of our country upholding certain humane values; we have no rich symbols, no colorful rituals. We have only a money-grubbing, industrial civilization. But we do have in the Negro the embodiment of a past tragic enough to appease the spiritual hunger of even a James; and we have in the oppression of the Negro a shadow athwart our national life dense and heavy enough to satisfy even the gloomy broodings of a Hawthorne. And if Poe were alive, he would not have to invent horror; horror would invent him.[102]

This passage brings to a climax the emergence of Richard Wright by suggesting his threefold claim to enduring importance — as social critic, as articulator of the black agony, and as American writer.

[102] *How "Bigger" Was Born*, p. 39.

# Epilogue

# FIVE

With the publication and favorable reception of *Native Son,* the emergence of Richard Wright was complete. His first two published books were among the three best of his entire career, the other being *Black Boy.* He was in 1940 both the leading black writer of the world and the foremost American novelist still attached to the Communist party. He had also achieved great popular success. Before essaying a brief description of the nature of Wright's achievement, both artistic and social, in his early career, it will be helpful to provide the additional perspective of a review of his withdrawal from the Communist party, which had nurtured his talent, and his expatriation from the land that had both maimed his spirit and provided the materials for his art.

The success of *Native Son* increased Wright's utility to the Communist party, and his name now appeared even more frequently on various statements and manifestos. He signed appeals on behalf of *New Masses,*[1] served as sponsor of a national photography contest[2] and the 1940 Book Ball[3] — both of which were also supported by

[1] Richard Wright et al., "To President Franklin D. Roosevelt," *New Masses,* XXXV (2 April 1940), 21; Richard Wright et al., "Writers Emergency Committee to Save New Masses," *New Masses,* XXXV (30 April 1940), 3.

[2] "Richard Wright Sponsors Youth Photo Contest," *Daily Worker,* 24 August 1940, p. 7. Wright's interest in photography had been stimulated by his friend Frank Marshall Davis. Letter from Davis to the author, 24 October 1964.

[3] "Book Notes," *Daily Worker,* 17 September 1940, p. 7.

non-Communists — and protested Red-baiting.[4] Perhaps most important, he issued a lengthy statement in support of the party presidential ticket of Earl Browder and James W. Ford.[5] As a national figure, Wright was elected one of the vice-presidents of the League of American Writers[6] and a member of the national council of the American Peace Mobilization,[7] groups under heavy party influence.

His party activity continued unabated in 1941. In February he congratulated *New Masses* on its thirtieth anniversary.[8] In March the International Publishers pamphlet edition of *Bright and Morning Star* appeared with a preface by Wright donating his royalties to the campaign to free Earl Browder, who had recently been imprisoned on the pretext of a passport violation but apparently for political reasons.[9] At the end of the year Wright was continuing his efforts on Browder's behalf.[10] He aided another imprisoned Communist — a college teacher of English — by contributing a foreword to his collection of letters written from the New York City jail.[11] He appeared as speaker or guest of honor at testimonial dinners for Mike Gold[12] and Vito Marcantonio,[13] and in June he spoke against American involvement in the war at the opening session of the fourth American Writers' Congress,[14] which chose *Native Son* as "the most distin-

[4] "Negro Leaders Protest Attacks against Communist Candidates," *Daily Worker*, 16 September 1940, p. 1; "Prominent Negroes Urge Ballot Rights for Communists," *Daily Worker*, 23 September 1940, p. 4.

[5] "Richard Wright's Statement Supporting Browder, Ford," *Daily Worker*, 30 September 1940, p. 5.

[6] "Writers League Elects Outstanding Authors as Vice-Presidents," *Daily Worker*, 5 August 1940, p. 7.

[7] "Officers of the American Peace Mobilization," *Daily Worker*, 3 September 1940, p. 4.

[8] "On New Masses' Thirtieth Anniversary," *New Masses*, XXXVIII (18 February 1941), 26. See also "Seven Prominent Americans Give Their Point of View," *New Masses*, XXXIX (6 May 1941), 15-16.

[9] Richard Wright, "A Letter to International Publishers," *Bright and Morning Star*, foreword by James W. Ford (New York, 1941), p. 3.

[10] " 'Let's Free Browder Now,' " *New Masses*, XL (16 September 1941), 20; "In the Name of Justice . . . ," *New Masses*, XLI (4 November 1941), 22.

[11] Morris U. Schappes, *Letters from the Tombs*, ed. Louis Lerman (New York, 1941).

[12] "Between Ourselves," *New Masses*, XXXVIII (4 March 1941), 2; (11 March 1941), 2.

[13] "Testimonial Dinner and Reception for the Hon. Vito Marcantonio," *New Masses*, XXXIX (1 April 1941), 29.

[14] Richard Wright, "Not My People's War," *New Masses*, XXXIX (17 June 1941), 8-9, 12.

guished American novel published since 1939."[15] In the last two
weeks of August he served as lecturer in the leftist White Mountain
Writers Conference in Jefferson, New Hampshire.[16] This year of
1941 was his last of intensive party activity.

In 1942 and 1943 his customary endorsement of the causes of the
Communist party was conspicuous by its absence. The last time a
piece by Wright appeared in a party publication was on 13 February
1942, when the *Daily Worker* printed his letter to Sender Garlin
concerning a recent controversy in the newspaper on the merits of
jazz. The letter was ostensibly friendly and congratulatory, but it
carried veiled signs of disaffection with the rigidities of hierarchical
party control of opinion: "I feel that this journalistic technique [con-
troversy through letters to the editor] can be extended to all depart-
ments of the Daily Worker, and I believe that there will accrue from
it a feeling that the Daily Worker is truly a people's paper." In calling for "multiple points of view, expressed from varied environmental class angles," Wright was implicitly rejecting autocratic party
control and the enforcement of intellectual uniformity. He concluded
his letter with this sentence: "The Communist Party is the only political party in America vitally concerned about culture and its problems, therefore let us encourage the expression of the opinion of the
man on the street; we can learn from him and he from us."[17] Wright
had deviated little from his original position upon entering the party
that Communist intellectuals could gain much from more exposure
to the masses,[18] but as in the earlier dispute concerning the abolition
of the John Reed clubs, the party was unwilling to be persuaded by
Wright. The difference was that in 1942 Wright was much less dependent on Communist support and guidance than in 1935.

Wright's public break did not come until two years later, when

[15] "Theodore Dreiser Gets Peace Award," *New York Times,* 7 June 1941,
p. 5; " 'Native Son' Wins Award for Novel," *New York Times,* 8 June 1941,
sec. 1, p. 46.
[16] A brochure concerning this conference, which was held under the auspices
of the League of American Writers, is deposited in the James Weldon Johnson
Memorial Collection of the Yale University Library.
[17] Richard Wright, "Richard Wright Lauds Controversy on Music," *Daily
Worker,* 13 February 1942, p. 7. Wright was one of the signers of the "Text of
National Call to Browder Congress," *Sunday Worker,* 15 February 1942, sec.
1, p. 3, but this seems to be the last party cause he officially supported.
[18] See above, p. 52.

he spoke against the party first briefly to a New York newspaper in July 1944,[19] and then at length in the *Atlantic Monthly*.[20] In the newspaper interview he attacked the party's intellectual rigidities, its intolerance of new ideas. The magazine article, originally part of his autobiography, treats his experiences with the party in Chicago. Although "I Tried to Be a Communist," as has been indicated,[21] is not without distortions of both chronology and fact, the general tone is one of regret and nostalgia rather than bitterness. Nevertheless, some of the biggest guns of the party were immediately trained on Wright — those of Benjamin J. Davis, Jr., Robert Minor, Samuel Sillen, and James W. Ford.[22] One of the blasts was a charge of both anti-black and anti-Semitic prejudice, which must have proved quite puzzling to both Wright and his Jewish wife, Ellen Poplar, who had been a party activist in Brooklyn.

Unlike some ex-Communists, however, Wright refused to make a career of anti-Communism or reaction. On the contrary, one of the sources of his disillusion with Communists was that they seemed no longer "effective instruments for social change."[23] As for himself, he stated: "I am as collectivist and proletarian in my outlook as when I belonged to the Communist Party...."[24] For the rest of his life Wright remained an independent radical, but during his life and even after his death he was regarded by the party as a renegade

---

[19] "Negro Author Criticizes Reds as Intolerant," *New York Herald Tribune*, 28 July 1944, p. 11.

[20] "I Tried to Be a Communist." This article was Wright's contribution to *The God That Failed* (1949).

[21] See above, pp. 63, 64-65, 67.

[22] Benjamin J. Davis, Jr., "New Times: A Few Words on Richard Wright and 'New Ideas,'" *Worker*, 6 August 1944, p. 9; Robert Minor, "To Tell the Truth: Mr. Wright Didn't Discover It," *Daily Worker*, 15 August 1944, p. 6; Samuel Sillen, "Richard Wright in Retreat," *New Masses*, LII (29 August 1944), 25-26; James W. Ford, "The Case of Richard Wright: A Disservice to the Negro People," *Daily Worker*, 5 September 1944, p. 6. In *Long Old Road*, p. 253, Horace Cayton recalled that he turned over one of his newspaper columns to Wright at this time. This piece must be Horace R. Cayton, "The Communists: War Relationship with Negroes Is Not Creditable," *Pittsburgh Courier*, 26 August 1944, p. 7, which attacked the Communist policy of deemphasizing efforts to achieve black rights for the duration so as not to interfere with the war effort. Benjamin J. Davis, Jr., unaware that Wright, not Cayton, wrote this, offered a rebuttal in "New Times: What Makes Mr. Cayton Tick," *Worker*, 3 September 1944, p. 11.

[23] "Negro Author Criticizes Reds as Intolerant."

[24] Webb, *Richard Wright*, p. 208.

deserving vigorous, often vituperative, attack in its journals.[25] For his own part, Wright depicted the Communist characters in his novel *The Outsider* (1953) as cynically intelligent votaries of a cult of power, unscrupulous assassins, or duped followers. On the other hand, to a French intellectual "he paid glowing tribute to the service of the Communist Party in the Negro cause and stressed that it had been popular among Negroes, particularly in Chicago."[26]

Wright was physically and mentally restless after his withdrawal from the Communist fold. In July of 1945 he took a holiday in Quebec.[27] This trip whetted his appetite for French civilization, and he began to think seriously of a trip to France. After corresponding with Gertrude Stein, that most venerable of American expatriates in Paris, and meeting Jean-Paul Sartre in New York early in 1946, Wright reached his decision to go and in March submitted his application for a passport. After considerable delay, occasioned by the reluctance of the State Department to permit an outspoken black radical to leave the country, Wright finally sailed with his wife and child on May Day 1946.[28]

He arrived in France as a celebrity. With the encouragement of Gertrude Stein, which Wright was at the time unaware of, the French government had extended to him an official invitation to make the trip with expenses paid.[29] More than a year earlier, French

[25] See, for example, Ward, "Five Negro Novelists: Revolt and Retreat"; S[idney] Finkelstein, "The Novel as Battleground," *New Masses*, LXIV (26 August 1947), 18-22; Doxey A. Wilkerson, "Negro Culture: Heritage and Weapon," *Masses & Mainstream*, II (August 1949), 3-24; and L. Barnes (pseud.), "The Proletarian Novel," *Mainstream*, XVI (July 1963), 51-57.

[26] Daniel Guerin, *Negroes on the March: A Frenchman's Report on the American Negro Struggle*, trans. and ed. Duncan Ferguson (New York, 1956), p. 125.

[27] Wright wrote Carl Van Vechten a postcard from Peironille, Quebec, post-marked 20 July 1945. He commented on his trip at some length in a letter to Gertrude Stein, 29 October 1945. Wright's letters to Van Vechten and Stein are deposited in the Yale University Library.

[28] Wright discussed his difficulties in arranging the trip in letters to Stein dated 15 March, 28 March, 12 April, and 30 April 1946. Dorothy Norman editorialized against the State Department's treatment of him in her column "A World to Live In — Operation: Richard Wright," *New York Post*, 17 June 1946, p. 34.

[29] See Claude Lévi-Strauss, "Letter to Richard Wright, 25 April 1946," *New Letters*, XXXVIII (Winter 1971), 130.

translations of his works had begun to appear,[30] and he was met in Paris "by Gertrude Stein, some French writers, two limousines and a battery of French reporters."[31] During the following months he was feted by French intellectuals, particularly those associated with Sartre, Simone de Beauvoir, and *Les Temps Modernes*. Ending his first taste of Europe with a three-week visit in London, he returned to New York, arriving in November, but Greenwich Village could not now compare to the Left Bank. In July 1947 he returned to Paris to establish permanent residence[32] and to begin the existentialist and third-world internationalist phase of his career. Despite some remarkable works written during the last thirteen years of his life, however, his importance in American literature and social protest resides chiefly in his experiences and achievements from 1908 to 1940, the years of his emergence. It remains to attempt a brief assessment of this importance.

As a writer of fiction, Wright's major achievements are *Uncle Tom's Children* and *Native Son,* the two books that established his early reputation and thus climaxed his emergence. Of the latter, R. P. Blackmur made a comment, quoted approvingly by Alfred Kazin and Frederick J. Hoffman,[33] that epitomizes the case against Wright's fiction: "*Native Son* is one of those books in which everything is undertaken with seriousness except the writing."[34] In one sense this objection has some validity; Wright was not in his early career, nor did he ever become, a consistently accomplished prose stylist. This is not to say that he was unaware of the importance of

---

[30] "Le Depart de 'Big Boy,' " trans. Marcel Duhamel, pref. Paul Robeson, *L'Arbalète,* IX (Autumn 1944), 237-66; "Le Feu dans la nuée," trans. Marcel Duhamel, *Les Temps Modernes,* I (1 October 1945), 22-47; (1 November 1945), 291-319.

[31] Smith, "Black Boy in France," p. 36.

[32] Ibid.

[33] Alfred Kazin, *On Native Grounds: An Interpretation of Modern American Prose Literature* (New York, 1942), p. 387; Frederick J. Hoffman, *The Modern Novel in America* (Chicago, 1956), p. 33. It is worth recording that Kazin's opinion of *Native Son,* as expressed in a more recent panel discussion, has improved. Comparing it favorably to *The Outsider,* he finds that it "still is a very powerful and enormously moving book." Alfred Kazin et al., "The Negro in American Culture," *Cross Currents,* XI (Summer 1961), 213.

[34] *Language as Gesture* (New York, 1952), p. 413.

style, for he recorded in "American Hunger" his painstaking efforts as he began to write in Chicago to achieve an adequate level of expression. He had a firm conception of his stylistic goal: "My purpose was to capture a physical state or movement that carried a strong subjective impression, an accomplishment which seemed supremely worth struggling for. If I could fasten the mind of the reader upon words so firmly that he would forget words and be conscious only of his response, I felt that I would be in sight of knowing how to write narrative. I strove to master words, to make them disappear, to make them important by making them new, to make them melt into a rising spiral of emotional stimuli."[35] At its best his prose acts in exactly this way, achieving the striking emotional force that characterizes his best fiction. At times, however, he slips into fine writing, into an inflated diction and a florid rhetoric that are seldom functional in the development of action, character, or theme.

Apart from this stylistic weakness — the frequency of which is easy to exaggerate — Wright was a much more careful literary craftsman than has customarily been recognized. As the analyses of *Uncle Tom's Children* and *Native Son* in this study have tried to show, his best fiction shows a firm if rather uncomplicated sense of structure, usually skillful employment of symbolism, adequate characterization, and gripping action. Above all, Wright's best writing has a dramatic quality of remarkably harrowing intensity.

It is this achievement which defines Wright's special place among American naturalistic novelists. He does not attempt Crane's stance of ironic detachment; nor does he usually work toward the cumulative effect of amassed detail that characterizes the writing of Dreiser and Farrell. Wright insists as much as these three on the deterministic influence of environment, but in his case the emphasis is on situations of violent crisis in the lives of his naturalistic protagonists, not on their slow deterioration.

Within the general naturalistic tradition, Wright has a special affiliation with the most distinctive literary movement of the decade of his emergence as a writer — proletarian fiction. It must be admitted that this movement produced very few works of enduring merit, but of these *Uncle Tom's Children* and *Native Son* are among the

[35] "American Hunger," p. 301.

best. Clearly Wright was the most accomplished writer of fiction developed by the Communist party. Compared to him, Mike Gold and Jack Conroy are quite deficient in literary technique. Of all the leftist writers of the thirties in America, Wright ranks with Farrell and Steinbeck, but he is without the former's dullness and the latter's sentimentality.

To relate Wright to naturalism and proletarian fiction is not to deny other relationships. If he read Dreiser and Sinclair Lewis as a youth in Memphis, he was soon also reading Dostoevsky, Conrad, James, Sherwood Anderson, Stein, Hemingway, Joyce, Proust, and others. The point is not that Wright's literary technique is as complex as that of most of these writers, for it is not, but neither is it limited to a pedestrian naturalism. Specifically, one may suggest that Wright's prose owes something to the laconic dialogue of Ernest Hemingway, the poetic vision of Sherwood Anderson and Gertrude Stein (especially in "Long Black Song"), and the polemical verve of H. L. Mencken and Sinclair Lewis. Further, Wright's psychological probing relates him to Dostoevsky, James, and Proust, just as his social documentation relates him to Dreiser, Dos Passos, and Farrell.

At the same time, Wright's work must be viewed in relation to Afro-American literature. Rebelling against what he considered the superficial exoticism of the Harlem Renaissance writers and the stultifying middle-class accommodation of such an earlier writer as Paul Laurence Dunbar, Wright represented the culmination of the tradition of vigorous racial and social protest espoused by writers such as Frederick Douglass and Claude McKay and by much black folklore. Wright in turn influenced a generation of black novelists of the forties and fifties, among whom Willard Motley, Chester Himes, Ann Petry, and William Gardner Smith are notable. Two of the most distinguished American novelists now living, Ralph Ellison and James Baldwin, began their careers under Wright's influence and personal encouragement, however much their subsequent work has diverged from the example of their mentor.[36]

Very early in his career Baldwin rejected the fiction of social pro-

---

[36] For a brief account of the Wright-Ellison relation, see above, pp. 71-72. Maurice Charney treats Wright and Baldwin in "James Baldwin's Quarrel with Richard Wright," *American Quarterly*, XV (Spring 1963), 65-75.

test in general and Wright in particular.[37] Another young black writer, Richard Gibson, made a similar case while still an undergraduate.[38] Characteristic of the politically exhausted literary climate of the McCarthy period, this position seems highly anachronistic today. Though many young black writers look immediately to Imamu Amiri Baraka as their literary big brother, Richard Wright is a father figure, just as W. E. B. Du Bois is a spiritual grandfather. Late in 1967 *Negro Digest,* perhaps the chief sounding board of the contemporary movement in black literature, conducted a poll of thirty-eight black writers, old as well as young, in which over half selected Wright as the most important of all Afro-American authors.[39] A year later the magazine devoted an entire issue to Wright, as did two organs of black literary scholarship, *CLA Journal* in June 1969 and *Studies in Black Literature* in the fall of 1970. Thus Eldridge Cleaver was speaking for many, probably most, of his colleagues when he stated: "Of all black American novelists, and indeed of all American novelists of any hue, Richard Wright reigns supreme for his profound political, economic, and social reference."[40]

The final and most important point to be made in a study of the emergence of Richard Wright, however, is not one of fictional technique or literary history. It is rather the point of the relevance of his work to American society, particularly, of course, to that social problem which has been the central "American dilemma" — the role of the black man in the national life. For Wright's chief subject is the racial problem, and his chief importance is as an interpreter of it in imaginative literature, an importance so imposing as to elicit Irving Howe's assertion that after "*Native Son* appeared, American culture was changed forever."[41] This claim may be excessive, but surely no black writer between Frederick Douglass and James Baldwin has

[37] See ibid., and James Baldwin, "Everybody's Protest Novel," *Zero,* no. 1 (Spring 1949), pp. 54-58, reprinted in *Notes of a Native Son,* pp. 13-23.

[38] Richard Gibson, "A No to Nothing," *Kenyon Review,* XIII (Spring 1951), 252-55.

[39] See Fuller, "A Survey: Black Writers' Views on Literary Lions and Values."

[40] *Soul on Ice* (New York, 1968), p. 108. Wright also influenced such African writers as Peter Abrahams and Ezekiel Mphahlele, as well as Frantz Fanon from Martinique.

[41] "Black Boys and Native Sons," p. 354.

offered so moving a testimony or uttered so scathing an indictment of the American racial situation to so large an audience as has Richard Wright. To have done so in spite of such enormous odds as Wright faced during his childhood and youth is not only a literary and social achievement, but also a profound witness to the capacity and endurance of an exceptional human spirit.

# Selected Bibliography

In addition to the sources cited, brief news items concerning Wright's American years may be found in such periodicals as *Baltimore Afro-American, Chicago Defender, Crisis, Daily* and *Sunday Worker, Left Front, Nation, Negro Digest, New Masses, New York Amsterdam News, New York Times, New York World-Telegram, Opportunity, Pittsburgh Courier, Publishers' Weekly, Soviet Russia Today,* and *Time.*

Aaron, Daniel. "Richard Wright and the Communist Party," *New Letters,* XXXVIII (Winter 1971), 170-81.
————. *Writers on the Left: Episodes in American Literary Communism.* New York, 1961.
Abcarian, Richard, ed. *Richard Wright's Native Son: A Critical Handbook.* Belmont, Calif., 1970.
Adams, J. Donald. *The Shape of Books to Come.* New York, 1944.
Advertisement for The Chicken Shack, *Chicago Defender,* 8 January 1938, p. 3.
Alexander, Margaret Walker. "Richard Wright," *New Letters,* XXXVIII (Winter 1971), 182-202.
Algren, Nelson. *Chicago: City on the Make.* Garden City, N.Y., 1951.
————. "Remembering Richard Wright," *Nation,* CXCII (28 January 1961), 85.
Allen, Walter. *Tradition and Dream: The English and American Novel from the Twenties to Our Time.* London, 1964.
*The American Negro Writer and His Roots.* New York, 1960.
"Another Book Soon by Richard Wright," *New York Amsterdam News,* 8 June 1940, p. 17.
"Another Mencken Absurdity," *Memphis Commercial Appeal,* 28 May 1927, p. 6.

Appel, Benjamin. "Personal Impressions," *New Letters,* XXXVIII (Winter 1971), 20-23.

*Arkansas: A Guide to the State.* American Guide Series. New York, 1941. (Compiled by the Arkansas Writers' Project of the Work Projects Administration.)

"Arraign Nixon's Accomplice in 2 Killings in West," *Chicago Sunday Tribune,* 26 June 1938, sec. 1, p. 7.

"At Funeral," *Chicago Daily Tribune,* 1 June 1938, p. 12. (Nixon case.)

" 'Bad Nigger,' " *Time,* XXXV (4 March 1940), 72. (Review of *Native Son.*)

Baker, Houston A., ed. *Black Literature in America.* New York, 1971.

Baldwin, James. "Everybody's Protest Novel," *Zero,* no. 1 (Spring 1949), pp. 54-58.

————. "Many Thousands Gone," *Partisan Review,* XVIII (November-December 1951), 665-80.

————. *Nobody Knows My Name: More Notes of a Native Son.* New York, 1961.

————. *Notes of a Native Son.* Boston, 1955.

————. "Richard Wright," *Encounter,* XVI (April 1961), 58-60.

————. "Richard Wright: A Personal Memoir," *New America,* 1 January 1961, pp. 3, 5.

————. "The Survival of Richard Wright," *Reporter,* XXIV (16 March 1961), 52-55.

Barnes, L. (pseud.). "The Proletarian Novel," *Mainstream,* XVI (July 1963), 51-57.

Bayliss, John F. "*Native Son:* Protest or Psychological Study?" *Negro American Literature Forum,* I (Fall 1967), 5-6.

"Beats Slayer of Wife; Own Life Menaced," *Chicago Daily Tribune,* 8 June 1938, pp. 3, 32. (Nixon case.)

Bennett, Lerone J. *Confrontation: Black and White.* Chicago, 1965.

Bernard, Harry. *Le Roman régionaliste aux États-Unis (1913-1940).* Montreal, 1949.

"Between Ourselves," *New Masses,* XXXVIII (4 March 1941), 2; (11 March 1941), 2.

Bilbo, Theodore G. Remarks on *Black Boy,* in *Congressional Record,* XCI (27 June 1945), 6808.

"Black Boy in Brooklyn," *Ebony,* I (November 1945), 26-27.

Blackmur, R. P. *Language as Gesture.* New York, 1952.

Blake, Nelson Manfred. *Novelists' America: Fiction as History, 1910-1940.* Syracuse, N.Y., 1969.

Bone, Robert A. *The Negro Novel in America.* New Haven, 1958.

————. *Richard Wright.* University of Minnesota Pamphlets on American Writers. Minneapolis, 1969.

Bontemps, Arna. "Famous WPA Authors," *Negro Digest,* VIII (June 1950), 43-47.

"Book Notes," *Daily Worker,* 17 September 1940, p. 7.

Bramwell, Gloria. "Articulated Nightmare," *Midstream,* VII (Spring 1961), 110-12.

"Brick Moron Tells of Killing 2 Women," *Chicago Sunday Tribune,* 29 May 1938, pp. 1, 5. (Nixon case.)

"Brick Slayer's Confession Up at Trial Today," *Chicago Daily Tribune,* 29 July 1938, p. 8. (Nixon case.)

"Brick Slayers Get a Day's Delay as One Seeks Lawyer," *Chicago Daily Tribune,* 14 June 1938, p. 7. (Nixon case.)

"Brick Slayers to Seek Trial outside County," *Chicago Daily Tribune,* 17 June 1938, p. 4. (Nixon case.)

"Brick Slayers' Trial Assigned to Judge Lewe," *Chicago Daily Tribune,* 19 July 1938, p. 6. (Nixon case.)

"Brick Slaying Confession Put before Jurors," *Chicago Daily Tribune,* 2 August 1938, p. 9. (Nixon case.)

Brignano, Russell Carl. "Richard Wright: A Bibliography of Secondary Sources," *Studies in Black Literature,* II (Summer 1971), 19-25.

———. *Richard Wright: An Introduction to the Man and His Works.* Pittsburgh, 1970.

———. "Richard Wright: The Major Themes, Ideas, and Attitudes in His Works." Doctoral diss., University of Wisconsin, 1966.

Britt, David Dobbs. "*Native Son:* Watershed of Negro Protest Literature," *Negro American Literature Forum,* I (Fall 1967), 4-5.

Browder, Earl. "Communism and Literature," *American Writers' Congress,* ed. Henry Hart. New York, 1935.

———. "The Writer and Politics," *The Writer in a Changing World,* ed. Henry Hart. New York, 1937.

Brown, Cecil. "The Lesson and the Legacy: Richard Wright's Complexes and Black Writing Today," *Negro Digest,* XVII (December 1968), 45-50, 78-82.

Brown, Deming. *Soviet Attitudes toward American Writing.* Princeton, N.J., 1962.

Brown, Lloyd W. "Black Entitles: Names as Symbols in Afro-American Literature," *Studies in Black Literature,* I (Spring 1970), 16-44.

———. "Stereotypes in Black and White: The Nature of Perception in Wright's *Native Son,*" *Black Academy Review,* I (Fall 1970), 35-44.

Brown, Sterling A. "From the Inside," *Nation,* CXLVI (16 April 1938), 448. (Review of *Uncle Tom's Children.*)

———. "Insight, Courage, and Craftsmanship," *Opportunity,* XVIII (June 1940), 185-86. (Review of *Native Son.*)

———. "The Literary Scene," *Opportunity,* XVI (April 1938), 120-21. (Review of *Uncle Tom's Children.*)

———. *The Negro in American Fiction.* Washington, 1937.

———, Arthur P. Davis, and Ulysses Lee, eds. *The Negro Caravan.* New York, 1941.

Bryer, Jackson R. "Richard Wright (1908-1960): A Selected Checklist of Criticism," *Wisconsin Studies in Contemporary Literature,* I (Fall 1960), 22-33.

Burgum, Edwin Berry. "The Art of Richard Wright's Short Stories," *Quarterly Review of Literature,* I (Spring 1944), 198-211.

———. *The Novel and the World's Dilemma.* New York, 1947.

———. "The Promise of Democracy and the Fiction of Richard Wright," *Science and Society,* VII (Fall 1943), 338-52.

Burke, Kenneth. *A Grammar of Motives.* New York, 1945.

———. *A Rhetoric of Motives.* New York, 1950.

Butcher, Fanny. "Negro Writes Brilliant Novel, Remarkable Both as Thriller and as Psychological Record," *Chicago Daily Tribune,* 6 March 1940, p. 19. (Review of *Native Son.*)

"Call for an American Writers' Congress," *New Masses,* XIV (22 January 1935), 20.

Calmer, Alan. "Books of the Day," *Daily Worker,* 4 April 1938, p. 7. (Review of *Uncle Tom's Children.*)

Cameron, May. "Prize-Winner Pens Novel," *New York Post,* 1 March 1940, p. 19. (Review of *Native Son.*)

Canby, Henry Seidel. "*Native Son* by Richard Wright," *Book-of-the-Month Club News,* February 1940, pp. 2-3.

———. "The Right Questions," *Saturday Review of Literature,* XXI (23 March 1940), 8. (Editorial on *Native Son* and *The Grapes of Wrath.*)

Carter, Elmer. "Richard Wright," *Opportunity,* XVIII (April 1940), 99.

Cash, W. J. *The Mind of the South.* Vintage ed. New York, 1960.

Cayton, Horace R. "The Communists: War Relationship with Negroes Is Not Creditable," *Pittsburgh Courier,* 26 August 1944, p. 7. (Richard Wright is the actual author of this essay.)

———. "The Curtain: A Memoir," *Negro Digest,* XVIII (December 1968), 11-15.

———. *Long Old Road.* New York, 1965.

———. "A Psychological Approach to Race Relations," *Présence Africaine,* no. 3 (March-April 1948), pp. 418-31; no. 4 (n.d.), pp. 549-63.

———, Herbert Hill, Arna Bontemps, and Saunders Redding. "Reflections on Richard Wright: A Symposium on an Exiled Native Son," *Anger, and Beyond: The Negro Writer in the United States,* ed. Herbert Hill. New York, 1966.

Chandler, G. Lewis. "Coming of Age: A Note on American Negro Novelists," *Phylon,* IX (First Quarter 1948), 25-29.

"Charge and Deny 3d Degree Used on Brick Slayer," *Chicago Daily Tribune,* 30 July 1938, p. 10. (Nixon case.)

Charney, Maurice. "James Baldwin's Quarrel with Richard Wright," *American Quarterly,* XV (Spring 1963), 65-75.

"Citizens Ask Horner's Aid in Nixon Case," *Chicago Defender,* 5 November 1938, p. 5.

Clarke, John Henrik, ed. *American Negro Short Stories*. New York, 1966.

Clay, E[ugene]. "The Negro in Recent American Literature," *American Writers' Congress*, ed. Henry Hart. New York, 1935. (See also the revised and expanded version: "The Negro and American Literature," *International Literature*, no. 6 [June 1935], pp. 77-89.)

———. "The Negro Writer and the Congress," *New Masses*, XIV (19 March 1935), 22.

Cleaver, Eldridge. *Soul on Ice*. New York, 1968.

Cohn, David L. "The Negro Novel: Richard Wright," *Atlantic Monthly*, CLXV (May 1940), 659-61. (Review of *Native Son*.)

"Confessed Brick Murderers Deny Crimes in Court," *Chicago Daily Tribune*, 15 June 1938, p. 12. (Nixon case.)

Conroy, Jack. "An Anthology of W.P.A. Writing," *New Masses*, XXIV (14 September 1937), 24-25.

———. "Personal Impressions," *New Letters*, XXXVIII (Winter 1971), 33-36.

C[ooke], M[arvel] J. "Dick Wright's 'Native Son' Praised Highly," *New York Amsterdam News*, 2 March 1940, p. 3.

———. "Prize Novellas, Brave Stories," *New York Amsterdam News*, 9 April 1938, p. 16. (Review of *Uncle Tom's Children*.)

Cowley, Malcolm. "The Case of Bigger Thomas," *New Republic*, CII (18 March 1940), 382-83.

———. "Long Black Song," *New Republic*, XCIV (6 April 1938), 280. (Review of *Uncle Tom's Children*.)

Creekmore, Hubert. "Social Factors in *Native Son*," *University of Kansas City Review*, VIII (Winter 1941), 136-43.

"Criminal or Victim?" *Times Literary Supplement*, 27 April 1940, p. 205. (Review of *Native Son*.)

"Crowd Hears Noted Author," *New York Amsterdam News*, 16 March 1940, p. 3.

Cruse, Harold. *The Crisis of the Negro Intellectual*. New York, 1967.

Daiches, David. "The American Scene," *Partisan Review*, VII (May-June 1940), 244-47. (Review of *Native Son*.)

"Dance Profits to Aid Nixon, Hicks," *Chicago Defender*, 20 August 1938, p. 5.

Daniels, Jonathan. "Man against the World," *Saturday Review of Literature*, XXI (2 March 1940), 5. (Review of *Native Son*.)

Davis, Benjamin J., Jr. "New Times: A Few Words on Richard Wright and 'New Ideas,'" *Worker*, 6 August 1944, p. 9.

———. "New Times: What Makes Mr. Cayton Tick," *Worker*, 3 September 1944, p. 11.

———. "Richard Wright's 'Native Son' a Notable Achievement," *Sunday Worker*, 14 April 1940, sec. 2, pp. 4, 6.

Davis, David Brion. "Violence in American Literature," *Annals of the Ameri-*

*can Academy of Political and Social Science,* CCCLXIV (March 1966), 28-36.

"Decision in Nixon Case Due April 12," *Chicago Defender,* 8 April 1939, p. 1.

Dickstein, Morris. "The Black Aesthetic in White America," *Partisan Review,* XXXVIII (Winter 1971-72), 376-95.

————. "Wright, Baldwin, Cleaver," *New Letters,* XXXVIII (Winter 1971), 117-24.

Donlan, Dan M. "The White Trap: A Motif," *English Journal,* LIX (October 1970), 943-44. (In *Native Son.*)

"Doomed Killer Nixon Will Be Put on Trial for Another Murder," *Chicago Daily Tribune,* 6 August 1938, p. 5.

Drake, St. Clair, and Horace R. Cayton. *Black Metropolis: A Study of Negro Life in a Northern City.* Rev. and enl. ed. 2 vols. New York, 1962.

Dugan, James. "New Negro Quarterly," *Daily Worker,* 25 October 1937, p. 7.

D[umay], R[aymond]. "WRIGHT (Richard): UN ENFANT DU PAYS traduit par Hélène Bokanovski [*sic*] et Marcel Duhamel," *La Gazette des Lettres,* III (23 August 1947), 10.

Ellison, Ralph. "The Art of Fiction VIII," *Paris Review,* III (Spring 1955), 55-71. (Interview of Ellison by Alfred Chester and Vilma Howard.)

————. "Hidden Name and Complex Fate: A Writer's Experience in the United States," *Shadow and Act.* New York, 1964.

————. "Recent Negro Fiction," *New Masses,* XL (5 August 1941), 22-26.

————. "A Rejoinder," *New Leader,* XLVII (3 February 1964), 15-22.

————. "Richard Wright's Blues," *Antioch Review,* V (June 1945), 198-211. (Essay-review of *Black Boy.*)

————. *Shadow and Act.* New York, 1964.

————. "That Same Pain, That Same Pleasure: An Interview," *Shadow and Act.* New York, 1964. (Interview of Ellison by Richard G. Stern.)

————. "'A Very Stern Discipline': An Interview with Ralph Ellison," *Harper's Magazine,* CCXXXIV (March 1967), 76-80, 83-86, 88, 90, 93-95. (Interview of Ellison by James Thompson, Lennox Raphael, and Steve Cannon.)

————. "The World and the Jug," *New Leader,* XLVI (9 December 1963), 22-26.

Emanuel, James A. "Fever and Feeling: Notes on the Imagery in *Native Son,*" *Negro Digest,* XVIII (December 1968), 16-24.

Embree, Edwin R. *13 against the Odds.* New York, 1944.

"Expect Brickbat Murder Case to Go to Jury Today," *Chicago Daily Tribune,* 4 August 1938, p. 7. (Nixon case.)

Fabre, Michel. "Black Cat and White Cat: Richard Wright's Debt to Edgar Allan Poe," *Poe Studies,* IV (June 1971), 17-19.

————, and Edward Margolies. "A Bibliography of Richard Wright's Works," *New Letters,* XXXVIII (Winter 1971), 155-69.

Fadiman, Clifton. "A Black 'American Tragedy,'" *New Yorker,* XVI (2 March 1940), 52-53. (Review of *Native Son.*)

Farnsworth, Robert M. "Introduction," *New Letters,* XXXVIII (Winter 1971), 5-7.

Farrell, James T. "Lynch Patterns," *Partisan Review,* IV (May 1938), 57-58. (Review of *Uncle Tom's Children.*)

"Fasten Double Murder in West on Brick Killer," *Chicago Daily Tribune,* 31 May 1938, p. 3. (Nixon case.)

Faulkner, William. "Letter to Richard Wright," *New Letters,* XXXVIII (Winter 1971), 128.

Fenwick, James M. "The Voice of Richard Wright," *New International,* VII (November 1941), 287-88.

Fiedler, Leslie A. *Waiting for the End.* New York, 1964.

Finkelstein, S[idney]. "The Novel as Battleground," *New Masses,* LXIV (26 August 1947), 18-22.

"First Prize Winner," *Story,* XII (March 1938), 1.

Fisher, Dorothy Canfield. Introduction to Richard Wright, *Native Son.* New York, 1940.

Flanagan, Hallie. *Arena.* New York, 1940.

Fontaine, William T. *Reflections on Segregation, Desegregation, Power and Morals.* Springfield, Ill., 1967.

———. "Toward a Philosophy of the American Negro Literature," *Présence Africaine,* n.s., nos. 24-25 (February-May 1959), pp. 165-76.

Ford, James W. "The Case of Richard Wright: A Disservice to the Negro People," *Daily Worker,* 5 September 1944, p. 6.

———. Foreword to Richard Wright, *Bright and Morning Star.* New York, 1941.

Ford, Nick Aaron. "The Fire Next Time? A Critical Survey of Belles Lettres by and about Negroes Published in 1963," *Phylon,* XXV (Second Quarter 1964), 123-34.

———. "*Lawd Today.* By Richard Wright," *CLA Journal,* VII (March 1964), 269-70.

———. "The Negro Novel as a Vehicle of Propaganda," *Quarterly Review of Higher Education among Negroes,* IX (July 1941), 135-39.

———. "The Ordeal of Richard Wright," *College English,* XV (November 1953), 87-94.

———. "Richard Wright, a Profile," *Chicago Jewish Forum,* XXI (Fall 1962), 26-30.

Foreman, Paul Breck. *Mississippi Population Trends.* Nashville, 1939.

"14 Years for Earl Hicks in Brick-Murder," *Chicago Defender,* 4 February 1939, pp. 1-2. (Nixon case.)

Franklin, John Hope. *From Slavery to Freedom: A History of Negro Americans.* 3rd ed. New York, 1967.

Frazier, E. Franklin. *The Negro in the United States.* New York, 1949.

French, Warren. "The Lost Potential of Richard Wright," *The Black American Writer,* ed. C. W. E. Bigsby. Deland, Fla., 1969.

———. *The Social Novel at the End of an Era.* Carbondale, Ill., 1966.

Freud, Sigmund. *The Basic Writings of Sigmund Freud,* trans. and ed. A. A. Brill. New York, 1938.

Fuller, Hoyt W. "On the Death of Richard Wright," *Southwest Review,* XLVI (Autumn 1961), vi-vii, 334-37.

———. "A Survey: Black Writers' Views on Literary Lions and Values," *Negro Digest,* XVII (January 1968), 10-48, 81-89.

Fullinwider, S. P. *The Mind and Mood of Black America: 20th Century Thought.* Homewood, Ill., 1969.

Gannett, Lewis. "Books and Things," *New York Herald Tribune,* 25 March 1938, p. 17 (review of *Uncle Tom's Children*); 1 March 1940, p. 17 (review of *Native Son*).

———. "*Lawd Today.* By Richard Wright," *New York Herald Tribune Books,* 5 May 1963, p. 10.

———. "Uncle Tom's Children by Richard Wright," *Book Union Bulletin,* April 1938.

Gautier, Madeleine. "Un Romancier de la race noire: Richard Wright," *Présence Africaine,* no. 1 (October-November 1947), pp. 163-65.

Gayle, Addison, Jr. "Richard Wright: Beyond Nihilism," *Negro Digest,* XVIII (December 1968), 4-10.

Gérard, Albert. "Humanism and Negritude: Notes on the Contemporary Afro-American Novel," *Diogenes,* no. 37 (Spring 1962), pp. 115-33.

———. *Les Tambours du neant: Le problème existentiel dans le roman américaine.* Brussels, 1969.

———. "Vie et vocation de Richard Wright," *Revue Générale Belge,* XCVII (January 1961), 65-78.

Gibson, Donald B. "Richard Wright: A Bibliographical Essay," *CLA Journal,* XII (June 1969), 360-65.

———. "Richard Wright and the Tyranny of Convention," *CLA Journal,* XII (June 1969), 334-57.

———. "Wright's Invisible Native Son," *American Quarterly,* XXI (1969), 728-38.

Gibson, Richard. "A No to Nothing," *Kenyon Review,* XIII (Spring 1951), 252-55.

Giles, Louise. "Wright, Richard. Lawd Today," *Library Journal,* LXXXVIII (1 April 1963), 1549.

Glicksberg, Charles I. "The Furies in Negro Fiction," *Western Review,* XIII (Winter 1949), 107-14.

———. "Negro Fiction in America," *South Atlantic Quarterly,* XLV (October 1946), 477-88.

———. "Race and Revolution in Negro Literature," *Forum,* CVIII (November 1947), 300-308.

Gloster, Hugh M. *Negro Voices in American Fiction.* Chapel Hill, N.C., 1948.
————. "Richard Wright: Interpreter of Racial and Economic Maladjustments," *Opportunity,* XIX (December 1941), 361-65, 383.
Gold, Mike. "Change the World," *Daily Worker,* 17 April 1940, p. 7; 29 April 1940, p. 7.
————. "Change the World," *Sunday Worker,* 31 March 1940, sec. 2, p. 7 (review of *Native Son*); 29 September 1940, sec. 2, p. 5.
————. *The Hollow Men.* New York, 1941.
"Grand Jury Acts to Speed Trial of Rapist Nixon," *Chicago Daily Tribune,* 9 June 1938, p. 7.
Green, A. Wigfall. *The Man Bilbo.* Baton Rouge, 1963.
Grennard, Elliott. "New Blues," *New Masses,* XLII (20 January 1942), 30-31. (Review of the Paul Robeson recording of Wright's "King Joe.")
Gross, Theodore L. *The Heroic Ideal in American Literature.* New York, 1971.
Grumbach, Doris. "Fiction Shelf," *Critic,* XXI (June-July 1963), 81-82. (Review of *Lawd Today.*)
Guerin, Daniel. *Negroes on the March: A Frenchman's Report on the American Negro Struggle,* trans. and ed. Duncan Ferguson. New York, 1956.
"Guggenheim Award to WPA Worker for His Brilliant Creative Writings," *Chicago Defender,* 8 April 1939, p. 4.
"Guggenheim Fund Names 69 Fellows," *New York Times,* 27 March 1939, p. 21.
"Guilty of Brick Murder; Gets Death in Chair," *Chicago Daily Tribune,* 5 August 1938, p. 2. (Nixon case.)
Guzman, Jessie Parkhurst, ed. *Negro Year Book.* Tuskegee, 1947.
Halper, Albert. *Good-bye, Union Square.* Chicago, 1970.
————, ed. *This Is Chicago.* New York, 1952.
Hand, Clifford. "The Struggle to Create Life in the Fiction of Richard Wright," *The Thirties: Fiction, Poetry, Drama,* ed. Warren French. Deland, Fla., 1967.
Hansen, Harry. "The First Reader," *New York World-Telegram,* 26 March 1938, p. 23; 9 September 1940, p. 17.
————, ed. *O. Henry Memorial Award Prize Stories of 1938.* New York, 1938.
Harper, Lucius C. "Dustin' Off the News: We Dwell amid Acres of Diamonds but Know It Not," *Chicago Defender,* 9 March 1940, pp. 1-2.
Harrington, Ollie. "The Last Days of Richard Wright," *Ebony,* XVI (February 1961), 83-86, 88, 90, 92-94.
Hart, Henry, ed. *American Writers' Congress.* New York, 1935.
————. *The Writer in a Changing World.* New York, 1937.
Herndon, Angelo. "Negroes Have No Stake in This War, Wright Says," *Sunday Worker,* 11 February 1940, sec. 1, p. 7.
Hicks, Granville. "Dreiser to Farrell to Wright," *Saturday Review,* XLVI (30 March 1963), 37-38. (Review of *Lawd Today.*)

————. *Part of the Truth*. New York, 1965.

————. "Richard Wright's Prize Novellas," *New Masses,* XXVII (29 March 1938), 23-24. (Review of *Uncle Tom's Children.*)

"Hicks Braced by a Letter from Mother," *Chicago Defender,* 10 September 1938, p. 6. (Nixon case.)

Hill, Herbert, ed. *Anger, and Beyond: The Negro Writer in the United States.* New York, 1966.

Hoffman, Frederick J. *The Modern Novel in America.* Chicago, 1956.

Holt, Arthur E. "The Wrath of the Native Son," *Christian Century,* LVII (1 May 1940), 570-72.

"Honored," *New York Amsterdam News,* 30 July 1938, sec. 2, p. 3.

Howe, Irving. "Black Boys and Native Sons," *Dissent,* X (Autumn 1963), 353-68.

————. "A Reply to Ralph Ellison," *New Leader,* XLVII (3 February 1964), 12-14.

————. "Richard Wright: A Word of Farewell," *New Republic,* CXLIV (13 February 1961), 17-18.

Hughes, Carl Milton. *The Negro Novelist: A Discussion of the Writings of American Negro Novelists, 1940-1950.* New York, 1953.

Hughes, Langston. "The Twenties: Harlem and Its Negritude," *African Forum,* I (Spring 1966), 11-20.

"Hunt Sex Moron for Assault on Woman in Park," *Chicago Daily Tribune,* 2 June 1938, p. 15. (Nixon case.)

Hurston, Zora Neale. "Stories of Conflict," *Saturday Review of Literature,* XVII (2 April 1938), 32. (Review of *Uncle Tom's Children.*)

Hyman, Stanley Edgar. "Richard Wright Reappraised," *Atlantic,* CCXXV (March 1970), 127-32.

"Indictment on New Murder Charge Nixon's Only Hope," *Chicago Defender,* 8 October 1938, p. 4.

"In the Name of Justice . . . ," *New Masses,* XLI (4 November 1941), 22.

"In the News Columns — Richard Wright," *Opportunity,* XVI (March 1938), 70.

Ivy, James W. " 'Whipped Before You Born,' " *Crisis,* XLVII (April 1940), 122. (Review of *Native Son.*)

Jack, Peter Monro. "A Tragic Novel of Negro Life in America," *New York Times Book Review,* 3 March 1940, pp. 2, 20. (Review of *Native Son.*)

Jackson, Blyden. "Richard Wright: Black Boy from America's Black Belt and Urban Ghettos," *CLA Journal,* XII (June 1969), 287-309.

————. "Richard Wright in a Moment of Truth," *Southern Literary Journal,* III (Spring 1971), 3-17.

Jackson, Esther Merle. "The American Negro and the Image of the Absurd," *Phylon,* XXIII (Fourth Quarter 1962), 359-71.

James, Charles L. "Bigger Thomas in the Seventies: A Twentieth-Century Search for Significance," *English Record,* XXII (Fall 1971), 6-14.

————, ed. *From the Roots: Short Stories by Black Americans.* New York, 1970. (See also *Notes for Teaching From the Roots: Short Stories by Black Americans.* New York, 1970.)

Jeffers, Lance. "Afro-American Literature, the Conscience of Man," *Black Scholar,* II (January 1971), 47-53.

Jenkins, Joseph H., Jr. " 'Saucy Doubts and Fears,' " *Phylon,* I (Second Quarter 1940), 195-97. (Review of *Native Son.*)

Jerome, J. D. "*Native Son.* By Richard Wright," *Journal of Negro History,* XXV (April 1940), 251-52.

Johnson, J. R. "Native Son and Revolution," *New International,* VI (May 1940), 92-93.

Johnson, Oakley. "The John Reed Club Convention," *New Masses,* VIII (July 1932), 14-15.

Jones, Howard Mumford. "Uneven Effect," *Boston Evening Transcript,* 2 March 1940, sec. 5, p. 1. (Review of *Native Son.*)

Kaempffert, Waldemar. "Science in Review: An Author's Mind Plumbed for the Unconscious Factor in the Creation of a Novel," *New York Times,* 24 September 1944, sec. 4, p. 11.

Kazin, Alfred. *On Native Grounds: An Interpretation of Modern American Prose Literature.* New York, 1942.

————, Nat Hentoff, James Baldwin, Lorraine Hansberry, Emile Capouya, and Langston Hughes. "The Negro in American Culture," *Cross Currents,* XI (Summer 1961), 205-24.

Kearns, Edward. "The 'Fate' Section of *Native Son,*" *Contemporary Literature,* XII (Spring 1971), 146-55.

Kent, George E. "On the Future Study of Richard Wright," *CLA Journal,* XII (June 1969), 366-70.

————. "Richard Wright: Blackness and the Adventure of Western Culture," *CLA Journal,* XII (June 1969), 322-43.

Key, V. O., Jr. *Southern Politics in State and Nation.* New York, 1949.

Kinnamon, Keneth. "*The Example of Richard Wright,* by Dan McCall," *Journal of English and Germanic Philology,* LXX (January 1971), 180-86; (October 1971), 753-54.

————. "*Lawd Today:* Richard Wright's Apprentice Novel," *Studies in Black Literature,* II (Summer 1971), 16-18.

————. "*Native Son:* The Personal, Social, and Political Background," *Phylon,* XXX (Spring 1969), 66-72.

————. "The Pastoral Impulse in Richard Wright," *Midcontinent American Studies Journal,* X (Spring 1969), 41-47.

————. "*Richard Wright: A Biography.* By Constance Webb," *American Literature,* XL (January 1969), 575-76.

————. "Richard Wright Items in the Fales Collection," *Bulletin of the Society for the Libraries of New York University,* no. 66 (Winter 1965).

————. "Richard Wright: Proletarian Poet," *Concerning Poetry,* II (Spring 1969), 39-50.

————. "Richard Wright's Use of *Othello* in *Native Son*," *CLA Journal*, XII (June 1969), 358-59.

Kirnon, Hodge. "Guest Editorial: Why No Criticism of 'Native Son'?" *New York Amsterdam News*, 11 May 1940, p. 16.

Kirwan, Albert D. *Revolt of the Rednecks, Mississippi Politics: 1876-1925.* Lexington, Ky., 1951.

Kostelanetz, Richard. "The Politics of Unresolved Quests in the Novels of Richard Wright," *Xavier University Studies*, VIII (Spring 1969), 31-64.

Ladner, Heber. "James Kimble Vardaman, Governor of Mississippi, 1904-1908," *Journal of Mississippi History*, II (October 1940), 175-205.

Las Vergnas, Raymond. "Richard Wright," *La Revue de Paris*, LXV (August 1958), 124-31.

Leavelle, Charles. "Brick Slayer Is Likened to Jungle Beast," *Chicago Sunday Tribune*, 5 June 1938, sec. 1, p. 6. (Nixon case.)

LeClair, Thomas. "The Blind Leading the Blind: Wright's *Native Son* and a Brief Reference to Ellison's *Invisible Man*," *CLA Journal*, XIII (1970), 315-20.

Lee, Carleton L. "Religious Roots of the Negro Protest," *Assuring Freedom to the Free*, ed. Arnold M. Rose. Detroit, 1964.

Lehmann, Rosamond. "New Novels," *Spectator*, CLXIV (19 April 1940), 574. (Review of *Native Son*.)

Lennon, Peter. "One of Uncle Tom's Children," *Manchester Guardian*, 8 December 1960, p. 8.

" 'Let's Free Browder Now,' " *New Masses*, XL (16 September 1941), 20.

Lévi-Strauss, Claude. "Letter to Richard Wright," *New Letters*, XXXVIII (Winter 1971), 130.

Lewis, Theophilus. "*Native Son*," *Interracial Review*, XIII (April 1940), 64-65.

————. "The Saga of Bigger Thomas," *Catholic World*, CLIII (May 1941), 201-6.

Littell, Robert. "Outstanding Novels," *Yale Review*, XXIX (Summer 1940), vi, viii, x, xii. (Review of *Native Son*.)

Littlejohn, David. *Black on White: A Critical Survey of Writing by American Negroes.* New York, 1966.

Locke, Alain. "Dry Fields and Green Pastures," *Opportunity*, XVIII (January 1940), 4-10, 28.

————. "God Save Reality! Retrospective Review of the Literature of the Negro: 1936," *Opportunity*, XV (January 1937), 8-13; (February 1937), 40-44.

————. "Jingo, Counter-Jingo and Us — Retrospective Review of the Literature of the Negro: 1937," *Opportunity*, XVI (January 1938), 7-11, 27; (February 1938), 39-42.

————. "The Negro: 'New' or Newer — A Retrospective Review of the Literature of the Negro for 1938," *Opportunity*, XVII (January 1939), 4-10; (February 1939), 36-42.

————. "Of Native Sons: Real and Otherwise," *Opportunity*, XIX (January 1941), 4-9; (February 1941), 48-52.

Lyons, Eugene. *The Red Decade*. Indianapolis, 1941.

McCall, Dan. *The Example of Richard Wright*. New York, 1969.

McCarthy, Harold T. "Richard Wright: The Expatriate as Native Son," *American Literature*, XLIV (March 1972), 97-117.

McIlwaine, Shields. *Memphis Down in Dixie*. New York, 1948.

McSorley, Joseph. *"Native Son*. By Richard Wright," *Catholic World*, CLI (May 1940), 243-44.

Margolies, Edward. *The Art of Richard Wright*. Carbondale, Ill., 1969.

————. "A Critical Analysis of the Works of Richard Wright." Doctoral diss., New York University, 1964.

————. *Native Sons: A Critical Study of Twentieth-Century Negro American Authors*. Philadelphia, 1968.

Marriott, Charles. "New Novels," *Manchester Guardian*, 16 April 1940, p. 3. (Review of *Native Son*.)

Marsh, Fred T. "Hope, Despair and Terror," *New York Herald Tribune Books*, 8 May 1938, p. 3. (Review of *Uncle Tom's Children*.)

Marshall, Margaret. "Black Native Son," *Nation*, CL (16 March 1940), 367-68.

Martin, Kenneth K. "Richard Wright and the Negro Revolt," *Negro Digest*, XIV (April 1965), 39-48.

"Martyr or Traitor?" *Times Literary Supplement*, 29 April 1965, p. 324. (Review of *Lawd Today*.)

Mason, Clifford. "Native Son Strikes Home," *Life*, LXVIII (8 May 1970), 18.

M[axwell], A[llen]. "Troubles of Negro in America Probed in Courageous Novel," *Dallas Morning News*, 3 March 1940, sec. 3, p. 14. (Review of *Native Son*.)

————. "*Uncle Tom's Children* by Richard Wright," *Southwest Review*, XXIII (April 1938), 362-65.

Mendelson, M. *Soviet Interpretations of Contemporary American Literature*, trans. Deming B. Brown and Rufus W. Mathewson. Washington, 1948.

"Midwest Club News," *Left Front*, I (May-June 1934), 21.

"The Midwest John Reed Conference," *Left Front*, I (September-October 1933), 11.

Miller, William D. *Memphis during the Progressive Era, 1900-1917*. Memphis and Madison, Wis., 1957.

Minor, Marcia. "An Author Discusses His Craft," *Daily Worker*, 13 December 1938, p. 7.

Minor, Robert. "To Tell the Truth: Mr. Wright Didn't Discover It," *Daily Worker*, 15 August 1944, p. 6.

Mitra, B. K. "The Wright-Baldwin Controversy," *Indian Journal of American Studies*, I (July 1969), 101-5.

Mizener, Arthur. *A Handbook of Analyses, Questions, and a Discussion of Technique for Use with Modern Short Stories: The Uses of Imagination.* 3rd ed. New York, 1971.

Moon, Henry Lee. "New Song of America," *New Challenge,* II (Fall 1937), 88-89.

M[orrow], E. F[rederic]. "*Uncle Tom's Children* by Richard Wright," *Crisis,* XLV (May 1938), 155.

Mullaney, Bernard J. "Approving Mr. Rascoe," *American Mercury,* L (July 1940), 377. (See Burton Rascoe, "Negro Novel and White Reviewers.")

Myrdal, Gunnar. *An American Dilemma: The Negro Problem and Modern Democracy.* New York, 1944.

Nagel, James. "Images of 'Vision' in *Native Son,*" *University Review,* XXXVI (December 1969), 109-15.

"*Native Son, a Novel.* By Richard Wright," *Christian Century,* LVII (24 April 1940), 546.

" 'Native Son' Author to Relate Birth of 'Bigger,' " *Chicago Defender,* 6 July 1940, p. 6.

"Native Sons," *Time,* LXXXI (5 April 1963), 106.

" 'Native Son' Sales Near Quarter Million within Two Weeks!" *New York Times Book Review,* 24 March 1940, p. 15. (Contains excerpts from reviews.)

" 'Native Son' Wins Award for Novel," *New York Times,* 8 June 1941, sec. 1, p. 46.

"Negro Author Criticizes Reds as Intolerant," *New York Herald Tribune,* 28 July 1944, p. 11.

"Negro Hailed as New Writer," *New York Sun,* 4 March 1940, p. 3.

"Negro Leaders Protest Attacks against Communist Candidates," *Daily Worker,* 16 September 1940, p. 1.

"A Negro's Tragedy in Eloquent Tale," *Springfield* (Mass.) *Republican,* 10 March 1940, sec. E, p. 7. (Review of *Native Son.*)

"Negro Writer Wins Story Contest," *New York Times,* 15 February 1938, p. 14.

Nelson, John Herbert, and Oscar Cargill, eds. *Contemporary Trends: American Literature since 1900.* New York, 1949.

"Nixon Arraigned for 1936 Slaying," *Chicago Defender,* 17 September 1938, p. 5.

"Nixon Carefree, Price Solemn Awaiting Death," *Chicago Defender,* 1 April 1939, p. 1.

"Nixon Dies in Chair," *Chicago Defender,* 17 June 1939, pp. 1-2.

"Nixon-Hicks Hearing Set for Monday," *Chicago Defender,* 23 July 1938, p. 7.

"Nixon on Trial Next Month for Unsolved Castle Murder," *Chicago Defender,* 13 August 1938, p. 1.

"Nixon Plea to Be Given to Governor," *Chicago Defender,* 15 October 1938, p. 6.

"Nixon's Death Date Extended to December 1," *Chicago Defender,* 19 November 1938, p. 4.

"Nixon to Die Oct. 21," *Chicago Defender,* 20 August 1938, p. 1.

"Nixon Wins Death Stay until Nov. 9," *Chicago Defender,* 29 October 1938, pp.1-2.

"Nixon Wins Delay of Execution," *Chicago Defender,* 22 October 1938, p. 2.

"Nixon Wins 4th Stay, Fate Rests with Supreme Court," *Chicago Defender,* 3 December 1938, p. 1.

"Nixon Wins Third Stay from Death," *Chicago Defender,* 12 November 1938, p. 8.

Norman, Dorothy. "A World to Live In — Operation: Richard Wright," *New York Post,* 17 June 1946, p. 34.

O'Brien, Edward J., ed. *50 Best American Short Stories.* Boston, 1939.

"Officers of the American Peace Mobilization," *Daily Worker,* 3 September 1940, p. 4.

Oliver, Clinton Forrest, Jr. "The Name and Nature of American Negro Literature: An Interpretative Study in Genre and Ideas." Doctoral thesis, Harvard University, 1965.

Orro, David H. "Nixon Denies Guilt; Re-imprison McCall," *Chicago Defender,* 11 June 1938, p. 1.

———. "Nixon Goes on Trial," *Chicago Defender,* 30 July 1938, pp. 1-2.

———. "Nixon Is Found Guilty," *Chicago Defender,* 6 August 1938, pp. 1-2.

———. " 'Police Beat Us' Say Hicks, Nixon," *Chicago Defender,* 18 June 1938, pp. 1-2.

———. " 'Somebody Did It,' So 2 Youths Who 'Might Have Done It' Are Arrested," *Chicago Defender,* 28 May 1938, p. 24. (Nixon case.)

Ottley, Roi. *'New World A-Coming.'* Boston, 1943.

———. *No Green Pastures.* New York, 1951.

Owens, William A. Introduction to Richard Wright, *Native Son.* New York, 1957.

"Parole Board O.K.'s Reprieve for Nixon," *Chicago Defender,* 10 December 1938, p. 1.

"Pass Courtney Moron Bill in Heated Debate," *Chicago Daily Tribune,* 8 June 1938, p. 1. (Nixon case.)

Patterson, Ray. "From Our Past: Roi Ottley — *Black Odysseus;* Richard Wright — *Native Son,*" *New York Citizen-Call,* 10 November 1960, p. 14.

Pettigrew, Thomas F. *A Profile of the Negro American.* Princeton, N.J., 1964.

"Pick Four Jurors to Try Brick Slayer of Woman," *Chicago Daily Tribune,* 27 July 1938, p. 9. (Nixon case.)

"Playing into the Hands of Slander," *Memphis Commercial Appeal,* 31 July 1927, sec. 1, p. 6.

"Pleads Guilty in Brick Killing to Escape Chair," *Chicago Daily Tribune,* 26 July 1938, p. 12. (Nixon case.)

Plessner, Monika. "Richard Wright, Vorkämpfer der Zweiten Amerikanischen Revolution," *Frankfurter Hefte,* XX (December 1965), 840-52.

Poore, Charles. "Books of the Times," *New York Times,* 2 April 1938, p. 13; 1 March 1940, p. 19.

Powell, Adam Clayton, Jr. "Soap Box," *New York Amsterdam News,* 16 March 1940, p. 13.

"Price Given Stay: Nixon Awaits Fate," *Chicago Defender,* 15 April 1939, p. 1.

Prisco, Michele. "I figli dello zio Tom hanno fatto la guerra," *La fiera letteraria,* 15 January 1950, p. 4.

"Prize-Winning Book by WPA Writer Published," *Crisis,* XLV (April 1938), 123.

"Prominent Negroes Urge Ballot Rights for Communists," *Daily Worker,* 23 September 1940, p. 4.

"Pulitzer Awards," *New Masses,* XXXV (14 May 1940), 26.

"The Pulitzer Prizes," *New Masses,* XXXIX (13 May 1941), 21.

"Push Fight to Save Nixon," *Chicago Defender,* 22 April 1939, p. 1.

Putnam, Samuel. "Literary Lookout," *Daily Worker,* 22 August 1944, p. 11.

R., B. P. "Regarding Richard Wright," *Daily Worker,* 18 August 1944, p. 7.

Radine, Serge. "Ecrivains américains non conformistes," *Suisse Contemporaine,* IX (June 1949), 287-95.

"Rapist Indicted for Slaying of Three Women," *Chicago Daily Tribune,* 11 June 1938, p. 2. (Nixon case.)

"Rapist Slayer Acts Out 2 More Savage Attacks," *Chicago Daily Tribune,* 4 June 1938, p. 6. (Nixon case.)

"Rapist Slayer Identified at Murder Trial," *Chicago Daily Tribune,* 28 July 1938, p. 3. (Nixon case.)

"Rapist Slayer of Three Women to Be Arraigned," *Chicago Sunday Tribune,* 12 June 1938, sec. 1, p. 6. (Nixon case.)

Rascoe, Burton. "Negro Novel and White Reviewers," *American Mercury,* L (May 1940), 113-16.

"Readers Discuss 'Native Son,'" *Daily Worker,* 26 April 1940, p. 7.

Record, Wilson. *The Negro and the Communist Party.* Chapel Hill, N.C., 1951.

Redding, Saunders. "The Alien Land of Richard Wright," *Soon, One Morning: New Writing by American Negroes, 1940-1962,* ed. Herbert Hill. New York, 1963.

———. "Richard Wright: An Evaluation," *AMSAC Newsletter,* III (30 December 1960), 3-6.

Reed, Kenneth T. *"Native Son:* An American *Crime and Punishment,"* *Studies in Black Literature,* I (Summer 1970), 33-34.

Reilly, John Marsden. Afterword to Richard Wright, *Native Son.* New York, 1966.

———. *"Lawd Today:* Richard Wright's Experiment in Naturalism," *Studies in Black Literature,* II (Autumn 1971), 14-17.

———. "Richard Wright: An Essay in Bibliography," *Resources for American Literary Study,* I (Autumn 1971), 131-80.

————. "Richard Wright's Apprenticeship," *Journal of Black Studies,* II (June 1972), 439-60.

————. "Self-Portraits by Richard Wright," *Colorado Quarterly,* XX (Summer 1971), 31-45.

"Reopen Hotel Rape Case as Killer Recants," *Chicago Daily Tribune,* 10 June 1938, p. 5. (Nixon case.)

"Rev. Austin Preaches on Wright's 'Native Son,'" *Chicago Defender,* 15 June 1940, p. 9.

Rexroth, Kenneth. *Assays.* Norfolk, Conn., 1961.

"Richard Wright Given Literary Post for Work," *New York Amsterdam News,* 25 June 1938, p. 6.

"Richard Wright's Native Son," *Chicago Defender,* 16 March 1940, p. 14.

"Richard Wright Sponsors Youth Photo Contest," *Daily Worker,* 24 August 1940, p. 7.

Rickels, Milton and Patricia. *Richard Wright.* Austin, Tex., 1970.

Riddell, Hugh J. "New Negro Playwrights Group Formed in Harlem," *Daily Worker,* 27 July 1940, p. 7.

Rideout, Walter B. *The Radical Novel in the United States, 1900-1954.* Cambridge, Mass., 1956.

Riesman, David. "Marginality, Conformity, and Insight," *Phylon,* XIV (Third Quarter 1953), 241-57.

"Robert Nixon Attacked by Irate Hubby," *Chicago Defender,* 11 June 1938, p. 6.

Robeson, Paul. "Préface," *L'Arbalète,* IX (Autumn 1944), 237-38.

Rogge, Heinz. "Die amerikanische Negerfrage im Lichte der Literatur von Richard Wright und Ralph Ellison," *Die neuren Sprachen,* no. 2 (1958), pp. 56-69; no. 3 (1958), pp. 103-17.

Rougerie, R. J. "*Les Enfants de l'Oncle Tom* par Richard Wright," *Présence Africaine,* no. 3 (March-April 1948), pp. 518-19.

Rugoff, Milton. "A Feverish Dramatic Intensity," *New York Herald Tribune Books,* 3 March 1940, p. 5. (Review of *Native Son.*)

Sartre, Jean-Paul. *What Is Literature?* trans. Bernard Frechtman. New York, 1949.

"Says 'Native Son' Fails Its Purpose," *Chicago Defender,* 25 May 1940, p. 7.

"Science Traps Moron in 5 Murders," *Chicago Daily Tribune,* 3 June 1938, pp. 1, 8, 38. (Nixon case.)

Scott, Nathan A., Jr. "The Dark and Haunted Tower of Richard Wright," *Graduate Comment* (Wayne State University), VII (July 1964), 93-99. (Reprinted in *Black Expression,* ed. Addison Gayle.)

————. "Judgment Marked by a Cellar: The American Negro Writer and the Dialectic of Despair," *Denver Quarterly,* II (Summer 1967), 5-35.

————. *Modern Literature and the Religious Frontier.* New York, 1958.

————. "Search for Beliefs: Fiction of Richard Wright," *University of Kansas City Review,* XXIII (Autumn 1956), 19-24; (Winter 1956), 131-38.

Seaver, Edwin. "Richard Wright," *Book-of-the-Month Club News*, February 1940, p. 6.

"Seven Prominent Americans Give Their Point of View," *New Masses*, XXXIX (6 May 1941), 15-16.

Shukotoff, Arnold. "Proletarian Short Stories," *New Masses*, XXX (3 January 1939), 22-23.

"Sift Mass of Clews for Sex Killer," *Chicago Daily Tribune*, 28 May 1938, pp. 1-2. (Nixon case.)

Silberman, Charles E. *Crisis in Black and White*. New York, 1964.

Sillen, Samuel. "The Meaning of Bigger Thomas," *New Masses*, XXXV (30 April 1940), 26-28.

————. " 'Native Son': Pros and Cons," *New Masses*, XXXV (21 May 1940), 23-26.

————. "The Response to 'Native Son,' " *New Masses*, XXXV (23 April 1940), 25-27.

————. "Richard Wright in Retreat," *New Masses*, LII (29 August 1944), 25-26.

————. "Richard Wright's 'Native Son,' " *New Masses*, XXXIV (5 March 1940), 24-25.

Skillin, Edward, Jr. "*Native Son*. Richard Wright," *Commonweal*, XXXI (8 March 1940), 438.

"Slayer Admits Rape: Another in Prison for It," *Chicago Daily Tribune*, 7 June 1938, p. 5. (Nixon case.)

Slochower, Harry. "In the Fascist Styx," *Negro Quarterly*, I (Fall 1942), 227-40.

Smith, William Gardner. "Black Boy in France," *Ebony*, VIII (July 1953), 32-36, 39-42.

————. "Richard Wright, 1908-1960: The Compensation for the Wound," *Two Cities*, no. 6 (Summer 1961), pp. 67-69.

Solotaroff, Theodore. Afterword to Richard Wright, *Native Son*. New York, 1964.

S[ordo], E[nrique]. "Richard Wright y la epopeya negra," *Cuadernos Hispanoamericanos*, no. 49 (January 1954), pp. 110-14.

Spear, Allan H. *Black Chicago: The Making of a Negro Ghetto, 1890-1920*. Chicago, 1967.

Stanford, Don. "*The Beloved Returns* and Other Recent Fiction," *Southern Review*, VI (Winter 1941), 610-28. (Review of *Native Son*.)

Starke, Catherine Juanita. *Black Portraiture in American Fiction*. New York, 1971.

"State Rests in Brick Slaying Trial of Rapist," *Chicago Daily Tribune*, 3 August 1938, p. 9. (Nixon case.)

"State's Case against Nixon, Hicks, Weaker," *Chicago Defender*, 25 June 1938, p. 2.

"State Will Seek Trial Today for 2 Brick Slayers," *Chicago Daily Tribune*, 29 June 1938, p. 8. (Nixon case.)

Stegner, Wallace. "The New Novels," *Virginia Quarterly Review,* XVI (Summer 1940), 459-65. (Review of *Native Son.*)

Sullivan, Richard. Afterword to Richard Wright, *Native Son.* New York, 1961.

"Supreme Court Halts Execution of Nixon," *Chicago Defender,* 17 December 1938, pp. 1-2.

Tarry, Ellen. "Native Daughter," *Commonweal,* XXXI (12 April 1940), 524-26.

Tatham, Campbell. "Vision and Value in *Uncle Tom's Children,*" *Studies in Black Literature,* III (Spring 1972), 14-23.

"Testimonial Dinner and Reception for the Hon. Vito Marcantonio," *New Masses,* XXXIX (1 April 1941), 29.

"Text of National Call to Browder Congress," *Sunday Worker,* 15 February 1942, sec. 1, p. 3.

Theis, E. "Un Ecrivain: Richard Wright," *Présence Africaine,* VIII-IX (March 1950), 141-48.

"Theodore Dreiser Gets Peace Award," *New York Times,* 7 June 1941, p. 5.

Thorpe, Earl E. *The Mind of the Negro: An Intellectual History of Afro-Americans.* Baton Rouge, 1961.

Timmerman, John. "Symbolism as a Syndetic Device in Richard Wright's 'Long Black Song,'" *CLA Journal,* XIV (March 1971), 291-97.

Tolson, M. B. "Richard Wright: Native Son," *Modern Quarterly,* XI (Winter 1939), 19-24. (This is actually the Winter 1940 issue.)

Torriente, Loló de la. "*Sangre Negra,* por Richard Wright," *Afroamerica,* I (January and July 1945), 102-4. (Review of *Native Son.*)

"To Take Plea for Nixon to Higher Court," *Chicago Defender,* 27 August 1938, p. 3.

Tourtellot, Arthur Bernon. "A Voice for the Negro," *Boston Evening Transcript,* 9 April 1938, sec. 3, p. 1. (Review of *Uncle Tom's Children.*)

Townsley, Luther. "Robert Nixon, Who Has Faced Chair Seven Times, Tells Just How It Feels," *Chicago Defender,* 11 February 1939, p. 5.

Turner, Darwin T. "*The Outsider:* Revision of an Idea," *CLA Journal,* XII (June 1969), 310-21.

Tuttleton, James W. "The Negro Writer as Spokesman," *The Black American Writer,* ed. C. W. E. Bigsby. Deland, Fla., 1969.

"2 Accuse Each Other in Brick Killing," *Chicago Daily Tribune,* 30 May 1938, pp. 1-2. (Nixon case.)

"2 Brick Slayers Lose Pleas for Separate Trials," *Chicago Daily Tribune,* 30 June 1938, p. 12. (Nixon case.)

Van Gelder, Robert. "Books of the Times," *New York Times,* 2 November 1936, p. 19.

———. "Four Tragic Tales," *New York Times Book Review,* 3 April 1938, pp. 7, 16. (Review of *Uncle Tom's Children.*)

"Victims Listed in 2 Year Wave of Sex Crimes," *Chicago Daily Tribune,* 28 May 1938, p. 2. (Nixon case.)

"Vigorous Stories Portray Tragedy of Southern Negro," *Dallas Morning News,*
27 March 1938, sec. 3, p. 10. (Review of *Uncle Tom's Children.*)

Vogel, Albert W. "The Education of the Negro in Richard Wright's *Black
Boy,*" *Journal of Negro Education,* XXXV (Spring 1966), 195-98.

Wallace, Margaret. "The Book of the Day: A Powerful Novel about a Boy
from Chicago's Black Belt," *New York Sun,* 5 March 1940, p. 34. (Review
of *Native Son.*)

Ward, Theodore. "Five Negro Novelists: Revolt and Retreat," *Mainstream,*
I (Winter 1947), 100-110.

Wartenweiler, Fritz. *Schwarze in USA.* Zurich, 1960.

Watson, Edward A. "Bessie's Blues," *New Letters,* XXXVIII (Winter 1971),
64-70.

Watteau, Maurice. "Situations raciales et condition de l'homme dans l'oeuvre
de J.-P. Sartre," *Présence Africaine,* no. 2 (January 1948), pp. 209-29;
no. 3 (March-April 1948), pp. 405-17.

Webb, Constance. *Richard Wright: A Biography.* New York, 1968.

————. "What Next for Richard Wright?" *Phylon,* X (Second Quarter
1949), 161-66.

Weigel, Henrietta. "Personal Impressions," *New Letters,* XXXVIII (Winter
1971), 17-20.

Weitz, Morris. *Philosophy of the Arts.* Cambridge, Mass., 1950.

Wertham, Frederic, M.D. "The Dreams That Heal," introduction to *The
World Within: Fiction Illuminating Neuroses of Our Time,* ed. Mary
Louise Aswell. New York, 1947.

————. "An Unconscious Determinant in *Native Son,*" *Journal of Clinical
Psychopathology and Psychotherapy,* VI (July 1944), 111-15.

West, Anthony. "New Novels," *New Statesman and Nation,* XIX (20 April
1940), 542-43. (Review of *Native Son.*)

West, Dorothy. "Dear Reader," *Challenge,* I (January 1936), 38; II (Spring
1937), 40-41.

————, and Marian Minus. "Editorial," *New Challenge,* II (Fall 1937), 3-4.

White, Grace McSpadden. "Wright's Memphis," *New Letters,* XXXVIII
(Winter 1971), 105-16.

White, Ralph K. "*Black Boy:* A Value-Analysis," *Journal of Abnormal and
Social Psychology,* XLII (October 1947), 440-61.

" 'White Fog,' " *Time,* XXXI (28 March 1938), 63-64. (Review of *Uncle
Tom's Children.*)

Wilder, Roy. "Wright, Negro Ex-Field Hand, Looks Ahead to New Triumphs," *New York Herald Tribune,* 17 August 1941, sec. 6, p. 4.

Wilkerson, Doxey A. "Negro Culture: Heritage and Weapon," *Masses &
Mainstream,* II (August 1949), 3-24.

Williams, John A. *The Most Native of Sons: A Biography of Richard Wright.*
Garden City, N.Y., 1970.

Williamson, Simon. "Guest Editorial," *New York Amsterdam News,* 25 May
1940, p. 8.

Wilson, Charles H. *Education for Negroes in Mississippi since 1910*. Boston, 1947.

Winslow, Henry F. "Nightmare Experiences," *Crisis,* LXVI (February 1959), 120-22.

———. "Richard Nathaniel Wright: Destroyer and Preserver (1908-1960)," *Crisis,* LXIX (March 1962), 149-63, 187.

Witham, W. Tasker. *The Adolescent in the American Novel, 1920-1960*. New York, 1964.

Work, Monroe N., ed. *Negro Year Book*. Tuskegee, 1925.

"A Work of Genius," *New York Amsterdam News,* 23 March 1940, p. 14. (Editorial on *Native Son*.)

Wright, Richard. "A. L. P. Assemblyman Urges State Control of Price of Milk," *Daily Worker,* 8 November 1937, pp. 1, 4.

———. "Adventure and Love in Loyalist Spain," *New Masses,* XXVI (8 March 1938), 25-26.

———. "Ah Feels It in Mah Bones," *International Literature,* no. 4 (April 1935), p. 80.

———. "Alger Revisited, or My Stars! Did We Read That Stuff?" *PM,* 16 September 1945, magazine section, p. 13.

———. "Almos' a Man," *Harper's Bazaar,* LXXIV (January 1940), 40-41, 105-7. (Reprinted as "The Man Who Was Almost a Man" in *Eight Men*.)

———. "ALP Assemblyman in Harlem Hails Unity of Labor at Polls," *Daily Worker,* 18 November 1937, p. 2.

———. "American Hunger," *Mademoiselle,* XXI (September 1945), 164-65, 299-301.

———. "American Negroes in Key Posts of Spain's Loyalist Forces," *Daily Worker,* 29 September 1937, p. 2.

———. "Ban on Negro Doctors Bared at City Probe," *Daily Worker,* 14 December 1937, pp. 1, 5.

———. "Bates Tells of Spain's Fight for Strong Republican Army," *Daily Worker,* 1 October 1937, p. 2.

———. "Between Laughter and Tears," *New Masses,* XXV (5 October 1937), 22, 25.

———. "Between the World and Me," *Partisan Review,* II (July-August 1935), 18-19.

———. "Big Boy Leaves Home," *The New Caravan,* ed. Alfred Kreymborg, Lewis Mumford, and Paul Rosenfeld. New York, 1936. (Reprinted in *Uncle Tom's Children*.)

———. "Big Harlem Rally for China Tonight," *Daily Worker,* 27 September 1937, p. 4.

———. *Black Boy: A Record of Childhood and Youth*. New York, 1945.

———. *Black Power: A Record of Reactions in a Land of Pathos*. New York, 1954.

———. "Blueprint for Negro Writing," *New Challenge,* II (Fall 1937), 53-65.

———. "Born a Slave, She Recruits 5 Members for Communist Party," *Daily Worker*, 30 August 1937, p. 3.

———. "Bright and Morning Star," *New Masses*, XXVII (10 May 1938), 97-99, 116-22, 124. (Reprinted in the second edition of *Uncle Tom's Children* [1940] and as a separate pamphlet [1941].)

———. "Browder Warns of Growth of Fascism in Latin America," *Daily Worker*, 23 October 1937, p. 5.

———. "C. P. Leads Struggle for Freedom, Stachel Says," *Daily Worker*, 9 August 1937, p. 2.

———. "Child of the Dead and Forgotten Gods," *Anvil*, no. 5 (March-April 1934), p. 30.

———. *The Color Curtain: A Report on the Bandung Conference*. Cleveland, 1956.

———. "Communist Leader Warns on Harlem Tiger Stooges," *Daily Worker*, 13 August 1937, p. 4.

———. "Correspondence," *Partisan Review and Anvil*, III (June 1936), 30.

———. "Le Depart de 'Big Boy,'" trans. Marcel Duhamel, pref. Paul Robeson, *L'Arbalète*, IX (Autumn 1944), 237-66.

———. "Down by the Riverside," *Uncle Tom's Children*. New York, 1938.

———. "Early Days in Chicago," *Cross-Section 1945*, ed. Edwin Seaver. New York, 1945. (Reprinted as "The Man Who Went to Chicago" in *Eight Men*.)

———. *Eight Men*. Cleveland, 1961.

———. "Les Etats-Unis sont-ils une nation, une loi, un peuple?" *La Nef*, XIV (November 1957), 57-60.

———. "The Ethics of Living Jim Crow," *American Stuff*. New York, 1937. (Reprinted in the second edition of *Uncle Tom's Children* [1940].)

———. "'Every Child Is a Genius,'" *Daily Worker*, 28 December 1937, p. 7.

———. "Everywhere Burning Waters Rise," *Left Front*, I (May-June 1934), 9.

———. "Le Feu dans la nuée," trans. Marcel Duhamel, *Les Temps Modernes*, I (1 October 1945), 22-47; (1 November 1945), 291-319.

———. "Fire and Cloud," *Story*, XII (March 1938), 9-41. (Reprinted in *Uncle Tom's Children*. Charles K. O'Neill made a radio adaptation of the story that appeared in *American Scenes*, ed. William Kozlenko. New York, 1941.)

———. Footnote to Kumar Goshal, "India and the Peoples' War," *Negro Quarterly*, I (Summer 1942), 140.

———. "Forerunner and Ambassador," *New Republic*, CIII (28 October 1940), 600-601.

———. "Foreword," *Illinois Labor Notes*, IV (March 1936), 2.

———. Foreword to Paul Oliver, *Blues Fell This Morning*. New York, 1961.

———. Foreword to Morris U. Schappes, *Letters from the Tombs*, ed. Louis Lerman. New York, 1941.

————. "Gouging, Landlord Discrimination against Negroes Bared at Hearing," *Daily Worker*, 15 December 1937, p. 6.

————. "Harlem, Bronx Sign Competition Pact," *Daily Worker*, 19 October 1937, p. 5.

————. "Harlem, East Side Honor Hero Who Died in Rescue of Negroes," *Daily Worker*, 7 December 1937, p. 4.

————. "Harlem Leaders Rap Amsterdam News' Stand for Mahoney," *Daily Worker*, 29 October 1937, p. 7.

————. "Harlem Negro Leaders Back Mayor for Liberal Views," *Daily Worker*, 20 October 1937, p. 4.

————. "The Harlems," in Federal Writers' Project, *New York City Guide*. New York, 1939.

————. "Harlem Spanish Women Come Out of the Kitchen," *Daily Worker*, 20 September 1937, p. 5.

————. "Harlem Vote Swings Away from Tiger," *Daily Worker*, 2 November 1937, p. 3.

————. "Harlem Women Hit Boost in Milk Price," *Daily Worker*, 3 September 1937, p. 1.

————. "Hearst Headline Blues," *New Masses*, XIX (12 May 1936), 14.

————. " 'He Died by Them' — Hero's Widow Tells of Rescue of Negroes," *Daily Worker*, 6 December 1937, pp. 1, 6.

————. "High Tide in Harlem," *New Masses*, XXVIII (5 July 1938), 18-20.

————. " 'Horseplay' at Lafayette Fun for Children and Grown-ups Alike," *Daily Worker*, 11 September 1937, p. 7.

————. "How 'Bigger' Was Born," *Saturday Review of Literature*, XXII (1 June 1940), 3-4, 17-20. (An enlarged version was issued by Harper's later in the same year as a separate pamphlet.)

————. "How He Did It — And Why the People Rejoice — And Oh — Where Were Hitler's Pagan Gods?" *Daily Worker*, 24 June 1938, pp. 1, 8.

————. "How Jim Crow Feels," *Negro Digest*, V (January 1947), 44-53.

————. "How 'Uncle Tom's Children' Grew," *Columbia University Writers' Club Bulletin*, II (May 1938), 16-18.

————. "Huddie Ledbetter, Famous Negro Folk Artist, Sings the Songs of Scottsboro and His People," *Daily Worker*, 12 August 1937, p. 7.

————. "I Am a Red Slogan," *International Literature*, no. 4 (April 1935), p. 35.

————. "I Bite the Hand That Feeds Me," *Atlantic Monthly*, CLXV (June 1940), 826-28.

————. "I Have Seen Black Hands," *New Masses*, XI (26 June 1934), 16.

————. "Inner Landscape," *New Republic*, CIII (5 August 1940), 195.

————. "Insect-Ridden Medicine Given in Hospital," *Daily Worker*, 4 September 1937, p. 5.

————. Introduction to Nelson Algren, *Never Come Morning*. New York, 1942.

————. Introduction to St. Clair Drake and Horace R. Cayton, *Black Metropolis: A Study of Negro Life in a Northern City.* New York, 1945.

————. Introduction to Howard Nutt, *Special Laughter.* Prairie City, Ill., 1940.

————. Introduction to J. Saunders Redding, *No Day of Triumph.* New York, 1942.

————. Introduction to "American Hunger," *The World's Best,* ed. Whit Burnett. New York, 1950.

————. "Is America Solving Its Race Problem?" *Negro Digest,* III (August 1945), 42-44.

————. "I Tried to Be a Communist," *Atlantic Monthly,* CLXXIV (August 1944), 61-70; (September 1944), 48-56. (Reprinted in *The God That Failed,* ed. Richard Crossman. New York, 1949.)

————. "I Wish I Had Written Early Days of a Woman from Melanctha by Gertrude Stein," *I Wish I'd Written That,* ed. Eugene J. Woods. New York, 1946.

————. "James W. Ford Celebrates 44th Birthday — Leads Progressives in Harlem Community," *Daily Worker,* 23 December 1937, p. 4.

————. "Joe Louis Uncovers Dynamite," *New Masses,* XVIII (8 October 1935), 18-19.

————. "King Joe," *New Letters,* XXXVIII (Winter 1971), 42-45.

————. *Lawd Today.* New York, 1963.

————. Letters to Carl Van Vechten. Deposited in the Yale University Library.

————. Letters to Gertrude Stein. Deposited in the Yale University Library.

————. *Letters to Joe C. Brown,* ed. Thomas Knipp. Kent, Ohio, 1968.

————. Letters to Langston Hughes. Deposited in the Yale University Library.

————. "A Letter to International Publishers," *Bright and Morning Star,* foreword by James W. Ford. New York, 1941.

————. "The Literature of the Negro in the United States," *White Man, Listen!* Garden City, N.Y., 1957.

————. "Long Black Song," *Uncle Tom's Children.* New York, 1938.

————. *The Long Dream.* Garden City, N.Y., 1958.

————. "Lynching Bee," *New Republic,* CII (11 March 1940), 351-52.

————. "The Man Who Lived Underground," *Cross-Section,* ed. Edwin Seaver. New York, 1944. (Reprinted in *Eight Men.* A shorter version, subtitled "Two Excerpts from a Novel," appeared in *Accent,* II [Spring 1942], 170-76.)

————. "Mrs. Holmes and Daughters Drink from the Fountain of Communism," *Daily Worker,* 7 September 1937, p. 5.

————. *Native Son.* New York, 1940.

————. *The Negro and Parkway Community House.* Chicago, 1941.

————. "Negro Leaders Hail Victory of A. L. P. at New York Polls," *Daily Worker,* 4 November 1937, p. 5.

————. "Negro Social Worker Hails Housing, Education in Spain," *Daily Worker*, 12 November 1937, p. 2.

————. "Negro Tradition in the Theatre," *Daily Worker*, 15 October 1937, p. 9.

————. "Negro, with 3-Week-Old Baby, Begs Food on Streets," *Daily Worker*, 4 August 1937, p. 3.

————. "Negro Writers Launch Literary Quarterly," *Daily Worker*, 8 June 1937, p. 7.

————. "Negro Youth on March, Says Leader," *Daily Worker*, 7 October 1937, p. 3.

————. "New Negro Pamphlet Stresses Need for U.S. People's Front," *Daily Worker*, 25 October 1937, p. 3.

————. "Notes on Jim Crow Blues," *Southern Exposure*. Keynote Recordings 107, 1941. (This article appears on the inside front jacket of this phonograph record album by Josh White.)

————. "Not My People's War," *New Masses*, XXXIX (17 June 1941), 8-9, 12.

————. "Obsession," *Midland Left*, no. 2 (February 1935), p. 14.

————. "Old Habit and New Love," *New Masses*, XXI (15 December 1936), 29.

————. "On New Masses' Thirtieth Anniversary," *New Masses*, XXXVIII (18 February 1941), 26.

————. "Opening of Harlem Project Homes Shows How Slums Can Be Wiped Out in New York," *Daily Worker*, 8 October 1937, p. 5.

————. " 'Opportunity for Soviet Youth Unlimited,' Says Negro Musician," *Daily Worker*, 24 August 1937, p. 6.

————. *The Outsider*. New York, 1953.

————. *Pagan Spain*. New York, 1957.

————. "Portrait of Harlem," in Federal Writers' Project, *New York Panorama*. New York, 1938.

————. "Pullman Porters to Celebrate 12th Year of Their Union," *Daily Worker*, 19 August 1937, p. 3.

————. "Randolph Urges Parley between CIO-AFL Unions," *Daily Worker*, 30 September 1937, p. 3.

————. "Rascoe-Baiting," *American Mercury*, L (July 1940), 376-77.

————. "Readers' Right: Writer Asks Break for the Negroes," *New York Post*, 5 April 1938, p. 30.

————. "Red Leaves of Red Books," *New Masses*, XV (30 April 1935), 6.

————. "A Red Love Note," *Left Front*, I (January-February 1934), 3.

————. "Rest for the Weary," *Left Front*, I (January-February 1934), 3.

————. "Richard Wright Lauds Controversy on Music," *Daily Worker*, 13 February 1942, p. 7.

————. "Richard Wright's Statement Supporting Browder, Ford," *Daily Worker*, 30 September 1940, p. 5.

————. "Rise and Live," *Midland Left,* no. 2 (February 1935), pp. 13-14.

————. "Santa Claus Has a Hard Time Finding Way to Harlem Slums," *Daily Worker,* 27 December 1937, p. 4.

————. *Savage Holiday.* New York, 1954.

————. "Scottsboro Boys on Stage Is Opposed," *Daily Worker,* 21 August 1937, p. 2.

————. "See Biggest Negro Parley since Days of Reconstruction," *Daily Worker,* 14 October 1937, p. 5.

————. "The Shame of Chicago," *Ebony,* VII (December 1951), 24-30, 32.

————. "A Sharecropper's Story," *New Republic,* XCIII (1 December 1937), 109.

————. "Silt," *New Masses,* XXIV (24 August 1937), 19-20. (Reprinted as "The Man Who Saw the Flood" in *Eight Men.*)

————. "Spread Your Sunrise!" *New Masses,* XVI (2 July 1935), 26.

————. "Strength," *Anvil,* no. 5 (March-April 1934), p. 20.

————. "Superstition," *Abbott's Monthly,* II (April 1931), 45-47, 64-66, 72-73.

————. "A Tale of Folk Courage," *Partisan Review and Anvil,* III (April 1936), 31.

————. "10,000 Negro Vets in N.Y. Silent, but They're Talking Up at Home," *Daily Worker,* 23 September 1937, p. 4.

————. "They Support the Soviet Union," *Soviet Russia Today,* X (September 1941), 29.

————. "Transcontinental," *International Literature,* no. 1 (January 1936), pp. 52-57.

————. *12 Million Black Voices: A Folk History of the Negro in the United States.* New York, 1941.

————. "Two Million Black Voices," *New Masses,* XVIII (25 February 1936), 15.

————. *Uncle Tom's Children: Four Novellas.* New York, 1938. (The second, enlarged edition is *Uncle Tom's Children: Five Long Stories* [1940].)

————. " 'U.S. Negroes Greet You,' Wright Cables to USSR," *Daily Worker,* 1 September 1941, p. 7.

————. "Walter Garland Tells What Spain's Fight against Fascism Means to the Negro People," *Daily Worker,* 29 November 1937, p. 2.

————. "We of the Streets," *New Masses,* XXIII (13 April 1937), 14.

————. "What Happens at a Communist Party Branch Meeting in the Harlem Section?" *Daily Worker,* 16 August 1937, p. 6.

————. "What Is the Stand of America's Largest Minority Group in Today's Warswept World?" *Coronet,* XI (April 1942), 78.

————. "What You Don't Know Won't Hurt You," *Harper's Magazine,* CLXXXVI (December 1942), 58-61. (Reprinted, in a revised version, as part of "Early Days in Chicago.")

————. *White Man, Listen!* Garden City, N.Y., 1957.

————. "Why He Selected 'How "Bigger" Was Born,' " *This Is My Best,* ed. Whit Burnett. New York, 1942.

————. "Why the Eyes of the People Turn to the Ring for the Title Bout at Yankee Stadium Tonight," *Daily Worker,* 22 June 1938, pp. 1, 4.

————. "Young Writers Launch Literary Quarterly," *San Antonio Register,* 10 July 1937, p. 4.

————, and Antonio R. Frasconi. "Exchange of Letters," *Twice a Year,* nos. 12-13 (Spring-Summer, Fall-Winter 1945), pp. 255-61.

————, and Paul Green. *Native Son (The Biography of a Young American).* New York, 1941.

————, and Langston Hughes. "Red Clay Blues," *New Masses,* XXXII (1 August 1939), 14.

————, Joseph Cadden, Roswell Rosengren, Barbara Allen, George Strayer, and Charles C. Glover III. "Can We Depend upon Youth to Follow the American Way?" *Town Meeting,* IV (24 April 1939), 3-28.

————, Elmer Carter, Irving Ives, and Jerry Voorhis. "Are We Solving America's Race Problem?" *Town Meeting,* XI (24 May 1945), 3-22.

————, Theodore Dreiser, George Seldes, Ruth McKenney, and William Blake. "Writers Emergency Committee to Save New Masses," *New Masses,* XXXV (30 April 1940), 3.

————, et al. "In Defense of Culture," *New Masses,* XXXIX (22 April 1941), 25.

————, et al. "Statement of American Intellectuals," *International Literature,* no. 7 (1938), p. 104.

————, et al. "To President Franklin D. Roosevelt," *New Masses,* XXXV (2 April 1940), 21.

————, et al. "Writers and the War," *New Masses,* XL (5 August 1941), 23.

————, et al. "The Writers Don't Want War," *New Masses,* XXXVI (25 June 1940), 21.

"Wright, Richard," *Current Biography, 1940,* ed. Maxine Block. New York, 1940.

"Wright Shows New Book," *Chicago Defender,* 24 February 1940, p. 22.

"Wright Wins a New Prize," *New York Amsterdam News,* 12 November 1938, p. 15.

"Writers League Elects Outstanding Authors as Vice-Presidents," *Daily Worker,* 5 August 1940, p. 7.

Wyke, Marguerite. "South Side Negro," *Canadian Forum,* XX (May 1940), 60. (Review of *Native Son.*)

# Index

*Abbott's Monthly,* 48
Abraham Lincoln Center (Chicago), 66
Abrahams, Peter, 161*n*
Africa, 15, 32
Africans, 15
Aggrey, O. Rudolph, 100*n*
Agrarians, 100
Al (in *Lawd Today*), 79
Alcorn Agricultural and Mechanical College, 25*n*
Alger, Horatio, 3, 27, 37
Algren, Nelson, 63*n*, 65*n*, 117*n*
Allen, Samuel, 32*n*
Alley, J. P., 42-43
American Guide Series, 73
*American Mercury,* 44, 146
American Peace Mobilization, 154
*American Stuff,* 73
*An American Tragedy* (Dreiser), 147, 151
American Writers' Congress, 16, 63-65, 68, 110, 154-55
Amherst College, 149
Anderson, Lewis, 39
Anderson, Sherwood, 44, 70, 107*n*, 160
"Another Mencken Absurdity" (editorial in *Memphis Commercial Appeal*), 41-42
*Anvil,* 50, 53, 55
Aptheker, Herbert, 149*n*

Aragon, Louis, 59
*Argosy All-Story Magazine,* 27
Arkansas, 4, 7, 11, 12, 17, 18, 19, 26, 29
"The Art of Fiction" (James), 119
Asia, 32
Atlanta, Georgia, 6
*Atlantic Monthly,* 44, 156
Attaway, William, 70
Austin, Reverend, 146-47

Babbitt, George F. (in *Babbitt*), 44, 77
Baldwin, James, 4, 16, 81, 82, 119, 132*n*, 160-61
*Baltimore Sun,* 41
Baraka, Imamu Amiri (LeRoi Jones), 161
Barbados, 15
Barbusse, Henri, 70
Basie, Count, 61
Beach, Joseph Warren, 71
Beale Street (Memphis), 8, 9
Beauvoir, Simone de, 31, 158
Berkman, Alexander, 51
*The Best Short Stories 1939,* 116
Bibbs, Miss, 120
Bibbs, Mrs., 35
Bilbo, Theodore Gilmore, 5, 6
Bill, 49
Birmingham, Alabama, 6
Black Belt. *See* Chicago
Black Legion, 125

*Black Metropolis* (Drake and Cayton), 121n

Blackmur, R. P., 158

Bluebeard, 26, 27, 36, 38, 43

Blum's (in *Native Son*), 131, 137

Bob (in "Down by the Riverside"), 87, 90, 92

Bob (in *Lawd Today*), 78

Bobo (in "Big Boy Leaves Home"), 83, 84

Bodenheim, Maxwell, 63n

Bolton, Mayor (in "Fire and Cloud"), 101, 102, 103, 104

Bonds, Deacon (in "Fire and Cloud"), 103

Bontemps, Arna, 54n, 66, 69-70

Booker (in "Bright and Morning Star"), 113, 115

Booker, Perry "Conkey," 39

*A Book of Prefaces* (Mencken), 43

Book-of-the-Month Club, 118, 143

Book Union, 109

Boston, Massachusetts, 117, 145

Bowman (in "Down by the Riverside"), 90, 92

Brinkley (in "Down by the Riverside"), 88, 92, 93

Britten (in *Native Son*), 132, 133

Brooklyn, New York, 14, 68n, 81n, 118

Brooks, Gwendolyn, 32n

Brooks, Van Wyck, 65n

Browder, Earl, 63, 65, 148, 154

Brown, Joe C., 30-31, 39

Brown, Lloyd W., 142n

Brown, Sterling A., 60, 109

Bruden, Chief (in "Fire and Cloud"), 102

Buckley (in *Native Son*), 132, 133, 137, 139

Burgum, Edwin Berry, 107n, 108n

Burke, Kenneth, 63n, 129

Caldwell, Erskine, 57n, 63n, 109

Canby, Henry Seidel, 143, 149

*Cane* (Toomer), 109

Cantwell, Robert, 63n

Carlisle, Harry, 65n

Carlton Avenue (Brooklyn), 68n, 118

Carter, Elmer, 17n

Castle, Florence Thompson, 125

Catholics, 40, 43

Cayton, Horace R., 17n, 29n, 32n, 121, 148, 156n

*Challenge,* 68-69

Chesnutt, Charles Waddell, 4

Chicago, Illinois: racial conditions in, 4, 11-14, 17, 120, 135; migration of blacks to, 11-12, 84, 85, 86; economic conditions in, 12, 13, 47; political conditions in, 12-13; Black Belt, 13, 14, 16, 62, 119; South Side, 13, 47, 62, 72, 77, 120-21, 127, 128; social conditions in, 13-14, 119; North Side, 14, 46; Depression in, 21, 47; black writers' group, 65-66, 68, 69; portrayed in *Lawd Today,* 75, 80; portrayed in *Native Son,* 120-21; mentioned, 19, 45, 46, 59, 61, 62, 65, 66, 67, 72, 76, 83, 96, 118, 123, 124, 125, 146, 156, 157, 159

Chicago Public Library, 80

*Chicago Tribune,* 121-23

The Chicken Shack (Chicago), 121

China, 72

Christ, Jesus, 93, 114, 116, 137

Civil War, 40, 77

*CLA Journal,* 161

Clarksdale, Mississippi, 23

Clay, Eugene, 65n

Cleaver, Eldridge, 161

Clurman, Harold, 117n

Coahoma County, Mississippi, 10

Cohn, David L., 145-46, 151

Cole, Joseph H., 150

Communism, 40, 116. *See also* Marxism

Communist party: in New York, 15; racial discrimination in, 16, 64; appeal to Wright, 31, 47, 50, 53, 54, 99, 100; Wright withdraws from, 31, 153, 155-56; Wright joins, 62; Wright's criticism of, 62, 67, 72, 155-57; Wright's activity in, 62-65, 72-73, 116-17, 153-55; in "Fire and Cloud," 101-2, 104, 106; in "Bright and Morning Star," 112, 114; in

*Native Son,* 119, 125-26, 134, 142, 147-50; responds to *Native Son,* 147-50; mentioned, 66, 160. *See also* Marxism
Conrad, Joseph, 44, 71, 160
Conroy, Jack, 50, 63n, 65n, 117n, 160
Constitution of the United States, 40
Cook County, Illinois, 124
Cooke, Marvel J., 109
Cossit Library (Memphis), 43
Courtney, Thomas J., 123
Cowley, Malcolm, 63n, 111, 144
Crane, Stephen, 4, 46, 159
Creekmore, Hubert, 122n
*Crime and Punishment* (Dostoevsky), 147
*Crisis,* 147
Crump, Edward Hull, 8

Dahlberg, Edward, 63n
*Daily Worker,* 14, 16, 63, 68, 70, 72-73, 110, 116, 149, 155
Dalton, Henry (in *Native Son*), 73, 128, 131, 133
Dalton, Mary (in *Native Son*), 120, 128, 130, 131, 133, 134, 135-36, 137, 139-41, 148, 149
Dalton, Mrs., 128, 131, 133, 135-36
Damocles, 115
Damon, Cross (in *The Outsider*), 138
Daniels, Jonathan, 144
Davis, Benjamin J., Jr., 15, 149, 156
Davis, Frank Marshall, 32n, 66, 70, 72n, 153n
"The Dead" (Joyce), 116, 137n
De Beauvoir, Simone. *See* Beauvoir, Simone de
De Kruif, Paul, 117n
Democratic party, 50
Depression, 13, 21, 47, 59, 60, 62, 69, 78, 81, 100, 127
DePriest, Oscar, 13
Desdemona (in *Othello*), 139
DeSheim, Charles, 66, 67n
Dickens, Charles, 44, 144
Doc (in *Native Son*), 133
Dorsey, George R., 147
Dos Passos, John, 160

Dostoevsky, Feodor, 46, 71, 143, 144, 160
Douglas Hotel (Harlem), 68
Douglass, Frederick, 105, 160, 161
Drake, St. Clair, 121n
Dreiser, Theodore, 3, 44, 63n, 144, 159, 160
Du Bois, W. E. B., 4, 105, 161
Dunbar, Paul Laurence, 4, 60, 160

Elaine, Arkansas, 10, 11, 18, 22
Eliot, T. S., 50, 70
Ella (boarder in Jackson), 26, 36, 38, 41
Ellison, Ralph, 4, 28n, 49, 71-72, 82, 147, 160
Emancipation Proclamation, 145
Embree, Edwin R., 3n, 36
Emerson, Ralph Waldo, 3, 4
Erlone, Jan (in *Native Son*), 126, 131, 132, 134, 136, 148, 149
Ernie's Kitchen Shack (in *Native Son*), 121
*Everyman,* 66, 67n
Existentialism, 31-32, 138, 158

Fabre, Michel, 39n, 48n
Fadiman, Clifton, 144
Fanon, Frantz, 161n
Farrell, James T., 63n, 81, 110-11, 159, 160
Faulkner, William, 108, 109
Federal Theatre, 66-67
Federal Writers' Project, 14, 66, 67, 68, 70, 73, 74, 109, 112
Fiedler, Leslie, 130n
*50 Best American Short Stories* (O'Brien), 116
Finn, Huck (in *Adventures of Huckleberry Finn*), 39, 85
Fisher, Dorothy Canfield, 143
Fisk University, 17
Flanagan, Hallie, 67n
*Flynn's Detective Weekly,* 27
Foley, Martha, 109
Foley's Woods (in "Bright and Morning Star"), 113
Ford, James W., 116, 154, 156

Ford, Nick Aaron, 81
France, 40
Frank, Waldo, 63n, 65n
Frederick, John T., 67n
Freeman, Joseph, 63n
French Guiana, 15
Freud, Sigmund, 78
Frost, Robert, 4
Fullerton Street (Chicago), 46

Gannett, Lewis, 80, 109, 144
Garlin, Sender, 155
Garrison, William Lloyd, 77
The Gay Woman (in Native Son), 127
Gellert, Hugo, 59
Genesis, 86
G.H. (in Native Son), 133
Gibson, Donald B., 142n
Gibson, Richard, 161
Giles, Louise, 80
Glicksberg, Charles I., 119
Gold, Mike, 63n, 148-49, 150, 154, 160
Gold Coast, 32
Gorky, Maxim, 70
Grannie (in "Down by the Riverside"), 87, 88, 91, 92
Grant, U. S., 40
The Grapes of Wrath, 144, 148
Green (in "Fire and Cloud"), 101-2, 103
Green, Paul, 66, 67n, 109
Greenley, Bob (Robinson), 57n
Greenville, Mississippi, 145
Greenwich Village, New York, 14, 17, 158
Greenwood, Mississippi, 23, 28
Gregory, Horace, 63n
Grey, Zane, 27, 37
Griffiths, Clyde (in An American Tragedy), 140
Gropper, William, 59, 79
Grumbach, Doris, 80-81
Guadeloupe, 15
Guerin, Daniel, 157
Guggenheim Fellowship, 118
Gus (in Native Son), 126, 127, 130-31, 133, 135, 142

Hadley (in "Fire and Cloud"), 101-2, 103
Haiti, 15
Halper, Albert, 76
"Hambone Meditations" (Alley), 42-43
Hammett, Dashiel, 117n
Hammond, Reverend (in Native Son), 133, 138
Handy, W. C., 8
Hansen, Harry, 112n
Harlem: Wright's journalism on, 14, 16, 72-73; cosmopolitanism of, 14-15; racial conditions in, 14-16; migration of blacks to, 15; political conditions in, 15; social conditions in, 69; mentioned, 68, 117, 118. See also New York, New York
Harlem Renaissance, 15, 69, 70, 160
Harper's, 118, 151
Harper's Magazine, 44
Harrison, 40-41
Harvard Law School, 149
Harvey, Jim (in "Big Boy Leaves Home"), 83, 85, 107
Harvey, Mr. (in "Big Boy Leaves Home"), 83
Hawthorne, Nathaniel, 4, 152
Hayden, Robert, 70
Heartfield, Mr. (in "Down by the Riverside"), 87, 88, 90, 91, 107
Heartfield, Mrs. (in "Down by the Riverside"), 87, 88, 89, 90, 92
Hellman, Lillian, 117n
Hemingway, Ernest, 33, 70, 107n, 111, 160
Henderson, Ernie, 121
Herrick, Robert, 65n
Hicks, Earl, 121-22, 123
Hicks, Granville, 63n, 80, 110, 117
Higgins, Doc (in Lawd Today), 76-77
Himes, Chester, 4, 150, 160
Hoffman, Frederick J., 158
Hoffman, Mr. and Mrs., 45
Holly Springs, Mississippi, 8
Holmes, Eugene, 150
Hopkins, Sam "Lightnin'," 61
Hoskins, Fred (uncle of Wright), 10, 18-19, 22, 28

Hoskins, Maggie (aunt of Wright), 10, 18-19, 20, 22, 23, 45, 46, 120
Howard, Sidney, 65$n$
Howard Institute, 25
Howard University, 150
Howe, Irving, 72$n$, 161
Howells, William Dean, 4
Huggins, B. Doc, 77$n$
Hughes, Langston, 4, 32$n$, 60, 63$n$, 70, 72, 112$n$, 117$n$
Humphries, Rolph, 117$n$
Hurston, Zora Neale, 70, 110
Hurstwood, George (in *Sister Carrie*), 140
Huxley, Aldous, 50
*Hymn to the Rising Sun* (Green), 66, 67$n$

Iago (in *Othello*), 139
Illinois, 12
*Illinois Guide*, 67$n$
Illinois Writers' Project, 67$n$
Indianapolis, Indiana, 62
Indonesia, 32
International Labor Defense, 123, 125, 126$n$
*International Literature*, 52, 60
International Publishers, 154
*Invisible Man* (Ellison), 49, 72
Italian Harlem, 15
Ivy, James W., 147

Jack (in *Native Son*), 127, 133
Jackson, Esther Merle, 138$n$
Jackson, Jake (in *Lawd Today*), 33, 76-82
Jackson, Lil (in *Lawd Today*), 76, 77, 78, 80
Jackson, Mississippi, 10, 11, 19-31 passim, 34, 36, 37, 38, 46, 120
Jamaica, 15
James, Henry, 71, 119, 152, 160
Jefferson, New Hampshire, 155
*Jennie Gerhardt* (Dreiser), 44
Jews, 40, 45, 77, 125, 146, 156
Jim Hill School (Jackson), 34, 35
Johnny-Boy (in "Bright and Morning Star"), 112-13, 114-15

John Reed Club, 50-52, 61-62, 64, 66, 126$n$, 155
Johnson, Elmer, 124$n$
Johnson, Florence, 121, 123, 125, 128$n$
Johnson, Jack, 40
Johnson, James Weldon, 4, 60
Jones, Howard Mumford, 145
Jones, LeRoi. *See* Baraka, Imamu Amiri
Jordan, Richard "Squilla," 39
Joyce, James, 70, 108, 116, 137$n$, 160

Kazin, Alfred, 158
Kennedy, Robert, 132$n$
Knipp, Thomas, 38
Kreymborg, Alfred, 67
Krutch, Joseph Wood, 50
Ku Klux Klan, 40, 42, 138
Kunitz, Joshua, 63$n$, 65$n$

La Guardia, Fiorello, 15
Lake Michigan, 45
Latin America, 72
Latura, "Wild Bill," 9
Lawson, John Howard, 63$n$
Leadbelly (Huddie Ledbetter), 61
League of American Writers, 65, 154, 155$n$
Leaner, Arthur, 39$n$
Leavelle, Charles, 122-23
*Left Front*, 52, 53, 62
Lehmann, Rosamond, 151
Lewe, John C., 124
Lewis, Sinclair, 44, 109, 160
Leyda, Jay, 117$n$
Liberty, Mississippi, 7$n$
Lincoln, Abraham, 40, 77, 78
*Literaturny kritik*, 112
Littell, Robert, 145
Locke, Alain, 109, 147
London, England, 158
London, Jack, 70
Los Angeles, California, 123
Louis, Joe, 61, 75$n$, 117
Lovett, Robert Morss, 65$n$
Lowe, Mr. (in "Fire and Cloud"), 102
Lumpkin, Grace, 63$n$
Lynching, 57-58, 83-85, 88, 93, 106, 107, 137, 138

McCarthy, Joseph, 161
McKay, Claude, 160
Mann (in "Down by the Riverside"),
87-94, 95, 107
Mann, Lulu (in "Down by the Riverside"), 87, 88, 91
Mann, Peewee (in "Down by the Riverside"), 87, 88
Marcantonio, Vito, 15, 154
Margolies, Edward, 142n
Marsh, Fred T., 111, 112n
Marshall, Margaret, 144
Martinique, 15
Marx, Karl, 78
Marxism: in Wright's poetry, 58, 60,
62, 63; Wright's adherence to, 62,
63; in "Blueprint for Negro Writing," 70-71; in "Fire and Cloud,"
106; in Native Son, 121, 127; mentioned, 82. See also Communism;
Communist party
Masters, Edgar Lee, 44
Max, Boris (in Native Son), 73, 125-
26, 129, 131, 132, 134, 136, 139,
140, 141-43, 149
Maxwell, Allen, 111
Meadman, Rose Dhima (first wife of
Wright), 151
Mears, Bessie (in Native Son), 127,
128, 130, 131, 132-33, 140
Melville, Herman, 3, 4
Memphis, Tennessee: economic conditions in, 7-8; racial conditions in, 7-
10, 14, 17, 22, 29; political conditions in, 8; violence in, 8-10; Cossit
Library, 43; mentioned, 12, 18, 19,
20, 21, 25, 26, 32, 39, 56, 112
Memphis Commercial Appeal, 9, 41-
43
Mencken, H. L., 27, 37, 41-44, 160
Methodists, 30
Mexico, 5, 17, 22, 151
Michael Reese Hospital (Chicago),
48-49
Miller, William D., 8
Minor, Robert, 156
Minus, Marian, 15, 69
Mississippi: political conditions in, 5;
social conditions in, 5-6; economic
conditions in, 5-7, 8; racial conditions in, 5-7, 10, 11, 13, 17, 18, 39,
82; population, 6; migration of
blacks from, 12; educational conditions in, 24-25; mentioned, 4, 32,
35, 41, 86, 94, 96, 119, 122n
"The Mississippi Flood" (Mencken),
41-42
Mississippi River, 1927 flood, 41-42,
56
Mooney, Tom, 51
Morrison, Big Boy (in "Big Boy
Leaves Home"), 33, 82-87, 95, 107,
135
Moscow, U.S.S.R., 117
Motley, Willard, 70, 160
Mphahlele, Ezekiel, 161n
Mumford, Lewis, 65n, 67-68
"Murders in the Rue Morgue" (Poe),
123
Murray, Elder (in "Down by the Riverside"), 89, 92, 93
Myrdal, Gunnar, 24

Nadir, Moishe, 65n
Nashville, Tennessee, 17
Natchez, Mississippi, 5, 7, 19, 22, 26
National Association for the Advancement of Colored People, 147
National Negro Congress, 66, 124, 125
Negro Digest, 161
The New Caravan, 67, 82, 108
New Challenge, 15, 68-72
New Deal, 74
New Hampshire, 17
New Masses, 52, 68, 79, 112, 116, 117,
149, 150, 153, 154
New Orleans, Louisiana, 6
New Republic, 73, 144
Newton, Herbert, 68n
Newton, Jane, 68n, 118
New York, New York: racial conditions in, 4, 14-17, 64; Wright moves
to, 68; Wright's writing on, 73-74;
mentioned, 63, 67n, 82, 146, 157,
158. See also Brooklyn; Greenwich
Village; Harlem
New York City Guide, 14, 73
New York City Writers' Project, 68

*New Yorker,* 144
*New York Panorama,* 14, 72-73
New York State Temporary Commission on Conditions among Urban Negroes, 73
*New York Times,* 111
Nexø, Martin Andersen, 70
Nixon, Robert, 119, 121-25, 128n
Norman, Dorothy, 157
Normandy, France, 100n
North, Joseph, 63n
North Side. *See* Chicago
Northwestern University, 66

O. Henry Memorial Award, 112
Olin, Mr., 40-41
Oliver, Paul, 61
136th Street (New York), 68
Orro, David H., 122n
Othello (in *Othello*), 139

Paris, France, 5, 17, 61, 81n, 86, 150, 157, 158
Parker, Dorothy, 117n
Patricia Hotel (Chicago), 46
Peggy (in *Native Son*), 131
Peironille, Quebec, 157n
*People's Voice,* 148n
Percy, Leroy, 5
Persons, Eli, 9
Petry, Ann, 160
Pettigrew, Thomas F., 21n
Phillips County, Arkansas, 10, 11, 25
"Playing into the Hands of Slander" (editorial in *Memphis Commercial Appeal*), 43n
Poe, Edgar Allan, 4, 48, 123, 136, 152
Poore, Charles, 111, 118n, 144
Populist party, 6
Pound, Ezra, 50
Powell, Adam Clayton, Jr., 148n
*Pravda,* 112
*Prejudices* (Mencken), 43
Proust, Marcel, 46, 70, 160
Pulitzer Prize, 111, 150

Quebec, 5, 157

Rascoe, Burton, 3n, 145, 146, 150-51
Reconstruction, 5, 8-9, 12
Redding, Saunders, 24n
Reid, Ira DeA., 32n
Republican party, 40, 50, 68, 77
Reva (in "Bright and Morning Star"), 113, 115
Rivera, Oscar Garcia, 15
Robeson, Paul, 60-61
Robinson, C. T., 39n, 57n
Robinson, Edwin Arlington, 3
Rosenfeld, Paul, 68
Roth, Joseph, 123, 125
Rugoff, Milton, 144

St. Louis, Missouri, 12
St. Nicholas Avenue (Harlem), 68
Sandburg, Carl, 3
Sanders, Will (in "Big Boy Leaves Home"), 84
Sarah (in "Long Black Song"), 94-99
Sartre, Jean-Paul, 24, 31, 150, 157, 158
*Saturday Review of Literature,* 151
Sawyer, Tom (in *The Adventures of Tom Sawyer*), 39
Schappes, Morris U., 154
Scherman, Harry, 109
Schmeling, Max, 75n, 117
Schneider, Isidore, 63n
Scottsboro case, 15, 51
Seaver, Edwin, 63n
Selassie, Haile, 75n
Seventh-Day Adventists, 4, 23, 25, 26, 30, 34
Shakespeare, William, 139n
Sharecroppers, 4, 6, 7, 10, 11n, 32, 73n, 99, 112, 114
Shaw, Irwin, 117n
Shaw, Joel, 150
Sherman, William T., 40
Shorty, 14, 40
Silas (in "Long Black Song"), 87, 94-95, 96, 98-99, 107
Sillen, Samuel, 143n, 149-50, 156
Simmons, Isaac, 7n
Sims, Frank, 39
*Sister Carrie* (Dreiser), 44

Slim (in *Lawd Today*), 78
Smith, Deacon (in "Fire and Cloud"),
    100, 101, 102, 103, 104-5
Smith, William Gardner, 160
Smith-Robinson School (Jackson),
    25n, 35, 36
Socialism, 40
*Southern Messenger,* 27
Southern Negro Youth Congress, 73
*Southern Register,* 26, 37
South Side. *See* Chicago
South Side Boys' Club, 62, 65, 66, 120
Soviet Union, 51, 65, 117n, 150
Spain, 72
Spanish Harlem, 15
Stanford, Don, 144-45
State Department, 157
Steffens, Lincoln, 63n
Stegner, Wallace, 145
Stein, Gertrude, 46, 70, 107n, 157,
    158, 160
Steinbeck, John, 144, 148, 160
*Story,* 17, 109
Stowe, Harriet Beecher, 146
Stribling, T. S., 109
Strong, Edward, 73
Stuart, Jesse, 116
*Studies in Black Literature,* 161
Sue (in "Bright and Morning Star"),
    112-16
Sug (in "Bright and Morning Star"),
    112, 114
Switzerland, 65

Taggard, Genevieve, 63n
Tallulah, Louisiana, 122
Taylor, Dan (in "Fire and Cloud"),
    100-106, 107, 108, 114
Taylor, Jimmy (in "Fire and Cloud"),
    101, 102, 103, 104, 105, 114
Taylor, May (in "Fire and Cloud"),
    101, 102, 103, 104
*Les Temps Modernes,* 150, 158
Tennessee, 4, 7, 11, 12
Texas, 12n, 17
*Their Eyes Were Watching God* (Hur-
    ston), 110n
*These Low Grounds* (Turpin), 71
Thomas, Bigger (in *Native Son*), 3,

33, 45, 62, 119-22, 124-43, 145-51
Thomas, Biggy, 130n
Thomas, Buddy (in *Native Son*), 130,
    132
Thomas, Mrs. (in *Native Son*), 130,
    132, 138
Thomas, Vera (in *Native Son*), 130,
    132
Tillie, 46
*Time,* 81, 111
*Times Literary Supplement,* 81, 82,
    151
Tom (in "Long Black Song"), 94, 96,
    98
Tom, Uncle (in *Uncle Tom's Cabin*),
    130n
Toomer, Jean, 109
Trachtenberg, Alexander, 63n
Trinidad, 15
*Trouble in July* (Caldwell), 57n
Turpin, E. Waters, 71
Twain, Mark, 3, 4

*Uncle Tom's Cabin* (Stowe), 146
University of Chicago, 121

Van Doren, Irita, 112n
Van Gelder, Robert, 111
Van Vechten, Carl, 17, 32n, 157n
Vardaman, James Kimble, 5, 6

Walker, Margaret, 66, 70
Wallingford, Get-Rich-Quick, 27
Ward, Essie Lee, 39n
Ward, Theodore, 66, 67n, 70, 82n
Washington, Booker T., 105
Washington Park (Chicago), 13
Webb, Constance, 28n, 38, 39, 112n
Weber, Max, 117n
Weeks, Edward, 112n, 143-44
Wertham, Frederic, 119, 120n
West, Anthony, 150-51
West, Dorothy, 15, 68-69
West, Nathanael, 63n
West Helena, Arkansas, 10, 20, 45,
    99n
West Indians, 15
Wheatley, Phillis, 4
White, Josh, 60, 61

White Mountain Writers Conference, 155

Whitman, Walt, 3

Whittier, John Greenleaf, 4

Whitton, John, 124n

Williams, John Sharp, 5

Wilson, Addie (aunt of Wright), 23, 26, 28, 30, 34, 38

Wilson, Charles H., 25n

Wilson, Clark (uncle of Wright), 23, 28

Wilson, Cleo (aunt of Wright), 45, 46-47

Wilson, Jody (aunt of Wright), 23, 28

Wilson, Margaret Bolden (grandmother of Wright), 11, 20, 23, 25, 26, 28, 30, 36

Wilson, Richard (grandfather of Wright), 11, 20, 23

Wilson, Tom (uncle of Wright), 20, 23, 26, 28, 35

Wilson, Velma (cousin of Wright), 39n

Winslow, Henry F., 56n, 100n

Winwar, Frances, 117n

Wirth, Louis, 121

Wirth, Mary, 121

Witt, Peter, 17

Wittenber, Jan, 126n

Workers Cultural Union, 51

Works Progress Administration, 66, 69-70

World War I, 5, 7, 11, 12

Wright, Alan (brother of Wright), 9, 10, 18, 20, 22, 23, 45, 47, 121

Wright, Ella (mother of Wright), 8, 9, 10, 18, 19, 20, 21-23, 24, 25, 26-27, 28, 29, 30, 37-38, 39, 45, 47, 120

Wright, Ellen Poplar (second wife of Wright), 156, 157

Wright, Julia (daughter of Wright), 157

Wright, Nathaniel (father of Wright), 4, 7, 8, 18, 19, 21, 22, 24, 25, 28

Wright, Richard: family disorganization, 3, 4, 17-18, 21-24, 25, 27, 39; education, 3, 4, 17-18, 24-27, 34-37, 39, 41-45; racial discrimination against, 3, 4-17, 18, 24, 27, 28-29, 39, 40-41, 48-50, 64; criminal activity, 3, 20; poverty, 3-4, 17-21, 24, 25, 27, 39; birth, 5; vacations in Mexico, 5, 17, 151; vacations in Quebec, 5, 157; jobs, 7, 13, 19, 20, 40, 46, 47, 48-49, 50, 62, 68; goes to Memphis, 7, 39; goes to New York, 14, 64, 68; Daily Worker journalism, 16, 68, 72-73; hunger, 18-19; attitude toward religion, 23, 26, 30, 138; reading, 26, 27, 36-37, 41-45; writing, 27, 37, 68; personality, 27-33; fear as personality trait, 28-29; alienation as personality trait, 29-32; joins Communist party, 31, 62; withdraws from Communist party, 31, 153, 155-57; attitude toward existentialism, 31-32, 138, 158; friends, 32-33, 37, 38-39, 50, 118; "Dick Wright Klan," 38-39; goes to Chicago, 45; joins John Reed Club, 50; as poet, 52-61; attends American Writers' Congress, 63-65; joins black writers' group in Chicago, 66; works in Federal Theatre, 66-67; rural attachment, 99-100; moves to Brooklyn, 118; wins Guggenheim Fellowship, 118; replies to attacks on Native Son, 151-52; supports Communist party, 153-55; goes to France, 157-58; prose style, 158-59, 160; relation to naturalism and proletarian fiction, 159-60; relation to Afro-American literary tradition, 160-61; as interpreter of American racial problem, 161-62

— WORKS: "Adventure and Love in Loyalist Spain," 116, 117n; "Ah Feels It in Mah Bones," 60; "American Hunger," 46n, 159; "Ban on Negro Doctors Bared at City Probe," 16; "Between Laughter and Tears," 110n; "Between the World and Me," 57-58, 61; "Big Boy Leaves Home," 39, 67-68, 73, 75n, 82-87, 107, 109; Black Boy, 7, 10, 11, 14n, 18-47 passim, 56, 73, 80n,

81, 85, 99, 153; *Black Power,* 80n; "Blueprint for Negro Writing," 60, 70-71, 76; "Bright and Morning Star," 91-92, 107n, 112-16, 136n, 137n; *Bright and Morning Star,* 154; "Child of the Dead and Forgotten Gods," 55; "Down by the Riverside," 56, 82, 87-94, 107; "Early Days in Chicago," 14n, 46n, 49n; *Eight Men,* 82n; "The Ethics of Living Jim Crow," 10, 40, 73, 85n, 112, 115; "Everywhere Burning Waters Rise," 55-57; "Fire and Cloud," 56, 91, 100-106, 107, 108, 109, 112, 113; "Gouging, Landlord Discrimination against Negroes Bared at Hearing," 16; "Harlem Women Hit Boost in Milk Price," 16, 72; "Hearst Headline Blues," 59, 60; "High Tide in Harlem," 116-17; "How 'Bigger' Was Born," 151; *How "Bigger" Was Born,* 118n, 120, 129, 142, 151; "I Am a Red Slogan," 54; "I Have Seen Black Hands," 52-54, 60; "Insect-Ridden Medicine Given in Hospital," 16; "I Tried to Be a Communist," 62n, 64, 65, 156; "King Joe," 60-61; *Lawd Today,* 11n, 39, 47, 65, 75-82, 99; "Long Black Song," 94-100, 107, 108, 109, 112, 160; *The Long Dream,* 39, 56, 85, 99, 134; "Lynching Bee," 57n; "The Man Who Lived Underground," 49, 115n, 135; "The Man Who Saw the Flood," 82n; "The Man Who Went to Chicago," 14n; *Native Son,* 3n, 16, 21, 39, 47, 56, 73, 75, 76, 79, 80n, 81, 85, 86, 108, 112, 115, 116n, 117, 118-52, 153, 154-55, 158, 159, 161; *Native Son* (play), 17; "Negro, with 3-Week-Old Baby, Begs Food on Streets," 16; "Notes on Jim Crow Blues," 61; "Obsession," 57n, 58; "Old Habit and New Love," 59-60; "Opening of Harlem Project Homes Shows How Slums Can Be Wiped Out in New York," 17; *The Outsider,* 24, 31, 39, 85, 108, 134, 138, 157, 158n; "Portrait of Harlem," 73-74, 75; "Red Clay Blues," 60, 61; "Red Leaves of Red Books," 54; "A Red Love Note," 54, 55, 57, 59; "Rest for the Weary," 54-55, 59; "Rise and Live," 56; *Savage Holiday,* 134; "A Sharecropper's Story," 73; "Silt," 56, 82n; "Spread Your Sunrise," 58-59; "Strength," 55; "Superstition," 47-48, 53; "Transcontinental," 59; *12 Million Black Voices,* 80n, 86, 99; "Two Million Black Voices," 66n; *Uncle Tom's Children,* 62, 66, 68, 73, 75, 79, 80n, 82-116, 118, 144, 158, 159; "The Voodoo of Hell's Half-Acre," 26, 37, 53; "We of the Streets," 59-60, 71; "What You Don't Know Won't Hurt You," 49n

Yerby, Frank, 70
Yergan, Max, 148n